Suburban Xanadu

Suburban Xanadu

THE CASINO RESORT ON THE
LAS VEGAS STRIP AND BEYOND

David G. Schwartz

ROUTLEDGE
NEW YORK AND LONDON

Published in 2003 by
Routledge
29 West 35th Street
New York, NY 10001
www.routledge-ny.com

Published in Great Britain by
Routledge
11 New Fetter Lane
London EC4P 4EE
www.routledge.co.uk

Library of Congress Cataloging-In-Publication Data

Schwartz, David G., 1973–
    Suburban xanadu: the casino resort on the Las Vegas strip and beyond/ David G. Schwartz.
        p.   cm.
    Based on his Ph.D. thesis in history, presented to the University of California, Los Angeles.
    Includes bibliographical references and index.
    ISBN 0–415–93556–3 (alk. paper) – ISBN 0–415–93557–1 (pb.: alk. paper)
    1. Casinos—Nevada—Las Vegas. 2. Gambling industry—Nevada—Las Vegas. 3. Suburban life—United States. 4. Lifestyles—United States. 5. Leisure—United States. 6. Las Vegas (Nev.)—Social life and customs. 7. United States—Social life and customs. I. Title: Casino resort on the Las Vegas strip and beyond. II. Title.
HV6721.N45S39 2003
307.74909793135—dc21   2003040927

Dedicated to the memory of
Joe Curinga, my grandfather,
Carmela Curinga, my grandmother, and
Sonny Schwartz, my father

and in honor of
Connie Schwartz, my mother.

Contents

Preface and Acknowledgments

I have no distinct memories of a life without casinos. I was barely five years old when Resorts International opened on the Atlantic City Boardwalk, less than three miles from where I lived, in 1978. Although I couldn't appreciate it, my hometown was undergoing a historic change. Even then, I wondered why the redevelopment of Atlantic City happened the way it did. Why did the law demand that each casino include a large contingent of hotel rooms, restaurants, and entertainment? When I asked, most people vaguely answered that large casino hotels were easier to regulate than small gambling rooms, or that they were better for the economy.

As a graduate student in American History at UCLA, I discovered that no one yet answered this question to my satisfaction. This book developed out of my doctoral dissertation and for me is a tale of three cities: Atlantic City, where I first learned to ask questions about casinos; Los Angeles, where I found the intellectual tools to seek an answer, and Las Vegas, where I discovered the solution. So while this book is, in large part, a history of the Las Vegas Strip, I would be remiss in not warning the reader that it is written to answer the questions raised by the growth of casinos elsewhere. For me, the archetypal casino is not the Mirage or Excalibur, but the Trump Taj Mahal, for the sole reason that I worked there for three years.

I would like to express my sincerest gratitude to everyone who helped me write this and my apologies for not being able to mention everyone. Dave McBride was very helpful to me at Routledge, walking a rather clueless first-time author through the manuscript process. It is to his credit that I worked my over-weight dissertation into a readable book. My mother Connie and my sister Pauline have given me constant encouragement. Everyone I worked with at the Trump Taj Mahal also deserves thanks, particularly Rick Santoro, Executive VP of Security and Community Affairs. The chair of my dissertation committee, Eric Monkkonen, provided the right amount of guidance; without him I could not have progressed as rapidly as I did, nor could I have made the transition from dissertation to book. In the department office, Beebe Bernstein and Shela Patel helped me through the process, and for that I am still grateful.

When I wrote my dissertation, the people at UNLV Special Collections were solicitous and encouraging; no matter where I had gone, I would owe them a debt of gratitude. Since joining the department as coordinator of the Gaming Studies Research Center, though, I've gotten to know everyone there as co-workers and friends. Peter Michel, the director, helped me refine many of my arguments and, with Manuscripts Librarian Su Kim Chung, admirably preserved through reading this book in several stages— both gave me excellent critiques. Toby Murray, Kathy War, Jonnie Kennedy, and Joyce Marshall each helped me in different ways. I also got to know people who just hung around Special Collections. Michael Green made it through a reading and helped by sharing his incredible knowledge of Southern Nevada's history. Hal Rothman helped me hone my analysis and gave me encouragement from his "office." The students in my "History of Casino Gaming in the United States" class let me work on developing my historical understanding of the gaming industry. Away from UNLV, Lisa Oliva gave me her support and kindness. Training at the Las Vegas Combat Club kept me grounded—no scholarly work compares to the challenges of countering a triangle choke, and I'd like to thank everyone there.

Finally, I'd like to thank you, the reader, for picking up this book, and ask only that you read it with an open mind. If you are curious about casinos and gambling, check out the Gaming Studies Research Center website, http://gaming.unlv.edu, which has been my second intellectual attempt to understand casinos and is a comprehensive source for information about gambling.

In Xanadu did Kubla Khan
A stately pleasure-dome decree:
Where Alph, the sacred river, ran
Through caverns measureless to man
Down to a sunless sea.
So twice five miles of fertile ground
With walls and towers were girdled round:
And there were gardens bright with sinuous rills
Where blossomed many an incense-bearing tree;
And here were forests as ancient as the hills,
Enfolding sunny spots of greenery. . . .

Kubla Khan, Samuel Taylor Coleridge, 1798

Kubla Khan, as a croupier might sum it up, has had it. His stately pleasure dome in Xanadu has been surpassed at least seven-fold by the posh hostelries that line a fabulous three-mile stretch of erstwhile desert south of Las Vegas. And if there is no sacred running Alph, there is at least a paved highway to Los Angeles along which flows a constant horde of tourists (some 8,000,000 a year) bent on seeing, if only briefly and from a safe distance, this latter-day eighth wonder of the world.

Kent Ruth, 1956 travel guide

Introduction
Enter the green felt garden:
new ideas about the history of casinos

A great number of Americans gamble although some, like me, don't. Those who don't gamble and don't live in a city with casinos have little reason to know much about the historical development of the gaming industry or how casinos work. Most of what they do know has been picked up from movies like *The Godfather* and *Casino,* and confirmed by the endless stream of "inside Las Vegas" specials that crowd extended basic cable programming like handbill hawkers along the Strip. Within this genre, the casino industry is dangerous and exciting, owing more to mafia capos than to the white-collar managers who actually run most casinos. Though the business is thoroughly mainstream today, it retains a flavor of its outlaw gangster past, and the paunch of disreputability protrudes from under corporate pinstripes, if only one looks hard enough. "The casino" is an essentially deviant spot in American life, bearing the same relationship to a sound economy that an adult bookstore does to great literature.

For those who live in cities with casinos, such an interpretation of the casino industry is pretty far from the truth. To us, "the casino" is not a sybaritic den of vice, but a place to work or go for entertainment: to see a movie, play bingo, hit the buffet, or gamble. In short, casinos form a normative part of the social and economic landscape, and they are usually neither dangerous nor exciting. Most of the people who work at casinos don't seem particularly deviant. They have mortgages and car payments. They are, for the most part, productive citizens. Most are a great deal like their neighbors, but instead of telemarketing or selling insurance they just happen to deal blackjack or work in casino promotions. For people who actually live in the shadow of the industry, the sensationalistic "insider" stories

1

circulating on extended basic cable are interesting tales, but they have little to do with the reality of everyday life, and they really don't explain much about the business that shapes their lives.

So in writing this book, I started from the point that neither casino operators nor patrons are fundamentally deviant, but are in fact more or less rational people acting to maximize their profit and vacation value, respectively. Surprisingly, this is a position articulated by few who have written about casinos. The glitter of the Las Vegas Strip is hardly conducive to clear-headed social analysis, but the superficial glibness of so much that has been written about the casino industry is still amazing. In the past twenty-five years, casinos have migrated from Nevada idiosyncrasy to near ubiquity. There are casinos, it seems, nearly everywhere—off the winding roads of northern San Diego County, in the shadow of the Civil War battlefield of Shiloh, and in downtown Detroit. But the even-tempered historical analysis of how and why this happened has been, for the most part, neglected.

Understandably, a faux medieval castle/4,000-room casino hotel standing next to a pyramid/3,000-room casino hotel (and across the street from a faux Manhattan skyline/2,000-room casino hotel) is a bit unnerving. But it should be no more distracting than the fact that, within any movie multiplex, the latest *Star Trek* movie is playing alongside a James Bond spy thriller, a feature-length cartoon, a teen slasher retread, and a period costume drama. We'd hardly accept a film historian concluding that today's movie industry is a surreal pastiche of consumer desire, shrugging her shoulders, and walking away. Rather, a student of American film would demand a well-reasoned study that charted the evolution of the art form and offered an explanatory framework. The seemingly inexplicable development of the casino resort as a premier American vacation attraction in an era of vehement moral and political campaigns against gambling demands no less rigor.

For those from jurisdictions that have hitched their economic futures to the wagon train of casino gaming, this book will hopefully help you understand a bit better the dynamics that created the casino resort and helped it grow into maturity. I chose to investigate the casino resort in response to unanswered questions I had about the development of the industry in my hometown, Atlantic City, New Jersey. Why, I wondered, did casinos with hotels, restaurants, and entertainment facilities receive the sanction of law? How did rational people decide that their best hope for a livable region was with gambling? Why were casino resorts on the Las Vegas Strip such promoters of growth? Why haven't other casino towns duplicated their runaway success?

There are no simple answers to these questions, but this book explains the creation and development of casino resorts as specific adaptations to specific circumstances during the years after 1945. These resorts evolved to fill a void created by the dramatic turn against urban gambling that peaked in the early 1950s, just as casino operators were creating the Las Vegas Strip. My thesis—that suburban Americans chose to gamble in insular resorts far from their homes in order to forestall the particular problems posed by widespread urban gambling—suggests that the current expansion of gambling will require yet another solution. Hopefully, a careful study of how the "greatest generation" solved their gambling "problem" will yield lessons for today.

The secret origins of Xanadu

What does a Samuel Taylor Coleridge poem have to do with gambling? Probably more than you might expect. I use the word Xanadu to describe the casino resorts of the Strip because it evokes an opulent, exotic locale, which is precisely what casino operators sought to do. As I did my research, I made two further discoveries. First, a travel writer in the 1950s had used Xanadu as a metaphor for the hostelries of the Strip. Second, a Xanadu Casino Hotel was actually planned by a prominent casino hotel architect, Martin Stern, Jr., though it was never built.[1]

If that explains Xanadu, what explains "casino resort"? I use the term to mean a complete vacation resort, a unified complex operated by a single entity centered on a gambling casino but also containing restaurants, entertainment venues, pools, spas, and retail shopping. The term first came to prominence in the early 1990s to describe megacasinos with extensive nongaming components, such as shopping malls or themeparks, but it is also the best way to describe earlier casino/hotel/vacation complexes. For several reasons, casino operators of the 1950s usually called their Strip properties hotels. At the time, the "hotels" of the Strip were understood to include all of the things that casino resorts do. But outside that context, that word means little more than a structure with rooms for rent. The word "resort" better captures what these properties actually were—sprawling complexes in which visitors were expected to vacation comfortably. "Casino," of course, reminds us of those resorts' featured, though often unstated, attraction: gambling.

Within this complex, dining and entertainment were relatively cheap, as even the gourmet room and superstar shows were well within the budget of virtually all guests, and they were often given free to favored players as comps. Then, with relatively small casinos, there was nowhere near the segmentation in high- and low-end play that is seen today. This created the illusion of a "classless" social milieu, in which stenographers and chief executive officers rubbed elbows. Contemporary writers remarked on the apparent absence of barriers to sociability within the casino, painting the picture of a place where everyone was as good as his last roll. This has inspired some to conclude that casino resorts are supremely democratic institutions that reflect the egalitarian nature of American society. Casino resorts are, it is true, reflections of American values and social expectations, but this surely means that they are imbued with unwritten, though very present, rules. The spontaneous freedom of the casino floor is in fact structured, and the democratic casino, admitting all gamblers from penny slot players to $20,000 per hand baccarat players, is in actuality brutally segmented.

From a seat at a high-limit table, the casino seems to be without limit. The privilege of high stakes gambling is well rewarded—premium players are given personalized customer contact, with a dealer serving them directly and high-level managers nearby. Cocktail servers bring complimentary beverages quickly, and, after the session is through, a casino host gladly arranges for complimentary food and entertainment. From a more crowded lower-limit table, the service is a little less crisp and the complimentaries less grand. Seated at a stool in front of a slot machine, the landscape is less inviting. If the high rollers at the tables are the landed gentry of the casino, free to repair to their palatial suites in lofty hotel towers, slot player are its tenant farmers, renting a stool in front of a slot machine by dropping coins. Contact with employees is less frequent and less personalized, as cocktail servers and slot attendants have an entire zone of machine players to serve. Complimentary meals no longer mean the gourmet room, but rather the buffet or coffee shop. On the casino floor, the patron knows exactly how much she is worth to the casino.

So the casino resort, despite its reputation as a carefree galaxy of lucky rolls and intuitive fortune, was always a tightly controlled space. The discipline imposed over employees extended to facial expressions and even to hand movements. Patrons, though they seemingly mingled with each other in a frenzy of speculative fantasy, actually closely followed a script of their own, one usually determined by their budget. There are few institutions more candidly reflective of American society than the casino resort.

Before seriously discussing casinos, I must clarify what I call what goes on there: gambling or gaming? Even members of the industry are sometimes unsure what to call their profession. A persistent myth states that the word "gambling" is the true, organic description of the activity, and that industry apologists use the word "gaming," hoping that through a feat of verbal crop-dusting, Americans will forget that the dice and slot machines in casinos are for gambling, and will overwhelmingly approve any initiatives for its expansion. In fact, according to Shannon Bybee's extensive historical and legal research into the gambling/gaming etymology, the word "gaming" is actually older than "gambling," and most dictionaries make no distinction in meaning between the two words.[5]

Within this book, I usually use "gaming" to describe the industry, and "gambling" to talk about the activity that takes place inside the casino. I follow the accepted rules of usage—industry leaders gather each Septem-

Casino work is the pits

A casino manager who was responsible for the daily operation of his or her shift as well as general casino policy stood at the apex of the casino's management hierarchy. The casino manager customarily worked swing shift, the consistently busiest shift throughout the week. A shift manager commanded the other two shifts. Shift managers had the authority of a Roman patriarch to make the final decision on any variety of actions, from player credit to employee discipline, ultimately accountable to only the shareholders or board of directors.

The table gaming area, or pits, consumed most of a shift manager's time and were the focal point of most of the "action" on a casino floor. A how-to guide for prospective cocktail waitresses summarized the word "pit" as "an arena," in which the lions and humans might be players or workers, depending on "which side thinks he's having the worst of it."[2] Between six and twelve table games constituted a single pit, and one to three pits were average for the Strip before the expansions of the 1960s.[3] A typical pit in an older Strip casino resort had either all craps tables or a mix of roulette, blackjack, and sometimes Big Six (a.k.a. the Wheel of Fortune). Baccarat tables, if they were featured at all, were typically in a separate pit, removed from the bustle of the central pits, befitting its reputation as a more refined, continental game of chance.

Casino employees within the pits were rigidly structured and supervised. A pit boss, who reported directly to the casino M.O.D. (manager on duty), superintended all of the action in his or her pit and acted as a middle manager, seeing that the directives of the M.O.D. were followed and company policy adhered to. Beneath the pit boss were floormen who directly supervised the dealers working at between two to six tables.[4] This floorman was responsible for maintaining the bankroll at his or her tables and assuring a smooth, honest flow of play. This position was analogous to that of a line manager, who directly supervised employees—in this case, dealers who dealt directly with the gambling public.

ber in Las Vegas for the Global *Gaming* Expo, and if they get bored they might wander over to the Hilton to *gamble* a little. I have never heard someone say, "I was out gaming until three last night," though within the United States most business and government entities profess to be in a slightly different field—New Jersey's Division of Gaming Enforcement might investigate a license application by Boyd Gaming. In addition, within Nevada and New Jersey, the word "gaming" has been understood to apply exclusively to the commercial casino industry, whose evolution this study concerns.

Why not a Pseudo-urban Shangri-La?

Even if it makes sense to call a casino resort Xanadu, how can it be suburban? After all, the Las Vegas Strip is one of the most well-known spectacles of high-rise construction in the world—hardly what one would consider suburban. And casinos, places with gambling, smoking, drinking, and assorted other adult mis-behaviors, seem to be antithetical to the culture of the postwar suburbs as it has typically been understood: conformity, homogeneity, and white picket fences, with the occasional Tupperware party or backyard cook-out to break up the tedium. Casinos seem jarringly out of place in this world.

I won't attempt to argue that casino resorts are suburban per se, but they are vitally connected to suburbia on several levels. The Las Vegas Strip, though it is currently the center of a 1.5 million person metropolitan concrete and asphalt oasis, was originally "settled" by casino operators as "virgin land," miles out of town on the Los Angeles Highway. Even today, the resorts of the Strip are not part of the City of Las Vegas, much to the consternation of municipal officials. From the start, they identified themselves as essentially antiurban, and leagues apart from the downtown gambling halls of Fremont Street. They were explicitly built and promoted as places for reasonably well-off Americans to vacation, much like themeparks.[6]

Calling Las Vegas casino resorts "Disneyland for adults" confuses the picture even more and is inaccurate: the Strip predates Disneyland by several years, so strictly speaking Walt's parks could be called "casino resorts for kids." But tying casino resorts to the suburbs, which they mined for consumers, makes sense, and permits students of history to see the rise of casino resorts within the perspective of other historical changes. It is no coincidence that, as upper- and middle-class Americans were moving to the suburbs in great numbers in the years after World War II, they did two things: they urged public officials to retain, and more strictly enforce, local antigambling statutes, and they began to patronize the resorts of the Strip. I see a deep connection between these two phenomena, and I believe that casino resorts reflected Americans' solution to the problem of perceived runaway urban gambling—to isolate gambling in space (distant Nevada) and in culture (posh vacation resorts). Within these confines, gambling was tolerable and even desirable. Outside of them, it was usually illegal and officially despised.

I use the word "suburban" a bit more loosely to refer to another aspect of casino resorts—their fundamental incompatibility with urban space.

True, suburban is not the right word for this—"nonurban" or "antiurban" would seem to be more accurate, and "pseudo-urban" probably the most apt. But *Pseudo-urban Xanadu* didn't quite have the ring of a page-turner to me, and such a title would obscure what I consider, in the broader context, the more important side of the story—the national social changes which influenced the casino resort's birth and development.

But the pseudo-urban nature of the casino resort is clear to most who have worked or lived around them. Casino resorts, from their first days, have been much like shopping malls, in the sense that visitors usually drive, park, and then enter them. "But wait," you might say, "aren't the casinos on the Strip connected by pedestrian walkways that span Las Vegas Boulevard? If that's not urban, what is?" True, the Strip of today hosts throngs of walking tourists with fanny packs and bottled water. But this is a recent phenomenon, hardly a decade old. For most of their histories, casino resorts on the Strip were isolated, insular patches of green and blue that stood in stark contrast to the desert scrub that surrounded them. The resorts of the Strip were designed to function as self-contained entities, in which guests could pursue all the pleasures of a complete vacation without leaving. And though most visitors to Las Vegas do visit more than one casino, it has long been the most sacred tenet of casino design, above all else, to keep guests in the complex and near the tables and slots.

Casino resorts have never really evolved out of this necessity to keep patrons inside the complex and near the casino, and casino operators created a series of inducements to retain their action. Lucky players were given free dinners for a reason: given a long enough stay in the facility, they inevitably would return to the tables, where the laws of probability (and the house advantage) would catch up with them. The worst nightmare of a casino manager has always been the spot player, the individual who bets large, gets lucky, and leaves. Though over the course of his career such a player should, theoretically, be a loser, on any particular night he can beat the house. To encourage him to "quit winners" by giving him no excuse to remain near the tables would be fiscal suicide. There is a reason that stand-alone casinos without surrounding resorts have consistently failed on the Strip—they are at a supreme competitive disadvantage.

Casino resorts built elsewhere have retained this law as their prime directive—keep the player in the house, or else. So they, like their Strip forbears, are self-contained mini-cities that purport to meet all their guests' needs. Indeed, this is what new casino employees are told during their orientation, when it is impressed upon them to remember the host of goods and services that a patron can procure just steps from the gambling action. What was true in 1941 is still true today. The vast increase in the size of casino resorts in the past fifty years has obscured the similarity in function between the earliest resorts and the latest megacomplexes. The MGM

Grand, for example, serves many of the same functions as the El Rancho Vegas—to provide dining, entertainment, and lodging for casino patrons. Considering entertainment in particular, the El Rancho Vegas had an intimate dinner theater that seated perhaps 100 patrons. The MGM Grand boasts, as of late 2002, no less than five venues, including a nightclub, a theater dedicated to the "EFX" stage spectacular, and a 17,157-seat multiuse arena. Both properties provided entertainment to guests, but on a drastically different scale. Similarly, while the structure of casino resorts has changed significantly, their basic functions remain the same. To really understand how casino resorts operate today, then, one must understand how these functions originally evolved.

It is because of the "casino prime directive" that casino resorts have evolved into such heady oases of pseudo-urbanity. If it takes a replica of the canals of Venice, a trendy nightclub, a bowling alley, or a place to buy lottery tickets to keep patrons near the slots, operators will provide them. Like shopping malls and theme parks, casino resorts are self-contained. But unlike other private spaces that increasingly function as public ones, casino resorts are not insular because their operators want to protect their patrons from outside undesirable elements. Rather, they are insular because their operators want to keep patrons inside. Bluntly speaking, they are not fortresses, but prisons.

Gardens out of the sand:
A new explanation of the casino industry's rise

When anticrime reporters Ed Reid and Ovid Demaris looked at the Las Vegas Strip in the early 1960s, they saw a civic nightmare where vice reigned and virtue was quiescent, a Hobbesean jungle world where life was nasty and brutish and gangsters openly controlled civic affairs. So they called their Las Vegas exposé *The Green Felt Jungle.* Even today, most writers agree that, before the influx of Wall Street capital and corporate respectability (usually dated to some unspecified moment in the Reagan years), the casino resorts of the Strip really were anarchic jungles where only the fittest (or most venal) survived.

The jungle metaphor, though, was never accurate. Rather than being a lawless jungle of opportunity and deceit, the Las Vegas Strip was always a garden of sorts: ordered, artificial, and well maintained (if not always well tempered). Even in the Strip's earliest days, visitors drove up to a casino resort, parked in a clearly demarcated space, and checked in at the hotel desk or simply entered the casino. Things were always in their place: entertainment in the showroom, fine dining in the restaurants, and gambling on the casino floor. Visitors to the casino resort could pick their path and find any number of safe adventures during their trip. Were they to gamble in the casino, they would have odds of winning that the casino's accountants had deemed acceptable. Whether they won or lost, they would be afforded complimentaries based on their expected level of play. The system was rough around the edges at times, but, from the start, casino resorts have always been intensely organized places. If there is a metaphor for the Las Vegas Strip of the past and present, it is that of a green felt garden.

That the pleasure palaces of the Strip were more like gardens than jungles doesn't mean that there wasn't a kernel of truth to the sensationalists' rants. Organized crime, quite clearly, profoundly influenced the casino resort's development. While to state that the gaming industry was subject to mob domination may be oversimplifying the picture, there was enough going on to attract considerable attention from crime reporters and law enforcement, and for good reason. Many "connected" men held points, furtively and openly, in Strip resorts, and many operating managers had criminal records (usually gambling convictions). Underworld overlords from Los Angeles, Chicago, Kansas City, and New York had varying amounts of influence in individual Strip casinos. The history of the gaming industry in Southern Nevada is riddled with shady dealing and disreputable characters. Many of the industry's icons were not nice guys. But to claim that the history of any business, political organization, or social movement is the story of nice guys is either naive or disingenuous. The complex reality of the casino industry's history is that of underworld influence and investment but not monolithic "control," and the tale is harder to sketch than the black and white saga of mob control yielding to corporate hegemony. The development of the casino resort is better understood as the product of individual ambition and opportunism rather than collective criminal conspiracy.

Some human achievements are so monumental that they invite attribution to a higher power. To some, the pyramids of Egypt are structures so imposing that they must have been the handiwork of visitors from outer space. Most archaeologists, though, can tell you that building the pyramids merely took a little human ingenuity and a sizable labor force. Likewise, some people look at the casino industry's incredible run of good luck over the past fifty years, as it has gone, in historian Hal Rothman's words, "from pariah to paradigm," and conclude that such a feat is beyond comprehension—it is simply impossible to imagine that honest businesspeople were able to take such a maligned business as gambling and turn it into the cornerstone of one of the world's largest tourist economies. It calls for secret, sinister forces operating outside the margins of spoken history—if not Knights Templar, surely shadowy mafia dons and corrupt public officials.

This book demonstrates exactly how more or less unexceptional people, acting rationally and responsibly, did the "impossible" within full view of the public. The process began humbly, and in my first chapter, "The Righteous and the Wicked," I discuss the conditions from which the casino resort would rise. During and after World War II, gambling operators first began to realize the possibilities of placing gaming in a new context, far from the cities but also away from the small downtown of Las Vegas. Before the war, Fremont Street gambling halls offered cheap, quick gambling action with few frills much like those in Reno, then Nevada's premier city. Tourists already in the region for other reasons (to see Hoover Dam, for example) visited these halls out of curiosity, lost a few dollars, and moved on. The concept of a pleasure trip to Las Vegas merely to gamble appealed to only a select breed of gambling habitué in the early 1940s. But by making gambling the centerpiece of a pleasure-filled vacation, operators opened up their trade to a burgeoning audience.

My second chapter, "The Unwholesome Allure," focuses on the first modest experiments that paved the way for later, more extravagant, operations that, though they still retained a taint of "unwholesomeness," attracted ordinary Americans to them. By 1947, three new casinos had opened on Highway 91 south of Las Vegas. They shared a common basic layout: a cluster of low-rise motel buildings set among expansive grounds, and a central structure housing a lobby, gaming casino, showroom, and restaurants. The integration of multiple tourist facilities within the complex obviated the need for patrons to rent rooms in the city or even to leave the premises for meals. Casino operators deliberately designed their resorts this way for two reasons. First, they distanced their luxury "carpet joints" from the hoi polloi of the downtown "grind" or "sawdust" (low-expense) gambling halls. Second, they kept patrons within the casino and near the gaming tables and machines for their entire stay, demonstrating the "casino prime directive" so well that they actually advertised their distance from downtown. This was a new and ironic twist on the conventional wisdom of the hospitality business; hotels traditionally promote their proximity to a city's major points, but the new resorts on Highway 91 conspicuously championed their self-sufficiency and isolation from the city while beckoning to Southern California for patrons. As that quintessentially suburban area blossomed, it was only natural that its inhabitants sought their recreation in a safe, familiar, but also exotic setting. With the existing latticework of Los Angeles's urban gambling shattered by anti-crime forces in the late 1930s and early 1940s, many of the city's illegal operators had begun to operate Las Vegas casinos.

With the success of the first casinos, other luxury resorts opened on Highway 91 in the early 1950s. They began to attract a national base of visitors, which led to increased development; by about 1952, the designation of Highway 91 as "the Strip" had become popularly accepted. Not coincidentally, in these same years, urban gambling operations throughout the nation succumbed to the attacks of anticrime/antigambling crusaders. This only spurred the success of the nascent Nevada industry. I devote chapter three, "A Fruitful Containment," to the paradox of the early 1950s—rapid growth on the Strip coupled with cresting national antigambling sentiment. The new casinos improved upon and expanded the basic designs of the innovators, which in turn increased startup costs. The informal coalitions and limited partnerships of earlier casinos did not have access to the capital now required for entering the field. Traditional sources of capital, such as commercial and investment banks, largely passed on opportunities to invest in the casino industry because of its unsavory image and doubtful future. As a result, prospective casino operators often turned to other sources, most notoriously former bootleggers and gambling operators with organized crime connections.

The presence of organized crime in casino resorts raised the ire of the Kefauver Committee in the early 1950s. In response, the state of Nevada, largely at the behest of the casino industry, adopted a new, active regulatory regime that proactively policed resorts for cheating and skimming violations and retained the right to revoke a casino's license. Both industry and government representatives argued for the imposition of stronger regulatory controls as necessary for both the continued operation of casino resorts and the ongoing financial health of the state. The state's increasing interest demonstrated how the casino industry in Southern Nevada and the economy of Nevada had become fused.

Opening casinos is one thing; running them is another. In "Organizing Luck," I discuss how casino operators developed workable systems to manage—and count—the incredible sums that passed through their doors, and how casino management and ownership have always been complex issues. Las Vegas's new success as a convention city, signified by the 1959 opening of the Las Vegas Convention Center, spurred an increase in the size of casino resorts. Casino operators now needed larger amounts of capital to build and maintain their resorts than traditional underworld sources could supply. The Teamsters Central States Pension Fund was a quasi-legitimate capital source that can be understood as a gateway to the subsequent entrance of mainstream capital into southern Nevada. In the 1960s, casinos sought more mainstream lenders and investors. With the successful implementation of stricter controls in the 1950s and a loosening of national cultural and social biases against gambling in Las Vegas (tied to the closure of illegal operations elsewhere), the future of the legal gaming industry in Nevada seemed secure and more palatable to mainstream business sensibilities. Casino ownership, too, changed in nature during these years. A simplistic "mobbed up/clean house" dichotomy does not do justice to the shifting patterns of ownership and investment in these years, nor does it recognize the achievement of casino managers in creating accurate accounting to meet the difficult reality of running a casino.

Having figured out how to profitably run casinos, operators soon enjoyed a golden age, an era that I discuss in chapter five, "Wiseguy Empire." In the early 1960s, the Rat Pack was the most visible symbol of casino culture, and its popularity explains in many ways how casino owners promoted themselves in that era. In these years, the resorts of the Strip abandoned earlier policies of racial segregation and enjoyed unprecedented profits and popularity. But the "Copa era" was soon over. The advancing age of the former bootleggers who had built the Strip and rising capital investment costs, not corporate or state strong-arming, forced the "mob's" decline in Las Vegas. At the same time, Caesars Palace brought a new level of themed extravagance to the casino resort, and the high costs and high profits of the Copa era forced the transition to a new ownership model.

In chapter six, "When the Suits Come Marching In," I explore exactly how the Strip "went corporate." Beginning in 1967, Howard Hughes bought six Las Vegas casinos that together represented one-quarter of the city's gaming business and, more important, the Nevada legislature amended the gaming code to allow for corporate ownership of casinos. Over the next decade, publicly traded national corporations would become the chief operators of Las Vegas casino resorts. Despite a few "skimming" and other mob scandals in the 1970s and 1980s, pundits declared Las Vegas free from underworld control. But what these pundits did not stress was the importance of continuity to the operation of casino resorts. Even when new owners arrived, they disdained the quick alteration of existing industry methods already in place. The changes in the casino industry in the 1970s were evolutionary rather than revolutionary and were more about scale than substance.

In 1976, the U.S. Commission to Review the National Policy on Gambling concluded that the casino resort model of legal gambling, pioneered on the Strip, was a basically innocuous form of public recreation that could be successfully harnessed for the public good. This positive verdict stands in stark contrast to the Kefauver Committee's unstintingly negative evaluation of Nevada gaming. Casino operators and the state of Nevada had combined to make the casino resort a form of gambling that, it was believed, positively benefited society.

This new acceptance of casino resorts as legitimate parts of a good economy fostered the expansion of the industry outside of Nevada, a process that I discuss in chapter seven, "The Casino Archipelago." With the casino resort model in mind, the voters of New Jersey agreed, in 1976, to legalize gambling within a set portion of the decaying seaside resort of Atlantic City. The enabling legislation that created the legal framework for the Atlantic City casino industry consciously borrowed from Nevada's regulatory structure, and actually superceded Nevada's code in stipulating that all gambling must take place within casino resorts. The voters and legislators of New Jersey believed that, through judicious use of the casino resort, Atlantic City could be redeveloped, the state's coffers would be enriched, and the industry would be kept honest. At this point, it is fair to say that the casino resort had arrived as an American institution.

In the 1980s, the casino resort prospered in its new home by the seashore while it gaudily stagnated in its desert greenhouse. By the latter years of that decade, the success of casino gaming in Atlantic City drew the interest of other economically troubled jurisdictions and resulted in the expansion of gaming on riverboats in the Midwest and South and on Indian land throughout the nation. And in 1989, the opening of the Mirage in Las Vegas cued a building boom that fostered a staggering increase in the size and polish of casino resorts on the Strip. In the 1990s, casino resorts cemented their status as respectably thriving institutions. Their Mojave fountainhead reached its fullest articulation, and by the end of the twentieth century the casino resort had reached a surprisingly even distribution throughout the continental United States; eleven states, from New Jersey to Michigan to Mississippi to Nevada, had commercial casino resorts, and at least twenty-seven states, spanning the country from Connecticut to California, had Indian-owned casino resorts on tribal land.

In an epilogue, "Odds against Tomorrow," I consider the ultimate impact of the evolution of the commercial casino industry in the United States, as well as the new challenges posed by new technologies, ranging from surveillance cameras and data mining to Internet gambling. Technology always changes society in ways that are unexpected and unintended, and the reality of Internet gambling, which can bring the equivalent of a casino into every home in America, certainly underlines the collapse of the casino resort model of gambling containment.

Looking at the evolution of the industry it is clear that the gaming industry is not really that exceptional—it has more similarities with other American industries than differences. It is not necessary to hypothesize about mob payoffs or political dirty dancing to understand the expansion of the gaming industry over the past thirty years. The industry has been able to capitalize on the placement of a popular activity, gambling, in what is seen as a socially innocuous and economically beneficial institution, the casino resort. Casino operators did not need to live by the "Mafia code of the jungle" to survive and thrive on the Strip; they only had to build and maintain better artificial gardens for their patrons.

CHAPTER 1

The Righteous and the Wicked
Gambling's popularity dooms it to exile in the Nevada desert

Attacks on gambling in general and legalized gambling in particular have recently been uttered by various public officials. . . . J. Edgar Hoover of the F. B. I. announced, "Gambling today is the nest egg of the criminal underworld." Gov. Thomas E. Dewey of New York declared, "The history of legalized gambling shows it has brought nothing but poverty, crime, and corruption. . . ."

In Nevada almost any kind of gambling is permitted, just so long as the Government gets its cut. Casinos are now more numerous and more glamorous than they were before the war. Estimated take this year: $1 billion dollars.
New York Times Magazine, 1950

The secret of Las Vegas's success is a combination of circumstances, sunshine, plus fate, topped by a curious grass-roots appeal. The visitor to Las Vegas finds himself whisked as if by rocketflight from the world of reality into a sun-baked neo-Klondike, as the Klondike might be depicted in a Hollywood musical with palm trees substituted for snow. The place roars with frontier atmosphere to a round-the-clock clink of silver dollars and the rattle of dice in a setting of bright lights, liquor, music, and dancing girls.
New York Times Magazine, 1953.

Americans have always been gamblers, and they have always struggled to control gambling. The frisson has produced the hallmark gambling form of contemporary America, the casino resort. The "pleasure palaces" of the Las Vegas Strip, first built during the twentieth century's largest antigambling movement, permitted Americans to contain gambling in both space and culture, and, in effect, to reserve public gambling for those with the means to travel to Las Vegas and the inclination to spend time in resorts that were isolated, exclusive, and safe. To unravel how and why the casino industry took shape in contemporary America as it has is to do more than chronicle the construction of the Strip's casinos. It is to delve deeper into the fabric of the suburbanizing nation that produced and nurtured a new institution, the casino resort, and added a chapter to the history of American gambling.

This industry didn't just spring up out of the Nevada desert. Its operators took advantage of several larger trends in American life that made their enterprises good gambles. Throughout America, citizens became increasingly anxious about the explosion of gambling in the cities. In the state of Nevada, hard economic times gave the business and political elite a license to construct the most ambitious regime of legal, regulated gambling ever seen in the United States. At the southern corner of the state, cunning operators hoped to take advantage of Las Vegas's relative proximity to Los Angeles by introducing a new kind of tourist experience centered on gambling in self-contained resorts outside of the city. Finally, as more Americans called the suburbs home, they naturally found appealing a gambling environment that reflected the suburban order. These factors combined to create the conditions needed for the new casino resort industry to prosper.

Rage against the machine: American gambling at midcentury

The casino resort emerged at a propitious moment, when the clash between gambling's popularity and its perceived social ill effects created a conflict that would only be solved by completely changing the cultural context of gambling. Gambling had long been a divisive issue. Americans, as far back as the pre-Columbian era, have always been a "people of chance" with a fondness for gambling. Yet, gambling, which offered simultaneously the promise of quick wealth and the threat of sudden ruin, ran counter to the Protestant work ethic—work hard, live prudently—that ostensibly formed the bedrock of social and economic order in the United States. Still, Americans loved to bet—on horse, dog, and foot races, on lotteries and the numbers, on cards and dice, on stocks and bonds, and even on presidential elections.[1] Where gambling remained predominantly a social activity conducted within a community, social pressures limited gains and losses and provided checks on dishonest behavior—someone who consistently beat his neighbors, through luck or cunning, would be subject to a range of sanctions.

But as the United States expanded throughout the nineteenth century, gambling became an increasingly commercial proposition. Itinerant professional gamblers, who more often than not cheated to win before moving on, could fleece townspeople and travelers indiscriminately without threat of social sanction. The rise of consistent winners meant a concomitant increase in consistent losers. As early as 1838, a Boston physician warned of the sad fate of unfortunates who, caught up in a gambling mania in the increasingly market-based economy, plunged into a sick world of debt, ruin, and death.[2] Loosed from the traditional strictures of family and community, some city dwellers could not refrain from literally gambling themselves to death. Notably, the frenetic, impersonal gambling that captured these unfortunates always took place in urban settings—taverns, pool halls, and the like. The temptation of chance was everywhere in early American cities and posed an unabating threat to even the unwary. While this gambling was usually illegal, payoffs to police and politicians ensured its quiet continuance.

Although reformers like Anthony Comstock raged against gambling, there was little reason for the populace in general to arm itself against the vice. Even though all social classes gambled, the high-stakes betting that horrified nongamblers was, for the most part, confined to the wealthy, as the less well off contented themselves with low grade forms of gambling such as lotteries, which represented a small, though continual, expense that seldom led to debt or serious social disruption. It was difficult for those who despised gambling to rally the masses in defense of wealthy fools who squandered their money gambling, and depriving the same masses of their own small-stakes gambling diversions would have been virtually impossible given the incredible popularity of technically illegal lottery-based games.

With expansions in technology came natural advances in gambling that would shift this precarious balance. The reel slot machine, which first appeared in the 1890s, was a radically new gambling technology that was phenomenally easy to play—one need only insert a coin, pull a handle, and wait for a lucky break. Other uncomplicated forms of gambling, such as lottery and numbers games, required long delays between the placing of a bet and the gambling decision. Not so with slot machines; they delivered instant gratification as readily as card and dice games. Even better (or worse), slot machines presented no skill barrier; with no rules to learn, as with card and dice games, a first-timer was just as proficient as an old pro. Like numbers games, they were small-stakes games, usually played for a penny or nickel at a time.

At the height of their urban popularity in the first half of the twentieth century, slots were identified almost exclusively with working- and lower-class gambling in bars, neighborhood hang-outs, and similar locales. The

Mills Novelty Company, incorporated in Chicago in 1891, was the largest slot machine company in the 1930s; other slot manufacturers operating out of the Chicago area included the Lion Manufacturing Company, A.B.T Manufacturing Company, and D. Gottleib and Company. In other areas of the country, Pacific Amusement Manufacturing Company and Exhibit Supply Company both produced slot machines.[3] The slot manufacturing company usually sold machines to a jobber or dealer who then installed them in public places, such as bars, restaurants, retail establishments, and fraternal halls, splitting the profits with the owner of the premises.

As near as the corner store, the slot machine brought gambling out of the backrooms and into the mainstream of urban life. It gave physical form to a new prevalence of gambling within the very fabric of the city. In the new American city, anyone could gamble, sometimes cumulatively large sums. A 1951 exposé of Brooklyn organized crime concluded that "the gamblers . . . infest the public school system like rats," with a system of bookies and runners divvying up the trade in every high school and junior high school in the borough, as students "pour out quarters in a desperate attempt to beat the odds." The gamblers, hovering "like vultures in tiny shops and stores off campus," also preyed on Brooklyn's three colleges, with predictable results: a number of Brooklyn College players admitted conspiring with gamblers to throw a game.[4] Gambling threatened even youths and young adults with temptation and corruption. No place in the city was free from its toxicity, and not even the most innocent could avoid its lure.

Gambling, around 1950, was seemingly everywhere in cities large and small but, because it was illegal, it was also nowhere. Contemporary accounts remarked on the disappearance of older casino-style "gambling hells," but even junior high students knew where to place a bet. One can read in the antigambling literature a distinct anxiety that gambling, from candy store slot machines to neighborhood bookies, was engulfing the cities. Unlike earlier antigambling crusaders, who implored their readers to weep for proud men, led by hubris, who squandered the fruits of their productive labor, the new antigambling forces decried the terrors of gambling unleashed on women and children. Both women and children had previously been discouraged from "serious" gambling (casino owners at Saratoga Springs, New York, even went so far as to post doormen to bar women and locals), but both groups found gambling at slot machines easy and fun.

Antigamblers did more than bemoan the loss of women and children to gambling; they actively exposed the "boss gamblers," those who ran citywide gambling empires and were usually linked to organized crime. The investment capital, distribution and maintenance network, and political protection needed for a successful slot operation discouraged individual operators and demanded the involvement of larger structures, namely, gambling syndicates. Often, these syndicates grew out of gamblers' groups formed to share the risks involved with accepting large wagers. As slot operations became more sophisticated and more lucrative, the bootlegging syndicates of the 1920s and 1930s often moved in, sometimes absorbing older gamblers' groups and sometimes supplanting them. Mark Haller concludes that bootleggers, as "ambitious men, primarily of Jewish and Italian backgrounds," used the 1920s as an opportunity to accrue "wealth, business experience, and political influence." During and after Prohibition, they supplied a number of locales with slot machines including illegal speakeasies. According to Haller, with Prohibition came a merger between the older gambling syndicates and the new ambitious bootleggers: bootlegging organizations for the most part subsumed the old gambling rackets into their vice fiefdoms while retaining members of the gambling syndicates as hands-on managers and operators.[5] This process combined the human capital of gambling experts with the finances, muscle, and political power of the new bootlegging syndicates.

Because of the larger scope of bootleggers' operations, they began to add slot machines to their portfolio of illegal gambling operations, which often already included the numbers racket and bookmaking. Bootleggers may have begun installing slot machines not as gambling devices per se, but rather as amusement devices. Frequently, gambling constituted only a minor part of the bootleggers' operations, which included the "coordination of the nightlife and commercialized entertainment of a city— nightclubs, bars, juke boxes, legal liquor distribution, and other related enterprises."[6] Since bootlegging syndicates were in the business of providing not only gambling but also alcohol and its ancillary vices, they may have evinced a greater partiality for the slot machine than those who specialized in traditional forms of gambling. In any event, the bootlegging combines of the East and Midwest, starting in earnest in the 1930s, brought gambling to a variety of social classes. Bootleggers simultaneously supplied New York bars and tobacco stores with slot machines and invested in high-class casinos of varying legality in Kentucky, Florida, and Havana. It is interesting to note that, for the most part, bootleggers avoided operating the urban "gambling hells" that previous generations had run, and they eschewed the city for backwater—and easily purchasable—jurisdictions. Eventually some members of these organizations would work in, manage, and hold points in Nevada's casino resorts—in many ways a natural progression.

Perhaps because of their popularity, many observers linked slot machines to both problem gambling and organized crime. Some even claimed

The integrated design of early casino resorts, though usually disguised by faux Wild West trappings, formed an ingenious system designed to keep patrons near the casino. The first casino on the Strip, the El Rancho Vegas, looks more like a suburban subdivision, with its sprawling bungalows, than "sin city." Courtesy UNLV Special Collections.

that all coin-operated machines were inherently corrupting. In 1948, Kings County, New York, district attorney Miles F. McDonald argued that pinball machines directly contributed to both juvenile delinquency and crime, a view that was, if not universal, certainly widely held, as New York's police commissioner Arthur W. Wallander and other law enforcement figures joined McDonald in blaming pinball machines for crime and delinquency. McDonald even promulgated a direct connection between pinball machines and Murder, Inc., the alleged underworld hit squad.[7] The anonymity of urban slots—the coins fed into them could end up anywhere, including in the pockets of known criminals—fueled public unease about this pastime.

Mayor Fiorello LaGuardia of New York City, facing a buffet of urban corruption, selected slot machines as the ultimate symbol of vice in the Big Apple. In the summer of 1934 he organized an all-out offensive against the pernicious devices. The mayor ordered slot machines removed from their establishments, loaded on a barge, and ultimately sent to sleep with the fishes. It is not standard procedure for a democratically elected official to reach out to constituents by attacking a popular pastime. Yet, a LaGuardia biographer suggests that it was the very popularity of slots that excited La-

Guardia's ire. Slots were, according to a LaGuardia biographer, "the more insidious because the public seemed ready to let itself be mulched by the unfavorable odds of these 'mechanical bandits.' They were placed in virtually every available retail outlet in working-class neighborhoods, often under the threat of property damage if rejected."[8] By smashing confiscated slot machines with a sledgehammer, the mayor could make a powerful statement against the "rackets" and bolster his reputation as a mayor who was graft-free and tough on crime.

Linking slot machines to the criminal underworld was no idiosyncrasy of LaGuardia. From their first appearance to the crest of the mid-century antigambling wave in the 1950s, reformers explicitly tied the two together, something that is hardly surprising given the fact that most gambling syndicates were typically involved with, or dominated by, other criminal syndicates. A 1949 *Collier's Magazine* exposé attributed over twenty deaths over a span of ten years to "slot machine wars." Slot machine operators and manufacturers, according to this article, used all their powers of gangland terror and police payoffs to continue their business. A Peoria locksmith who invented a device for opening slot cash boxes without a key was reported "promptly shot to death," and readers were warned ominously: "The police are often in too deep."[9]

Collier's further described those who played slot machines as having the "stoic calm of real addicts" and related horror stories of compulsive gamblers, such as the Oklahoma retiree whose obsession for slots drove him to wipe out his bank account, mortgage his house, and beg small change from former associates, or the Washington housewife who drained her family bank account. Readers learned the sad tale of a Montana woman who allegedly perished from "slot machinitis," a fatal infection brought on by an overworked right arm.[10] Some medical attempts to weigh in on the slot machine controversy bordered on, to contemporary audiences, the absurd. A sympathetic physician reported curing a Long Beach, California, woman of a slot machine addiction by "injections of glutamic acid" while a Chicago heart specialist declared the excitement of the gaming tables to be a leading cause of heart disease.[11] If these authors were to be believed, gambling was a tremendous social problem, requiring a complete ban.

Gambling, particularly slot machines, received more attention after World War II because of its apparently increased popularity. One source estimated that, in 1948, Americans put more than three billion dollars into over 200,000 machines nationwide.[12] Other forms of gambling, from illegal lotteries and sports betting to legal parimutuel horseracing, were also popular. In 1950, the *New York Times* estimated the amount spent on gambling, legal and illegal, to be $15 billion.[13] Clearly, Americans liked to gamble. But as gambling became increasingly impersonal, and as the cost to individuals became more apparent, the desire to stifle gambling grew. In the late 1940s, the idea of pathological or compulsive gambling gained currency, as is seen by the organization of Gamblers Anonymous by a "reformed gambler."[14]

Americans wrestled with the problems created by expanded urban gambling in less than effective ways. Voters chose to keep gambling illegal and to demand occasional police enforcement of antigambling statutes, but they also gambled. This fractured approach, brought to a head during Prohibition, was rapidly losing its charm as the nation, fresh from the struggle of World War II, endured the uncertainty of demobilization before embarking on the confusing journey of postwar economic prosperity and cold war anxiety. With the Great Depression looming none too distantly in the rear view mirror, it seemed prudent to wonder aloud whether the best solution to the problem of a "vice" like gambling might be to legalize and tax it, thereby diverting at least some of its loss to the public gain.

But there were obstacles to a coherent gambling policy. With organized crime groups apparently diversifying from gateway vices like prostitution, extortion, and labor-management racketeering to more hard-core societal ills like narcotics, dropping nickels into illegal slots became morally less defensible. Gadfly columnists, investigative reporters, and members of Congress fueled public debate about the existence of an organized national criminal conspiracy that wet its beak in all forms of crime and deviance. Gambling illegally became now less a question of lining the pockets of a neighborhood big man and more one of actively abetting a clandestine national criminal enterprise. The demand for gambling refused to die, and yet the existing system for satisfying that demand was becoming less and less attractive to the public.

In retrospect, the most rational policy might have been the federalization of gambling; that is, its legalization and regulation at the national level, which would have limited opportunities for local corruption and should have provided for a well-formulated, consistent development of gambling policy. However, such a policy was not articulated to any great degree due to the division of police power—and gambling law—in the United States among local, state, and federal authorities.[15] Although many Americans actively gambled, a similarly large percentage opposed the legalization of gambling for moral reasons. The midcentury anticrime, antigambling scare represents the crest of antigambling sentiment in the twentieth century. But still, gambling remained popular. As citizens, most Americans opposed the legalization of gambling. But as private men and women in search of a good time, many of them chose to gamble. To resolve the conflict between private desire and public good, these Americans would abandon the corner store slot machines that had come to define American gambling and, instead, would open themselves to a new concept—gambling as vacation entertainment—in the unlikeliest of places, the forbidding desert of Southern Nevada.

The Silver State's peculiar institution

Although casino-style gambling was illegal in the rest of the United States until the 1970s, Nevada stands out for having long reached an apparent rapprochement with gambling. For most of its history, Nevada has permitted legal gambling. The state had eked its way into the union because a Republican Congress, eager for another two senatorial votes in the coming debate on post–Civil War reconstruction, hastily authorized Nevada's statehood in 1864.[16] Because miners, not farmers or ranchers, dominated Nevada at that time, its laws reflected the political, economic, and cultural mores of a mining population—a group that, on the whole, favored gambling.

In Nevada, gambling, along with prostitution and drinking, was part of male frontier mining culture from the beginning. The mania for gambling manifested itself in card and dice games as well as "speculative fever" centered on stock certificates.[17] It would have been unusual indeed for the atomistic, transient, predominantly male miners to embrace "family values." As was the norm across the mining frontier, there was a noticeable lack of adequate law enforcement. In an area where the police authority was stretched to the limit in dealing with felonies against property and person, "victimless crimes" such as gambling were assigned low priority.

Before the organization of Nevada Territory, gambling was a legal, public activity that took place without shame or fear of prosecution. When the territorial legislature first met in 1861, however, it banned all gambling. The transplanted Easterners who comprised Nevada's first territorial government brought with them their notions of propriety, and it is no surprise that they sought to have them read into law as a step toward the normalization and Americanization, as well as Republicanization, of the Nevada Territory.

But the criminalization of gambling was difficult for Nevadans to digest, and in 1869 the legislature passed, over Governor Blasdel's veto, a law that legalized gambling and provided for the payment of license fees by gambling operators. Paradoxically, though, some proponents of the measure sought to discourage, rather then accept, gambling in their state. They viewed license fees as a legal mechanism to allow diligent marshals to prosecute gamblers for failure to pay.

Gambling flourished, although it continued to be a "backroom" industry hidden in the backs of bars and hotels, away from delicate women and impressionable minors. Control over gambling was remarkably lax; county officials, rather than state officers, collected the license fees, and the monies collected enriched county treasuries as well as state coffers. The only income that the state itself received under the first regime of legalized gambling resulted from a 1907 edict that taxed slot machines at the state level.[18]

As the nineteenth century progressed, the emphasis of Nevada's control ceased being more-or-less punitive in nature and took the first steps toward bona fide regulation. Amendments to gambling legislation set penalties for underage gambling and mandated which areas of a business might house gambling. These changes sought to maintain legal gambling while restricting it to the upstairs and backrooms of drinking establishments and hotels. After the Comstock Lode waned in the 1870s, a statewide depression gripped Nevada. This depression lasted until the early years of the twentieth century. Counties and the state together scrambled in this period to extract additional revenue from the state's remaining inhabitants, and gambling taxes were one way of doing this.

With the discovery of new sources of gold, silver, and other metals around 1900, the state's economic picture brightened considerably. It is probably not coincidental that during the Progressive era, a women's Civic League and an Anti-Gambling League sought to ban gambling. In 1909, the state legislature passed a law making gambling a felony, hoping that the draconian fines enacted would drive gamblers out of Nevada. A purely economic interpretation might read that, with plenty of money coming in from new mineral strikes, the citizens of Nevada no longer felt the need for the "dirty money" of gambling taxes to fund their schools, hospitals, and police agencies.

The restriction of gambling, however, proved entirely ineffective, and pragmatic legislators began almost immediately to roll back the complete ban on gambling. In 1915, the law was amended to allow games played for drinks, cigars, or sums under $2, as well as nickel slot machines. Higher stakes games remained technically illegal. In this ambiguous atmosphere, illegal and unlicensed casinos flourished, and Nevadans presumably got the worst of both worlds: a thriving gambling subculture that contributed nothing to the state and, indeed, actively corrupted local law enforcement officers.

Still, Nevadans seemed content with the status quo until the Great Depression's choke on the economy convinced citizens that gambling prohibition, like the nation's experiment in obligatory temperance, had clearly failed. Gambling opponents had handily defeated bills to liberalize the gaming laws in the 1925 and 1927 Nevada legislature, and pro-gamblers did not even introduce a bill in the 1929 session.[19] But by 1931, Nevada's economic situation was so grim that a bill to legalize "wide-open" gambling passed over the objections of nongamblers, and it was signed into law by Governor Fred Balzar on March 19, 1931. According to Nevada historian Eric N. Moody, who has given the 1931 gambling bill its most thorough study, the gambling law passed because "certain business interests" (those who stood to profit from gambling and tourism) were able to secure "strong support . . . in influential financial and political quarters," and because of the fiscal exigencies of the Great Depression.[20]

One might look at one of the staunchest proponents of "wide-open" gambling and see a true visionary. Thomas N. Carroll, a Las Vegas real estate developer, purchased newspaper advertisements in late 1930, arguing strenuously for the bill in language that, today, seems prophetic. Carroll proposed making Nevada the "Playground of the United States" by legalizing gambling and encouraging horse racing. These activities, combined with the "scenic outdoor attractions" of the state, would draw wealthy tourists to Nevada. Carroll pleaded for Nevadans to permit legal gambling, which he claimed would form the underpinning of an industry that would bring "millions" into the state.[21]

This is precisely what happened in the early 1950s, thanks to Strip casino resorts. But in 1931 the notion of gambling as the state's primary industry was considered fanciful. Indeed, gambling was only one strategy Nevada used to lure tourists and economic development in this period. Before the 1960s and the general easing of family law throughout the United States, the state's relatively liberal marriage, divorce, and adoption laws were also great attractions (a six-week divorce bill having also been passed in 1931). Gambling was just another pragmatic attempt to lure tourism and investment, such as earlier prize-fighting and later right-to-work laws. It would be a mistake to consider the 1931 gambling enactment a decisive stroke that destined the casino industry in the state for greatness. Rather, the operators who built the casinos of the Strip intrepidly took advantage of "wide-open" gambling and local boosters who facilitated development of tourism.

Above all, it is clear that though some Southern Nevadans actively worked for gambling legalization and other pro-tourism measures, business interests in the north of the state dominated the state legislature and helped to pass the bill because they thought it would help Reno. Indeed, the relaxed gambling and family laws initially boosted Reno's star. In the late 1930s, Reno billed itself as America's divorce capital and actively courted divorcés and divorcées to live (and spend) there for the six weeks residency required for a "quickie" Nevada divorce. Legislators and business leaders who favored the legalization of gambling surely assumed that Reno, the state's largest city, would reap the windfall of increased tourism. But for a variety of reasons, Reno gambling would remain in a holding pattern, chugging along profitably but not spectacularly, and would soon surrender its ascendancy to spectacular new resorts outside a little-known southern town.

The unlikely oasis

Before it hosted casino resorts and became the world's gaming and entertainment capital, Las Vegas was chiefly a place where travelers stopped on their way to somewhere else. It derived its name, Spanish for "the meadows," from the oasis that a group of springs created at the site, which became a welcome stopping-point for trade caravans.[22] Failing as a Mormon outpost and modestly successful as a ranch, the area that is now the Las Vegas Valley was somnolent until the turn of the twentieth century, when the extension of the national railroad network created both opportunity and exploitation in Southern Nevada. Although the first major wave of national railroad building and consolidation had bypassed the area, by the turn of the century booming Los Angeles demanded a direct rail line. William Clark, mining magnate and senator from Montana, created the San Pedro, Los Angeles, and Salt Lake Railroad to fill that need. Although a court battle with the rival Oregon Short Line forestalled development of the line, work began on the railroad after a 1902 legal settlement.

The town of Las Vegas began life with a land auction on May 15, 1905. In 1909 residents succeeded in bisecting the southern portion of Lincoln County to create Clark County, named after the railroad baron. Las Vegas became the new county's seat of government. In the same year, the SP, LA, and SL Railroad built maintenance and machine shops in the town. The construction of schools, churches, hotels, and commercial enterprises signaled the town's permanence. It was dusty and lacked air conditioning, but it functioned as the economic, political, and cultural hub of Clark County. Outside of the business brought to town with the railroad, Las Vegas remained devoid of true industrial development.

The town remained an obscure railroad stopover until the construction of the Hoover Dam on the Colorado River. From the summer of 1930 until President Franklin D. Roosevelt officially dedicated the dam on September 30, 1935, a torrent of construction workers and curiosity seekers transformed Las Vegas into a desert boomtown. The contract for the dam's construction was awarded to Six Companies, Inc., an entity formed by the merger of six prominent western construction and engineering companies.[23] During the dam's construction, workers frequently visited Las Vegas, filling the town's "bars, gambling halls, and fleshpots." The project boosted Las Vegas's economy, and the town doubled in size to 10,000 by 1934.[24]

Once completed, the dam provided Southern Nevada with Lake Mead, a 115-mile long artificial lake, flood control for the Colorado River Valley, and a prime tourist attraction. Contrary to popular belief, the cheap electricity produced by the dam's hydroelectric generators does not power Las Vegas; due to the town's negligible development when the dam compact

Casino resorts promised their patrons relaxing vacations in settings far removed from the grind of furtive illegal casinos or downtown Las Vegas's rough-hewn gambling halls. This Dunes publicity photo, circa 1956, is from a series called "Water Wake-up," in which the guest slid from his room (via the slide visible in the upper left) into the pool, where he received coffee, breakfast, and a morning paper—all the accoutrements of a respectable middle-class morning routine. Courtesy UNLV Special Collections.

was signed, Las Vegas was allotted a pittance of electricity in the agreement. The dam's biggest impact came from the impetus it gave to the town's nascent hospitality industry, as tourists stopped in the town on the way to seeing this modern-day wonder.

By the 1930s, Las Vegas was a regional commercial and political center. Already, the twin engines of the city's economy in the postwar period, gaming-related tourism and federal spending, were in evidence, albeit on a minor scale. The influx of visitors to the dam and workers at other federal projects demanded a more vibrant nightlife. Gambling hall owners began to dress up their unpretentious venues while civic leaders hoped that someone would build a "luxury" hotel.

All of the ingredients needed for a tourist economy were present in Las Vegas as early as this time—a unique local attraction in the Hoover Dam, a salubrious climate (for most of the year, at least), and bountiful gambling along Fremont Street. But the town had no real identity—some citizens had seriously toyed with the idea of renaming it "Hoover City" to greater enhance its cultural proximity to the dam. There was little entertainment to speak of in the city's clubs and scant reason to visit outside of the gambling and the dam. Though it was still the closest legal gambling spot to Los Angeles, Las Vegas played second fiddle to Reno until the early 1950s—nearly twenty years after the town became nationally prominent. As late as that time, it was still confused at times with Las Vegas, New Mexico. Still, the region south of this city would produce a powerful alchemy, one that created a new gambling institution and almost let vacationers forget that gambling was a vice.

Craps for the crabgrass frontiersmen (and women)

Vacationers would gladly travel to casinos nowhere near anything because, as the century reached its midpoint, gambling in the big cities was drying up. Those Americans who gambled once did so as part of a larger assortment of urban nightlife—bars, hotels, and restaurants. But the spread of gambling throughout the city, both spatially and culturally through the slot machine, upset the applecart, transforming city gambling from an exclusive diversion to mass entertainment. In other nations, the problem of how to reserve gambling for those who, in the eyes of policymakers, could afford it required a solution based frankly on social class: casinos were explicitly reserved for "gentlemen," whose stringent rules and costly membership fees kept the less well-off punter at his local bookie and away from high-stakes gambling.

An American solution could not be so frankly based on wealth and class; if gambling was a right claimed by the rich, they should hold no monopoly on it. Instead, gambling followed the same rules that were changing how and where Americans lived: it became a suburban activity. This is not to say that, when planning subdivisions, planners outside of major American cities began to include casinos in their developments; the process was far more subtle. Instead, in a stumbling, haphazard way, Americans realized a solution that would hold for a generation, namely, the isolation of gambling spatially and culturally in ways that would implicitly reserve it for those who could afford it.

The process was haphazard because there was no grand design, public debate, or legislative action that mandated it. Rather, the solution to the mid-century "gambling problem" was the end result of two seemingly antithetical, but actually intertwined, actions: the crumbling of local urban gambling, which was the direct result of public fervor against "boss gamblers" and rampant gambling in the cities, and the growth of casino resorts as vacation destinations that offered gambling. While urging local officials to curtail semilegal gambling in their own cities, Americans who could afford vacations to the Strip, predominantly upper- and middle-class Americans (who were predominantly suburbanites), gave the casino resorts of the Strip the ultimate vote of approval—they spent money there.

The new resorts created outside of Las Vegas worked because they fused public and private space in telling ways. As originally built, their public space (inhabited, not owned, by the public) took the form of the central casino/restaurant/lounge building, the swimming pool and its environs, and possibly a golf course. The guest rooms, housed in drive-up low-rise motel wings and cottages, obviously enfolded private space. Following Sharon Zukin's model, these resorts served the functions of earlier middle-class urban institutions such as tea rooms, restaurants, department stores, and hotels in "expanding once exclusive means of market consumption to a broader public."[25] But although casino resorts expanded the privilege of spa-like vacation pleasure to the "masses," they also served to restrict casino-style gambling to those who could afford to visit them.

The geographic and cultural setting of this innovation on the Las Vegas Strip is of far greater significance than is usually imagined. In a sense, an in-depth look at exactly how the casino resort was created stands traditional thinking about the historical role of that institution in Nevada's development on its head. Whereas Eugene Moehring[26] and other historians posit that the casino resort created Las Vegas, it is equally true (and far more important in the national perspective) that Las Vegas created the casino resort. The largest determinant for the success of Strip casinos never really was who controlled the action, or what kind of regulation it was subject to, but rather *where* the casinos were and to *whom* they catered. Suburban Americans fundamentally wanted to gamble in suburban resorts, and the new casinos of the Strip fit this need.

Looking at other features of American life that became prevalent in the same period, one can see certain similarities between casino resorts and suburban shopping malls. Both are places of both collective and individual consumption. Zukin's description of shopping malls as loci of "the collective rites of hunting and gathering, but also sites of personal desire," is also completely true of casino resorts. One shared in the group delights of an afternoon by the swimming pool and thrilled with others to Joe E. Lewis or Danny Thomas in the theater restaurant before stepping up to the gaming tables. Like Zukin's shopping centers, casino resorts fuse the material and the symbolic by giving "material form to a symbolic landscape of consumption."[27] Casino resorts did this in more vividly jarring ways than did shopping centers. At the resorts one could observe the public profligacy of others, or flaunt one's own consumption, at much higher stakes. That middle-class Americans overwhelming rejected the idea of urban gambling halls, and, instead, confined gambling to the landscapes of pleasure found within the suburban space of the new resorts in Southern Nevada, is entirely in conformity with other trends in suburban commercial culture.

The essential sub-urbanity of casino resorts is even more obvious in comparison with other suburban developments, both residential and commercial. Herbert Gans's landmark study *The Levittowners* revealed a community of men and women who, for the most part, lived happily in a prefabricated community; these suburbanites also enjoyed visiting the casino resorts of the Las Vegas Strip, which were "instant resorts" that sprouted from the desert almost overnight, much like suburban developments in the erstwhile fruit orchards of New Jersey, Illinois, or California. Thrown together in unfamiliar surroundings and unconstrained by tradition, vacationers could enjoy a social surrounding both similar to and different from those at home. Gans's description of Levittown's social structure as "open, universalistic, and achievement-oriented" fits the ephemeral social life of Strip vacationers aptly. Assuming their fellow vacationers to be members of the broad American middle class who could pass the admissions bar, vacationers judged their fellows on "what they did, not what they were."[28] Gambling with verve and proving oneself a "sport" by graciously winning or losing was more important then whether one was a bank officer from Evansville or a sales manager from Dallas.

Although on the surface they appeared to be progressive, forward-looking institutions, casino resorts, like other suburban developments, frequently served as bulwarks of privilege for the middle class. For some, de facto exclusion was obvious: the casino resorts of the Strip, until 1960, officially barred African Americans from enjoying their facilities. When outsiders raised the issue, operators would usually disavow any personal support for segregation and claim to be merely following (white) public opinion. In that year (not coincidentally the same year that New Jersey's Levittown began to integrate), casino operators on the Strip chose to integrate their facilities; however, much like the pattern in other suburban developments, casino resorts still retained a fairly exclusive clientele, thanks to the filter of geographic distance. In race, as in other areas, the evolution of the casino resort mirrored developments in suburban America.

That the first casino resorts catered almost exclusively to guests from Southern California was no idiosyncrasy. Southern Nevada was indebted to its prosperous western neighbor for, among other things, the human capital of Los Angeles gaming operators, investment capital, and a ready market of tourists. The location of the new gambling ventures on lonely Highway 91, also known as the Los Angeles Highway, outside the city limits was doubly significant. It signaled a practical desire to eschew potentially costly municipal taxes and meddlesome or venal city officials as well as a hunger for space and independence that echoed throughout the nation as large sections of the country became suburban.

As America became suburban, urban entertainments became scarce. In *Fantasy City*, John Hannigan telescoped Anthony Downs's forty theories of urban decline into three explanations for the decline of urban entertainments from the 1950s to the 1970s: demographic and lifestyle changes, competition/substitution, and disamenity/avoidance. The first explanation, demographic change, is simple to understand: more Americans lived in the suburbs, and they chose to spend their leisure time away from cities. The second explanation, competition/substitution, affirms that suburbanites began to frequent nonurban entertainment venues, from suburban drive-ins to destination theme parks such as Disneyland, instead of patronizing downtown movie theaters and amusements. The third explanation, disamenity/avoidance, is perhaps the most germane to the question of urban gambling's decline: suburbanites avoided the city out of fear.[29]

Suburbanites strangled urban gambling out of a dual fear. First, their general avoidance of downtown negated any possibility for development of urban gambling halls catering to the well-off. Second, they sought to prevent those who remained in the cities from gambling from fear that runaway urban gambling would lead to increased crime, decreased productivity, and rampant political and police corruption. Because of this double-edged panic, the cities of America became inhospitable for casino-style gambling. While illegal numbers games and sports betting could flourish, casinos, which required a relatively well-off clientele with an evening of leisure to spare, were doomed to extinction, at least within the confines of traditional downtowns. Unlike movie theaters and department stores, however, gambling did not, for the most part, make the jump to the suburbs. It was still tied too closely to political malfeasance and public disorder. Denied a place in the cities and the suburbs, casino-style gambling could flourish only in a place where it could be accessed by suburbanites and not the teeming masses of the cities.

The distant isolation of casinos on the Strip, which early promoters probably considered their greatest drawback, was paradoxically its salvation. Because the "wide-open" action of the Strip was located at a safe distance from the teeming masses of urban America, there was no great outcry over it. Few do-gooders complained about Strip casinos' impact on public morality or individual finances. The public knew that whoever came to Las Vegas resorts to gamble had the means and inclination to travel a great distance to satisfy their desire to wager, and, if they lost money, it was no one's fault but their own. Thus, from the start the casino resort was an institution that stood in sharp contrast to urban gambling.

The keynote of the campaign against urban slots, a desire to protect penny-ante gamblers from their own spendthrift plunging reminiscent of the Progressive tradition, could hardly be sounded in defense of jet-setting vacationers. Las Vegas gamblers were almost always middle-class Americans out for fun. Noel Coward, after making his American nightclub debut at the Desert Inn in 1955, remarked that visitors to Las Vegas were, "the most ordinary people out to enjoy the amenities of the last word in luxurious holidaymaking." He characterized the patrons as, "Mr. and Mrs. Everyman, Mr. and Mrs. America."[30]

This was a startling reversal of the earlier public discourse on gambling. The opponents of casino resorts, not their devotees, were the deviants. Most middle-class suburbanites remained forthrightly opposed to the expansion of gambling, illegal or legal, near their homes, but they now welcomed the possibility of escape to the "luxurious holidaymaking" that casino resorts afforded them. They could both indulge the urge to gamble and feel good about suppressing gambling in the cities. In so doing, they forged a containment of gambling that kept it confined to the suburban holiday resorts of the Strip while barring it from the nation's major metropolitan areas. By default, the state of Nevada had solved the national debate over gambling policy. Gamblers would no longer contribute to urban corruption and gambling; rather, those with the means to travel to the desert could now be parted from their money in sunny, state-regulated casinos. The shame of the cities would become a paradise for suburbanites.

CHAPTER 2

The Unwholesome Allure
Far from urban America, gambling casino resorts make gambling safe for some

Other years saw other near ventures, but never did Las Vegas see a completed resort hotel until 1940 when hotel man Tom Hull and a friend were driving from Las Vegas down the now-paved Highway 91 towards Los Angeles. On the edge of city limits, Mr. Hull had a flat tire, and while his friend hitchhiked back into town for help, Mr. Hull stood on the highway and counted the cars. An hour of this and he became convinced that the mesquite and sage-stippled fright of a desert behind him was a mighty wholesome spot for a luxury hotel.
Las Vegas travel guide, 1955

The Strip is basically unwholesome. . . . Remember, however, that what you see meets with the approval of the sovereign people of Nevada, and that some millions of visitors drop in each year without coaxing to try their luck. The long and short of it is that the Strip exists because most of us like to gamble. . . . Try to look upon the place simply as a phenomenon.
Harper's Magazine, 1955

The apocrypha about the birth of the Strip in the travel guide plays on one of the most common tropes of casino legend, stumbling into success.[1] Civic boosters sang breathless chansons of casino owners who fell into the Southern Nevada casino industry by accident, building a casino on a whim before being overwhelmed by the profits. These operators were depicted as lucky travelers who, entirely extemporaneously, had gambled big and won. Hopeful tourists, boosters imagined, would consider the lessons of the

Strip's heroes and come to town for their own stab at glory, hopefully leaving behind some gambling losses. But, as a well-worn aphorism states, luck is the residue of design, and to ascribe the creation of the Strip and the casino resort to happy fortune is disingenuous. The second quote reveals the larger regional and national patterns that gave the Strip life: Americans wanted to gamble without bringing "unwholesomeness" into their own cities, so they gladly experienced the "phenomenon" of the Strip's casino resorts.

These resorts were no phenomena of nature, but had in fact been carefully designed by very human hands. The first resorts, built during and immediately after World War II, effectively wove together the quilt of gambling, dining, and entertainment that remained the pattern for casinos into the next century. By the end of the 1940s, each of the first three casino resorts produced sufficient innovations to establish the casino resort as a proven institution. Casino resorts—the El Rancho Vegas's inward-looking design, the Hotel Last Frontier's emphasis on the total vacation experience, and the Flamingo's elevation of all-star entertainment—would create a powerful allure, one that would ease the acceptance of a new gambling form in a nation officially opposed to gambling's expansion.

"Stop at the sign of the windmill"

In the early 1940s, Las Vegas appeared to be a minor resort town hungry for further commercial development. Though not completely insulated from the Great Depression, the city enjoyed the boon of the Hoover Dam and, consequently, it did not suffer as badly as other regions of the state, particularly Reno, during the lean years of the 1930s. Furthermore, Las Vegas benefited from the explosive growth of Los Angeles; as Southern California increased in population and wealth, Las Vegas's tourist base grew. The city had vague possibilities as a hospitality center, but it needed attractions that appealed to the new breed of suburbanites who drove the freeways and peopled the subdivisions of Los Angeles.

Befitting their proximity to Los Angeles, the new resorts in Las Vegas spiraled in a suburban direction; they were not centered on the town's downtown but on its major southern artery, Highway 91. This roadway segued into Fifth Street to the north and meandered south about 300 miles across the Mojave to Southern California, thus its alternate designation as the Los Angeles Highway. There had been minimal development on Highway 91 before the early 1940s, but for a town priming itself as a tourist destination for Southern Californians, it seemed too good a stretch of land to leave unexploited.

On April 3, 1941, Thomas Hull opened the El Rancho Vegas just south of the city limits (then San Francisco Avenue, later rechristened Sahara Avenue) on Highway 91. Thomas Everett Hull had operated El Rancho chain motels in most of the major urban centers of California, including San Francisco, Fresno, Sacramento, and Los Angeles, before setting his sights on Las Vegas. Hull decided to open a franchise in Las Vegas after consulting a number of local business leaders.[2] It is inconceivable that Hull could have had anything but the Los Angeles trade on his mind when he planned his resort on the highway to Los Angeles.

Hull built his resort complex in a frontier/Spanish mission style, and its conception and execution owed a debt to the "Hollywood back-lot" school of design; the casino's structures were built primarily for impressive show rather than efficient function. The casino, in which patrons gambled at craps, black-jack, roulette, and slot machines, exuded an old Western ambience, replete with archaic firearms and cowboy hats. In this, it was unremarkable; almost all existing Nevada gambling halls, as "authentic" Western places, toed the line of wild Western décor. The casino wasn't the largest in Nevada, or even in Las Vegas, and its accommodations, although more extravagant than the sprin-kling of motor courts to be found near Fremont Street, were relatively unpre-tentious. Yet the El Rancho Vegas was groundbreaking for two reasons—its location on the Los Angeles Highway, outside of town, and its structure.

The physical structure of the El Rancho Vegas set the rough pattern for Strip casino resorts until the high-rise era, with a central structure housing the casino, restaurants, and theater surrounded by motel wings. The motel portion consisted of sixty-five bungalow-style rooms in a number of inde-pendent structures. The resort recalled a suburban subdivision rather than existing urban gambling milieus. Each "cottage" was directly accessible to automobiles via paved and lighted streets. Although the complex boasted public restaurants and recreation facilities, the presence of private lawns, porches, and kitchens in the El Rancho Vegas's vacation "cottages" suggests the private space of the suburbs.[3] Considering the high proportion of "ex-tended-stay" guests at the El Rancho Vegas (including but not limited to divorcees living their six weeks at the resort to establish Nevada residency), the blurring of vacation resort and quasi-domestic space is not surprising. As resorts became larger, the "residential density" of hotel rooms in-creased; the barracks-like motel wings of the Stardust, the last Strip resort built on the El Rancho Vegas paradigm, have a cookie-cutter impersonality far removed from the El Rancho Vegas's winding lanes and isolated bunga-lows. But the original purpose of the El Rancho Vegas remained—to allow guests to escape from the rigors of suburban life by relaxing in a facsimile of it.

Hull's resort featured a prescient focus on creating a uniformly tranquil vacation experience for his guests. Its managers touted customer service as its premium attraction. According to Guy Landis, an El Rancho Vegas em-ployee, the casino pioneered the idea that "all of a guest's needs could be found on the [property's] premises."[4] Among the services that the El Rancho featured were a travel agency, retail shops, and nightclub-style entertainment, as well as a steakhouse, swimming pool, and spacious lawns.[5] Employees were instructed to make guests "feel both welcome and excited about visiting the El Rancho Vegas." Rather than keeping an eagle eye on the bottom line, this was their "most important task,"[6] and it marked an important development for a hospitality industry that had no tangible services or products. It was the overall vacation experience, rather than simply winning or losing at the tables, that the El Rancho Vegas and later resorts stressed and delivered. This was a significant point for an industry that is statistically dependent on sending most of its patrons home unsatisfied, if not unhappy.

In its earliest years, the El Rancho Vegas was successful at keeping its patrons happy. Cocktail waitress Goldie Spicer described the large numbers of patrons drawn from the nearby Basic Magnesium Plant. Wartime federal projects in the area, such as the airfield north of Las Vegas, also kept the motel reasonably filled.[7] A modest regional advertising campaign, which would become national in the 1950s, encouraged visitors to "stop at the sign of the windmill." This is instructive, because it accurately imagined road-weary travelers happening upon the El Rancho Vegas, a full two miles out of town, and stopping. Nothing says more about the resort's promotion or its appeal.

The resort's casual Western decor seems to reflect less a deliberate marketing scheme than a lack of imagination. Though Hull's El Rancho Vegas hardly catered to the boots and jeans crowd, his resort's casino looked much like the Nevada gaming halls that did. In retrospect, it is clear that Hull, the first real builder on the Strip, crossed into a new frontier of design with dated ideas of what a gambling space should be. The El Rancho Vegas was definitely not a "gambling hall" like those of downtown Reno or Las Vegas; neither was it exactly a dude ranch nor a motor court. It was a combination of all these things, plus a dinner theater and nightclub.

If its theming and conception borrowed from the existing vocabulary of Nevada gaming, the El Rancho Vegas's self-contained, insular nature fixes it as the first suburban casino resort. The hotel was never promoted as having the best service in Las Vegas; it was merely assumed that guests, with their needs already met, would never even think to enter the city. The El Rancho Vegas marks the dawn of the suburban casino resort both because it was physically aloof from its surrounding cityscape and because it catered to middle-class suburbanites on vacation rather than workaday city dwellers. In a quadrant of the nation in which the automobile was the preeminent factor in residential and commercial development, and in an age when urban gambling came under increasing fire, this was a logical and natural adaptation. Significantly, a renovation of the late 1940s hardened the boundary between the El Rancho Vegas and its surroundings by replacing the corral fence that had originally circumscribed the property with a solid wall. Perhaps this constituted an unconscious reflection of the El Rancho Vegas's shift in identity from desert frontier outpost to suburban neighbor.

Some have wondered about the significance of Hull's decision to build his resort on the Los Angeles Highway. Would the Strip have become the Strip anywhere else? This question is partially answered by previous experiments in gambling entertainment around Las Vegas. In the 1930s, the Boulder Highway featured a few prominent nightspot/gambling dens, but the thoroughfare to the Hoover Dam was soon eclipsed by the Los Angeles Highway, primarily because the Strip developments incorporated hotel accommodations and therefore had captive audiences that isolated nightspots lacked. The Boulder Strip, as it was in the 1930s, may have had something of a low-rent stigma, given that most of the clubs catered to rough-and-tumble Hoover Dam workers, eager to let off some steam before returning to their hard labor.[8] Even if Hull had built his integrated resort on the Boulder Highway, it seems inevitable that some enterprising operators would have tried to scoop up the Angeleno trade by building along the more accessible Highway 91. So it is Hull's concept, coupled with its location, that marks the true birth of "the Strip" and the casino resort.

Drive-through gambling for a suburban nation

While Hull was unsuccessful as an absentee owner (he sold the property in the mid-1940s), his idea was, of course, a winner. As an institution, it arrived at just the right time; promoters would experiment with the casino resort until, in the early 1950s, they reduced the essentials of casino resort design to a formula, just in time to capture the tourist dollars of millions of Americans suddenly hungry for a casino vacation. In the years following World War II, middle-class Americans increasingly lived in suburbs. Casino resorts on the Strip provided a needed counterbalance to the staid mores of most bedroom suburbs. They served as the hedonistic antipodes to the nation's safe but unadventurous domestic bulwark against communist aggressors, creeping socialism, and cosmopolitan limousine liberals. Elaine Tyler May argues convincingly in *Homeward Bound* that the suburbs offered a security against outside aggression, a form of domestic containment. The ideal home "would fulfill all its members' personal needs through an energized and expressive personal life."[9] Yet, however nice a home entertainment center the average middle class family might own, it could not possibly supply every adult entertainment need. The casino resort served as a variant of the consumerism in which many suburban

Americans found their purpose in these years. Within the contained extravagance of the El Rancho Vegas and other casino resorts, suburbanites could indulge themselves in ways that could only be imagined in their homes.

Building away from the small but developing urban center of Fremont Street, which the El Rancho Vegas signaled, was entirely in keeping with larger trends in American metropolitan growth. After World War II, suburbs increased in population and political importance at the expense of the central cities, particularly in the "new cities" of the Sunbelt west. This is chiefly attributable to two factors: these cities came to maturity in the automobile age and developed as sprawling metropolises, and these cities lacked powerful downtown elites to champion an inner-city business district.[10]

In Las Vegas, casino resorts rather than industrial or residential movers led the way toward growth, something that is entirely understandable, given the city's surfeit of industrial development and, in the years before air conditioning, lack of promise as a great residential center. The profit-making motivations of Tommy Hull and those who followed him on the Strip are not unique to the Mojave. They can be subsumed under Mark Gottdiener's explanation of suburbanization as "a long, protracted story of bold quests to acquire wealth through the development of fringe area land and individual or group pursuits of a residential vision that would solve the problems of city living."[11] The description is apt for casinos if one substitutes a "commercial" vision for the residential one, as the resorts were of course commercial and not residential enterprises. The builders of Strip resorts acted from the same motivation as suburban developers around the nation, namely, to get rich. They did so in ways that mirrored the ongoing process of suburbanization, which, even as casino resorts began rising, was changing how Americans lived.

The supply side half of this argument is obvious: casino owners built on the Strip because by doing so they could eschew the payment of city taxes, take advantage of cheaper land prices, and keep their patrons near their casinos and out of rival operations. The demand side is less immediately clear but equally compelling. The actual suburban location of casino resorts emphasized their role as self-contained hedonistic zones. By indulging here, and not at home, suburbanites could keep their home communities free from "vice" and thus better places for family living. In the late 1940s and early 1950s, when the tenor of the national debate about urban gambling became increasingly strident, this made the resorts of the Strip not only tolerable but actually desirable for many Americans. As *Harper's* reminded its readers, "millions of visitors drop in each year without coaxing to try their luck . . . the Strip exists because most of us like to gamble."[12] The resorts of the Strip were acceptable to the broad center of American society precisely because they allowed middle-class suburbanites (and of course those who were even wealthier) to indulge a yen for gambling without imperiling their homes or travel to potentially dangerous inner-city gambling spots in their own hometowns.

Even as they were emerging outside of Las Vegas, casino resorts reflected a key trait of what John Hannigan identifies as "Fantasy City": solipsism, by which he means "isolated from surrounding neighborhoods physically, economically, and culturally."[13] Hannigan has examined later developments, such as Urban Enterprise Districts and casino resorts in Atlantic City, and he has concluded that this solipsism served chiefly to ignore social and economic problems already in large cities. However, casino resorts did not initially evolve as inward-looking places where the intent was to snub their neighbors. Rather, it was because their operators wanted to keep their visitors as close to the tables as possible. One might also argue that casino resorts evolved as self-contained entities on the Strip because operators, public officials, and patrons wished to contain the perceived social toxin of gambling within isolated resorts. Again, if one wants to make an extreme metaphor, casino resorts were not fortresses against unfriendly urban locales but rather quarantine wards, which kept gambling far from the vulnerable urban cores of American cities.

One of the more interesting questions bedeviling the history of the casino resort is why it originated in underdeveloped Las Vegas and not Reno, then the preeminent city in Nevada in population and political importance. Already well known as "The Biggest Little City in the World," Reno was the nation's acknowledged divorce capital in the 1930s and a thriving gambling center in the 1940s. Its agglomeration of gambling operators could have provided the human capital for a gambling boom, and the natural beauty of nearby Lake Tahoe provided an additional tourist attraction. Why did Las Vegas and not Reno witness the birth of the casino resort and become the nation's undisputed casino capital?

As noted, Las Vegas's proximity to Los Angeles accounted for much of its popularity, but the suburban nature of the casino resort as it developed on the Strip is also responsible for vaulting Southern Nevada's gaming industry ahead of that of the north. In Reno, gambling was confined to a five-block downtown area. Most of the casinos had no attached hotel. The containment of casinos within this red-lined zone was originally de facto, but by the 1950s it became calcified into law. This arrangement satisfied several groups. Downtown businesspeople adjacent to the red-lined district felt secure from the rising rents and speculation that would accompany an expansion of the casino zone. Renoites who opposed gambling were secure in the vice's physical separation from the rest of the city. Finally, established gambling operators enjoyed a near monopoly on the gambling trade; with a limited number of casinos, not even the most enterprising outsider could hope to compete against existing casinos.[14]

Thus, a prospective casino operator could choose between Reno, where he would have to buy out an existing owner and squeeze into an already overcrowded market, or Las Vegas, where land on the Strip was plentiful and the existing business culture welcomed outsiders with money into town. The rational choice was obvious. The mainstream business and gambling elites of Reno discouraged new development, whereas those of Las Vegas welcomed it. By allowing casino operators to build their own self-contained resort suburbs, rather than forcing them into an urban gambling district, Las Vegas's promoters actually aided the growth of the city and the region.

Even outsiders picked up on the differences between the two gambling havens and unconsciously revealed why the Strip casino resort became the favored paradigm for legal casino gaming. Ernest Havemann, in a 1954 article for _Life_, painted a vividly horrid picture of Harolds Club, then Reno's largest and most famous casino:

> Harolds is strictly assembly-line gaming. . . . There's nothing fancy about Harolds. Indeed Harolds is as garish and nakedly ugly as an unshaded light bulb hanging from the ceiling in a flophouse dormitory. There wasn't even a comforting drink to be bought at Harolds until the management was finally forced to relinquish some of the precious gambling space to keep up with the competitors—and even now only a small proportion of Harolds' single-minded patrons waste any time hanging around the bars. . . . There is still no lunch counter, much less a restaurant.[15]

This kind of hard-sell focus on gambling was anathema on the Strip, where early resorts relied more on the implicit promise of gambling than the explicit promotion of it. Most early Strip resorts didn't even use the word "casino" or "club" in their name, preferring the more elegant sounding "hotel," which on the Strip was a code word for a casino resort. Loath to mention their gambling, they preferred instead to wax poetic in their advertising copy about the pools, dining, and "excitement" of a Strip vacation.

It is easy to see why casino resorts were so much more attractive to vacationers than Reno gambling halls. In Strip casino resorts, vacationers tried their luck in between jaunts to "their" resort's yacht on Lake Mead, the swimming pool, and the dinner theater. In their suburban setting, casino resorts offered a complete vacation experience that Reno gambling halls, no matter how astute their owners or how beneficial their pay-outs, could not. The soft-sell approach of casino resorts made patrons feel it was almost their responsibility to "be a sport" and gamble a little—after all, it was the least they could do for the resort that had given them such a superlative vacation value. Of course, they more often than not dropped more at the tables than their entertainment, food, and lodging would have cost, but they felt good about it. Casino resorts on the Strip could give their suburban patrons gambling without guilt, something that no-frills gambling halls could not do.

The idiosyncratic geographic location of Strip casino resorts accounts for their relative invisibility in historical scholarship on national suburban trends. Because until 1978 they could be found only in two metropolitan regions within a sparsely populated state, casino resorts usually struck scholars as aparadigmatic, extravagant glitter palaces with little relevance or connection to the rest of American postwar society. But if casino resorts are seen as a variant of the shopping center, they fit perfectly into the suburban history defined by Kenneth Jackson, that is, they provided a collection of services in a single-stop, drive-in location.[16] Casino resorts actually leapfrogged the development of shopping centers. Jackson traces the evolution of local, then regional, and ultimately national megamalls; casino resorts, from the start, catered to a fly-in as well as a drive-in clientele.

Casino resorts did not flourish in complete isolation amid the sagebrush. The free-standing pleasure palaces off the highway were soon surrounded by a connective tissue of motels, gas stations, bars, and restaurants. However, the social space of these diverse institutions paralleled suburban commercial strips rather than traditional urban space. Certainly by 1950, Highway 91 possessed all of the landmarks of a typical commercial strip as enumerated by strip scholar Richard Horwitz. These included a roadway, copious signage, ample parking, and a standardized architecture enclosing "a massive, low space within rectangular walls and a flat roof," architecture whose utility is belied by the application of superfluous decorative flourishes—Venturi, Izenour, and Scott Brown's famed "decorated shed."[17] The casino resort led to the creation of a new suburban space that became the most famous apotheosis of a national phenomenon, namely, the commercial strip.

Early resort operators were often more involved in real estate than gambling. The Desert Inn complex, for example, also included the Desert Inn Golf Course and Desert Inn Estates. Students of suburbanization are familiar with the pattern of speculation, subdivision, and development that spawned both the golf course and the Estates, high-priced housing adjacent to the golf course. To coordinate their real estate developments, Moe Dalitz and his associates formed the Paradise Development Company, which developed middle- and high-income properties, professional commercial space, and retail centers. Having built one suburban entity, a casino resort, the syndicate easily moved into more mainstream suburban development.

The Desert Inn is an extreme example (it not only looked like a subdivision; it *was* a subdivision) but the case of the Estates and the Paradise Development Company shows just how in step with suburban life the "gamblers" of the Strip were. Such projects became the norm for casino operators. Bill Moore, who continued to design, build, and operate casinos after selling his interest in the Last Frontier, retired completely from the gaming industry by the early 1960s to engage full-time in noncasino real estate development. He eschewed the supposedly easy money of gambling for a distinctly unpoetic career as a developer. In his oral history, Moore proudly recalled having "promoted a number of subdivisions in town, and bought property . . . in some cases sold lots to developers; some cases, built the homes and/or business establishments on the property."[18] Had Moore and his fellow developers built Levittown or analogous suburban communities anywhere else in the United States, they would have earned faint praise. However, because they also operated casinos some authors have read sinister intent into their self-interested suburban projects. Antigambling writers saw the real estate speculations and developments of the Desert Inn syndicate as a series of ingenious fronts for "mob" money, but they can also be viewed as the machinations of a group of wealthy capitalists bent on becoming wealthier. Their behaviors are more typical of suburban developers than criminal deviants.

By the early 1950s, Highway 91 had been unequivocally transformed from a desert highway into a tourist-oriented strip. One account describes the scene's beginning:

> de luxe motels—with swimming pools, room service, lounges, terraces, patios—flamboyant gasoline stations, resplendent bars, smart restaurants, chic shops, and lustrous nightclubs started sprouting along [the highway's] glittery white way like jeweled daisies in a neon corn patch.[19]

This quote reflects design standards that would make Robert Venturi proud and critics of the Blake school wince. In most areas, motels, bars, gas stations, and tourist trap shops would be derided as suburban sprawl gone horribly wrong, as "God's Own Junkyard" incarnate. But some considered it a genuine civic accomplishment. Tommy Hull's successors had succeeded in bringing a piece of suburban America to the unlikeliest of locations, the Mojave Desert.

Clearly, the developers who created and managed Strip casino resorts thought about land, investment, and recreation in suburban terms. The really revolutionary thing about the casino resorts on the Las Vegas Strip was not that they featured legal gambling; Reno had, in the 1940s, the superior gambling halls. Resorts such as the El Rancho Vegas changed Amer-

Why not the Las Vegas "Gay White Way?"

The Los Angeles Highway, or Highway 91, was originally called "the Strip" in facetious reference to a famous Hollywood landmark. As the most widely quoted creation myth has it, Guy McAfee, an Angeleno who followed a career in law enforcement with one as a gambling operator and who, by the 1940s, ran the 91 Club (formerly the Pair-O-Dice), began to jokingly call the barren stretch of highway in front of his club "the Strip" after the bustling Sunset Strip.[20]

But the roadway had other designations. Some likened the road to the "Great White Way" of Broadway, and a travel guide dating from 1950 advertises the few hardy hotels on the "Gay White Way," a reference to the neon signs that towered over early resorts. In oral history interviews, most locals who were around in the early 1940s describe the Last Frontier and El Rancho Vegas as being "on the highway," "out of town," or "on the Los Angeles Highway." Most resort advertisements of the late 1940s and early 1950s gave their addresses on "Hiway 91."

However, the idea of Highway 91 as a "Strip" stuck, perhaps as an acceptance of the roadway's suburban nature. As the casino resorts blossomed on the Strip, the original irony was lost. At some unheralded moment in the early 1950s, the highway acquired the requisite commercial critical mass and eclipsed its namesake as the preeminent strip of America; local boosters confidently argued the merits of the "Las Vegas Strip" without apology or comparison to the Sunset Strip or Broadway. By the string of casino openings of 1955, the Las Vegas Strip was a fait accompli, not an inside joke.

ican gaming because they were not gambling halls but rather complete resort destinations that "just happened" to include a casino. Here visitors could engage in gambling as part of an otherwise relaxing vacation, with ample sunshine, food, and entertainment, in which it could be viewed as a diversion in a suburban setting practiced by patrons who were surrounded by fellow suburbanites.

Crafting a "period replica" heritage

As sunny as the poolside lounging was, and as easy as the action played in the casino, some promoters still wanted a "hook" to get people to vacation in the desert. Most other vacation areas relied upon their location to draw tourists, but the casino resorts of the Strip were deliberately isolated from the modest attractions of downtown Las Vegas and significantly off the beaten path of vacationers. The area boasted natural wonders no more attractive than those found elsewhere in the American Southwest. Promoters of casino resorts needed to create an instant cultural context that would ease tourists into relatively novel destinations. Within ten years, thanks to strenuous publicity and marketing efforts, Strip casino promoters exceeded even their own boosterish expectations. Seemingly relentless campaigns assuaged the American public into accepting that the resorts of what would become the Strip were indeed the playtopias it needed. In this world, the marketer, not the casino boss, was the real hero.

For many casinos, a theme of some sort became the preeminent marketing tool. This process started early. The Hotel Last Frontier, which opened about a half-mile south of the El Rancho Vegas site in 1942, carried the standard of "Western" theming into the postmodern age. R. E. Griffith, the proprietor of a chain of movie theaters in Texas and Oklahoma, built the Last Frontier. His nephew, architect Bill Moore, designed the complex, supervised its construction, and became the casino's chief operator after Griffith's demise, before selling the casino in 1951 to a group including Guy McAfee, Beldon Katleman, and Jake Kozloff and concentrating his energies on his real estate projects before and after returning to the business with the Showboat casino on Boulder Highway.[21]

Moore's first casino, the Last Frontier, was relatively straightforward. The hotel's name conspicuously evoked the Old West. The complex was "conceived to be as near Western as we [Griffith and Moore] could make it," said Moore. As he related in his oral history:

> The lobby had extremely high ceilings with the fireplace running right up through the middle of it—actually two fireplaces in the lobby, in the form of an octagon. The ceilings were of hewn timbers—logs—rough-sawed boards antiqued [sic] in such a way as to look many years old. And the whole structure was laid out on that basis.[22]

The casino's western décor also featured buffalo heads, saddles, and other "genuine" pioneer fixtures displayed prominently throughout the complex. The sandstone patios and fireplaces were hewn by Ute Indians brought in from New Mexico for both their skill and the "authentic" Western flavor of their work.[23]

The Gay Nineties Bar, a featured attraction at the Last Frontier, encapsulates Moore's approach to history. It was in fact much of the former Arizona Club of Block 16, Las Vegas's prewar red-light district. Moore simply bought up the bar and its leaded-glass front entrance and put it into the hotel as the Gay Nineties Bar. Moore was largely faithful to the original design, but he added a Western flourish:

we did add some saddle bar stools made out of leather in the form of a western saddle. Naturally, we had to make it comfortable. We didn't use the complete saddle design, but looking at the rear of the bar stool was like looking at the rear of a saddle. So in some cases there were stools big enough for two people because you would actually be—what looked like—seated on the side of the saddle.[24]

No comment could reveal more about the Western nature of the Last Frontier. As "the Old West in Modern Splendor," it gave patrons the trappings of the frontier West along with the comfort expected of a resort hotel. Where the real Western town of Las Vegas was not "West" enough, Moore embellished. This approach would dominate among Western-themed casinos in Las Vegas for a generation.

But the most outstanding feature of the resort was the Last Frontier Village. This complete re-creation of a "genuine" Western village boasted a variety of "old West" and Chinese artifacts. The origins of the village lay in the memorabilia collection of Nevada gambler and casino owner Robert F. Caudill, better known by his colorful nickname "Doby Doc." In 1947, Griffith and Moore convinced Cauldhill to open his heretofore private collection to public view as the Last Frontier Village. The village was designed to display artifacts so that, "the public would be allowed to see it and use it and actually were not charged for viewing it." But Moore's interest extended beyond mere historic preservation. He admitted candidly that the village served as "an advertising method in order to induce people to come to the hotel and stay there—patronize the hotel, patronize the village."[25]

The Last Frontier Village included a mix of museum pieces, "authentic" Western working attractions, and retail establishments. It included three "complete railroad outfits, with engine, tracks, and the usual accessories." The village featured a drug store, general store, post office, schoolhouse, and jail, as well as the "original printing plant of the venerable *Reese River Reveille*, Nevada's oldest newspaper."[26] In addition, patrons could relive the old West through purchases at retail establishments like a rock shop and an art gallery that featured paintings of "Western subjects": landscapes, mining towns, horses, and cowboys.

Moore and his compatriots transcended dry historic preservation by offering gambling within this faux Western village. The Silver Slipper Saloon and Gambling Hall, which opened in 1951 within the village, allowed guests to wager at various games, including an antique Wheel of Fortune reportedly used in nineteenth-century mining camps. It was considered a "genuine" reconstruction of an Old West watering hole. A group of dancers called the "Flora-Dora girls," outfitted in period costumes, performed nightly in the Old Bar.[27] The Last Frontier Village was to provide guests with a total entertainment experience centered upon, of course, gambling.

To modern ears, the Last Frontier Village sounds like an unapologetic commercialization of the Wild West. But many experienced hands believed that the village was not commercial enough. In his oral history, casino veteran Mort Saiger recalled that Bill Moore concentrated his efforts in building attractions "for the community" like the village and a racetrack instead of focusing on the casino and building a larger hotel to accommodate more gamblers.[28] Still, the Last Frontier Village was an important symbol of the power—and limitations of—the earliest attempts to sell the casino experience as entertainment.

A gas station operated by Texaco on the grounds of the village crystallized Moore's use of history to market the gaming experience even more than the Gay Nineties bar. The obvious anachronism of a gas station in the Old West was assuaged by the use of "period replica" design. In other words, the building was a reproduction of what an Old West filling station would have looked like had the internal combustion engine been in use a generation earlier, an interesting commentary on the selective historicism of the Last Frontier Village. Within this gas station, faux Western design was neatly merged with customer service and astute marketing. William Moore described the gas station's genesis:

> Originally, because Texaco [had] been using a fire chief—old, you might say, western-type advertising on their stations and promotion—we felt that it was a good tie-in with the old fire engine and tied in with Texaco's advertising. . . . Part of the idea was to put showers, restrooms, and so forth that would be inducive [sic] to the people cleaning up after a drive across the desert. The restrooms were rather elaborate—[and] the people would have the service that could be advertised on the road.[29]

By Moore's admission, the gas station was a tourist trap, as was the village that surrounded it. Still, it presaged both Disneyland and the elaborately themed casino resorts began to rise out of the Nevada desert in the 1960s.

Themes have been a tangential part of casino resorts almost since their origins. While all resorts had some kind of theme that suggested an exotic locale, there was little effort to match the zeal, amounting very nearly to obsession, of the Last Frontier's promoters in creating an artificial space. It is problematic to draw a straight-line progression from the modestly themed Sands to the more suggestive Caesars Palace to the "you-are-there" faux historicity of the Venetian. In fact, most subsequent resorts presented more subdued themes than the Last Frontier. So, was the Last Frontier's creation of a "period replica" tradition a successful marketing effort? On the surface, no. The Last Frontier, thanks to an unwieldy design, struggled against the increased competition of the early 1950s. After changing hands, its new owners completely rebuilt it in 1955, closing the Last Frontier and opening the space age New Frontier. But the notion that casino promoters could create, and patrons would buy into, themes was crucial to the establishment of casino resorts as national centers for adult vacationing.

As themed environments, casino resorts fall into one of John Hannigan's features of "Fantasy City:" theme-o-centrism.[30] From the Last Frontier, it has been more common than not for Strip resorts to have themes, even if they haven't always been very good or well-developed ones. Indeed, the Strip began to get interesting, architecturally and culturally, around the time that builders decided that the best way to lure visitors was to look like anything but the faux Old West Last Frontier. This is a bit out of step with most vacation destinations: hotels in Miami, for example, tried their best to fit the local style. In a market with little to work with in the way of a local vernacular architectural style, dominated by out-of-towners, it is easy to see how casino builders came to the conclusion that it was best to suggest that their patrons were in the Caribbean or the Riviera rather than the Mojave Desert. Themes served this purpose well.

But if casino resorts were theme-o-centric, they didn't truly exhibit another one of Hannigan's features, namely, aggressive branding.[31] Well into the 1960s, there was no idea of "brand loyalty" in the casino industry; players made decisions to gamble at a particular casino based on personal ties to managers or employees rather than devotion to a particular "brand." When cross-ownership of Strip properties became the norm after 1955, few visitors knew that the owners of the Sands also managed the Dunes, or that the Flamingo's syndicate also controlled the Riviera. Even today, few tourists walking the Strip know that MGM Mirage owns the MGM Grand, New York-New York, Bellagio, Mirage, and Treasure Island; whereas the properties share some centralized management functions, there is little attempt to raise public awareness of their common parent company. Casino companies that do emphasize the corporate brand rather than a specific property theme tend to have casinos in different markets, such as Harrah's Entertainment and Isle of Capri. Both of these companies stress overall brand loyalty (Harrah's quite aggressively through their unified Total Rewards player's card system) rather than individual properties, something that suits the less theme-o-centric nature of their markets well.

Still, themes are the norm on the Strip, and when most casual visitors imagine a trip to a casino, particularly a Strip casino, they picture the pseudo-Roman Caesars Palace, the tropical Mirage or Mandalay Bay, or the faux-city New York-New York ("the greatest city in Las Vegas"), Paris, or Venetian. This is because many casino operators, such as Bill Moore, have found that the best way to attract visitors to an otherwise unexceptional stretch of highway is to convince visitors that they are, in fact, going somewhere else.

With rows of slot machines surrounding the core of table games, this was the typical Strip casino. Casino resorts successfully marketed themselves as places where women and men could gamble without intimidation. Note the presence of peepholes above the table games. These were the precursors of the surveillance cameras that are ubiquitous in casinos today. Courtesy UNLV Special Collections.

Way out west

The "authentic replica" Last Frontier Village served as a touchstone for several trends in American life. As suburbs sprawled across the American landscape, popular culture returned to the frontier as a defining American experience. It probably is no coincidence that in the same years that the United States became an increasingly suburban nation, the idea of the frontier returned to the forefront of American popular culture with a vengeance. Through cinematic and television portrayals of the Wild West, America's frontier mythology emerged as a language through which Americans could make the changes in their everyday life understandable.

Indeed, some have drawn parallels between the suburban experience and the frontier. Richard Horwitz, for example, tags the suburban strip as a modern-day frontier in no uncertain terms:

The strip is a site for such common American experiences or plain adventures. Instead of covered wagons limping to a trading post of Fort Laramie, we speak of Ford wagons and Holiday Inns. Even strip regulars tell tales that recall the frontier. Strips are the unfordable rapids and towering peaks of rush-hour traffic. We rely on local scouts to recommend a bypass, a tangle of side streets like some obscure mountain pass between beds and jobs.[32]

Although Horwitz's conflation of the strip and the frontier is accomplished through literary parallel, it does cast some light on how people conceptualized commercial suburbia.

In addition to overt marketing purposes, the Last Frontier Village and Western theming in general served a less obvious but equally important function by identifying gambling with the frontier tradition. Like Gilded Age Republicans "waving the bloody shirt," casino owners used their Western identity to rally supporters and shout down opposition. If gambling was an inextricable part of the virile frontier past, anyone who opposed it could not be a genuine American. By conflating gambling with the all-American West, casino operators could shrug off antigambling foes as effete cosmopolitans out of touch with their nation's raw frontier tradition. In doing this, casino operators were chillingly successful. Before the emergence of the casino resort on the Strip, "gambling" for most middle-class Americans summoned up images of back alley craps games and threatening urban slot machines, both frequently linked to Italian, Jewish, and African-American crime syndicates. In its earliest years, the casino resort on the Strip stood as a striking contrast. Here, gambling took place in a milieu that recalled the rugged frontiersmen of the mythic American West. Without a doubt, the overriding factor in the acceptance of the casino resort was its isolated location and suburban orientation, but at the same time, the earliest resorts, because they were redolent of the frontier past, subtly reminded Americans that gambling, in one form or another, was a hallowed American pastime.

However, later casino resorts jettisoned the Wild West, something that certainly makes sense within the inner world of casino marketing but also offers clues as to how American perceptions of gambling had shifted. After the major wave of antigambling sentiment had crested in the early 1950s, the Old West lost ground to modern, desert, and Caribbean motifs in Strip casino resort theming. Perhaps having established their legitimacy as solidly American, casino resort operators felt free to leave the frontier.

The Last Frontier used as its marketing slogan "The Old West in Modern Splendor." This pithy phrase neatly sums up the marketing strategies of the earliest, Western-themed, casino resorts. They wanted their patrons to *see* the Old West, but not necessarily to *smell* it, so to speak. The operators of these casinos envisioned visitors basking in the ambience of the Old West while demanding all of the "modern" comforts of the atomic age. There is deep historical irony in resorts like the El Rancho Vegas, Last Frontier, and Thunderbird simultaneously evoking the old frontier West and offering their patrons a complete travel experience in air-conditioned safety. A travel guide of the period captures the irony implicit in the dualistic promotion of the Strip:

> Tourists enjoy the Chuck Wagon suppers, served from ten in the evening till seven the next morning—price, $1.50—and breakfast is served twenty-four hours a day. Nowhere in the world is there anything quite like it—this informal magnificence at multi-million dollar hotels at little more than motel rates; and you can take your choice of nearly a dozen of the nation's top-flight shows for the price of a drink. Of course, the casinos carry the load.[33]

This is a unique construction of the frontier West: promiscuously free-flowing food, lodging, and quality entertainment, with nary a frontier hardship in sight. It captures, though, the free-wheeling but comfortable ambience that casino operators successfully engineered on the Strip.

John Findlay is the one of the most recent and most eloquent writers to have connected gambling with the Western strain in American culture. The flourishing gambling subculture in virtually all major U.S. cities, east or west, since before the Continental Congress would seem to belie such a connection, but it retains a cogency in both scholarly literature and popular perceptions. In arguing that the western location of the twentieth-century gambling mecca Las Vegas was "not incidental," Findlay notes:

> The qualities that identified Americans as a people of chance stood out most boldly on western frontiers where gambling tended to flourish and where distinctly American betting games emerged for the first time. The affinity between gambling and frontiers has been forceful from the time that lotteries funded the first permanent English settlement in North America to the years when Las Vegas casinos, embodying Southern California culture, emerged as stunning new landmarks of United States civilization.[34]

The inclusion of casino operators and patrons as "people of chance" might be overstating the argument—the one constant of tourist-oriented casino resorts is that they have been promoted not as temples of chance, but as places of fun and relaxation. Findlay masterfully traces the development of frontier gambling, but many innovations in American gaming, the most important of which was the slot machine, had a decidedly urban genesis.

Though gambling occupied a central position in the myth and realities of the West, its history is national rather than sectional. The West needed gambling more than gambling needed the West.

The legacy of frontier gambling as part of the larger Western heritage for the casino resort was, therefore, more ideological and thematic than historic. Early operators genuinely believed that resorts would best prosper by clinging to frontier imagery, and the latter provided small but incalculable assistance in their marketing efforts. But the casino resort defies explanation as a solely Western product. Although the first resorts capitalized on a mythic "period replica" frontier heritage, nothing intrinsic to the design or operation of casino resorts identifies them as products of the American West. In fact, the resorts of the Strip would most deeply affect the American psyche only after abandoning, at least partially, the comfortable nostalgia of a departed frontier for the atomic—and automobile—age.

The Flamingo fantasy and the Bugsy Myth

Although both the El Rancho Vegas and the Last Frontier offered genuine innovations in resort design and themed ambience, they have been largely neglected as Strip pioneers. This was partially because Hull, Griffith, and Moore lacked any real background as "gamblers," that is, casino operators. These operators were, for the most part, hotel promoters. While they had original ideas about the general concept of a casino resort, they made mistakes that "casino men" would not have. For instance, Moore's design for the Last Frontier made the casino almost inaccessible from the main lobby, something that doomed the casino to failure.[35] Thus, the succeeding generation of Strip "pioneers" viewed these first resorts with contempt and wrote them out of the Strip's history.

Probably of greater import is the fact that these resorts were largely regional, in both their promotion and their ownership. Hull was from California and Griffith and Moore came from Texas. With the arrival of investors, operators, and managers from the East, Strip resorts would soon become national in scope. Two resorts pioneered in this regard: the Flamingo and the Desert Inn. The Flamingo is more infamous, though the Desert Inn was more influential. But in the standard telling of the history of Nevada gaming, the Desert Inn is regarded as far less significant than "Bugsy's Flamingo," which is held up as the true beginning of the Las Vegas Strip.

The belief that Strip history—and the casino resort—started with the Flamingo is confused by a host of inaccuracies. The mythic narrative of the Flamingo relates that it was the first true Strip casino, and that it was the exclusive brainchild of Ben "Bugsy" Siegel, who stuck to his dream of building a pleasure palace in the Nevada desert though it cost him his life.

He brought Hollywood glamour and sex appeal to the once-desolate desert. After his death, according to the story, the success of the Flamingo and the burgeoning Strip vindicated Siegel. More than anyone, he was the true father of the modern commercial casino industry.

This is misinformation. The Flamingo was not the inspiration of Siegel, but rather that of Billy Wilkerson, a founder of the *Hollywood Reporter*, Southern California restaurateur and compulsive gambler. His vision was that of superimposing Beverly Hills upon the barren desert. Work began on the casino in 1946. It was to offer both gambling and a "quiet oasis for visitors who did not wish to gamble," and Wilkerson turned to architect George Vernon Russell and decorator Tom Douglas, both of Los Angeles, to design his casino.[36] It was to be extravagant, with facilities modeled on the Beverly Hills Hotel and Paris's Moulin Rouge, and was to cater exclusively to the wealthy elites of Southern California who, Wilkerson hoped, were as desperate to gamble as he was.

Wilkerson's reach exceeded his grasp, however. His vision of an elegant resort proved too costly for his limited capital resources and, following a pattern in early casino finance, he turned to unorthodox sources of capital, namely, criminal syndicates. Siegel fronted for investors who bought into the project before eventually assuming control of it. The Del Webb Company of Phoenix, which later built the Sun City planned retirement suburb and is perhaps the best-known Sunbelt developer, served as chief contractor for Siegel, who fired designers Russell and Douglas and replaced them with Webb and Richard Stadleman.[37]

Siegel began to demand luxury on a scale that dwarfed even Wilkerson's grandiose plans. The project was beset by cost overruns attributable to theft, wartime shortages, the requisite black marketeering, and the sheer extravagance of the planned construction. Overindulgence in the scale, pace, and execution of the casino's fabrication was widely reported. According to mob legend, Siegel himself siphoned a portion of the construction funds to Virginia Hill (or she pilfered them from him, depending on the "reliable source"). Whatever the reason, the casino's costs ballooned from a projected $1 million to over $3 million; one source puts the total tab at $7 million.[38] According to the popular lore, this was what cost Siegel his life. The capital invested in the Flamingo came from underground sources, and those who lent the money were supposedly displeased with the difficulties involved in the casino's construction and Siegel's subsequent skimming of the profits.

The casino opened inauspiciously on December 26, 1946. Because of construction delays, the hotel portion of the complex was unfinished and remained closed. The weather was cold and rainy, but still a delegation of B-list Hollywood celebrities and members of the press attended, signaling the link between the resort and Hollywood that Wilkerson had sought.[39] A local resident described the opening as "posh," and she believed that the "elegant hotel" contrasted sharply with the "informal" El Rancho Vegas and Last Frontier: the Flamingo had "a different style, knee-deep carpeting and elegant draperies."[40] But fate conspired against the house. Good luck and novice dealers helped gamblers carry away tremendous sums from the Flamingo's tables. Rather than remaining at the casino to gamble their winnings back, most gamblers cashed out their chips and left the property. Because the hotel had not been opened, all of the casino patrons had lodgings elsewhere; many returned to their rooms at the El Rancho Vegas and Last Frontier, where they gambled away their Flamingo winnings. This was disastrous for the Flamingo, but vindicated the concept of a self-contained casino resort. In addition to the lack of hotel accommodations, a "no hats" policy irritated "come as you are" natives, who disliked having to remove their hats indoors. Due to these and other intangibles, the Flamingo quickly closed for business, pending completion of its motel wings.

According to Mafia aficionados, the Flamingo's initial failure sealed Siegel's death warrant, and at a mob "council" in Havana, the edict to have Siegel "rubbed out" was handed down. Siegel's partners may also have been angered by alleged skimming. Siegel, however, lived to reopen the casino and inaugurate the now-finished hotel in March. By May, the casino was turning a healthy profit. On June 20, 1947, Siegel was gunned down at 810 North Linden Drive, the Beverly Hills home of Virginia Hill, who was vacationing in Paris at the time.

The reasons for Siegel's assassination could only be speculated at even then; the passage of time has made their decryption even less likely. Some cling to the disgruntled gangster financier hypothesis, whereas others claim that Nevada gambling operators, leery of the law enforcement presence he would attract into town, killed Siegel. After a cursory investigation, Beverly Hills and Los Angeles police deemed the Siegel slaying unsolvable. Suffice it to say that the Flamingo was only one of Siegel's many enterprises and that, during his violent life, he aroused the ire of many dangerous people. Siegel's death is important for the understanding of the development of the casino industry in southern Nevada inasmuch as it has become an integral part of the Las Vegas legend.[41]

The Flamingo cast a long shadow across the Strip, but the iconic role that Ben Siegel's detractors and admirers cast for him is an injustice. Siegel, by all accounts, was a complete failure as impresario of the Flamingo, offending rather than welcoming patrons and terrorizing staff and guests alike. He was not a bold visionary who stuck to a dream when all others forsook him—he essentially hijacked another man's project and nearly drove it into the ground. He was not an exceptional manager. Hardly a "people person," he used terror rather than charm to achieve his ambitions, and his ideas about how to build and operate a casino resort often bordered on the whimsical.

Even more telling, Siegel's death neither retarded nor advanced the development of the casino resort. Before the revision of Las Vegas's history in the 1970s, Ben Siegel was notorious rather than legendary; his story was known but accorded no special significance. Journalist Dick Pearce, as familiar with Las Vegas as any of the journalists who were regularly assigned there to cover the nuclear tests to the town's north, conceded that Siegel's death had prompted Nevada to "clean up its gambling law," but he identified Siegel merely as a "New York hood who promoted the Flamingo."[42] Rightly, he reserved no special place for Siegel in the coterie of operators drawn to promoting casino resorts.[43]

It is also interesting that even Estes Kefauver, whose zeal to tarnish the image of Strip resorts and Nevada gambling was second to none, did not single out Siegel as the founder of the Strip, or even the Flamingo. He was aware that Siegel was a chief investor and boss in the Flamingo, a fact well established by the testimony of private detective Barney Ruditsky, but he didn't follow up on this angle, being more concerned with the wire service.[44] When confronting witness Moe Sedway, a former partner of Siegel's, Kefauver tried to establish conclusively that Siegel was killed "in connection with the wire service," but Sedway, of course, would not corroborate this or speculate at all about Siegel's demise, outside of changing the topic to discuss Siegel's apparently devoted work for charities.[45]

Kefauver would have made a significant point about the inherent corruption of the Strip, something he fervently believed in, by identifying Siegel as its founding father and by claiming that his murder was indicative of mob influence on the Strip. That he did not, despite access to the most current information, real and exaggerated, about the "inner workings" of American criminal syndicates, suggests that Siegel was not regarded as particularly tied to the Strip at that time. An anticrime writer working at the same time pulled Siegel's murder in yet another direction, alleging that it was the consequence of his designs on monopolizing the Tijuana heroin trade.[46] The idea that he founded the Flamingo and the Strip is, then, most likely a later invention.

But the Bugsy Myth still has an inexplicable hold on many. For feature filmmakers, pulp novelists, and mafia antiquarians, this Flamingo narrative is heaven-sent manna. Gangsters make far better romantic figures than theater-chain owners, architects, or motel operators. Siegel's life, his rise to wealth and power through crime, his vision, his ruthless persistence, his final betrayal and ultimate vindication, touch upon larger themes within the American consciousness. The image of Siegel as the hitman entrepreneur with a winning vision is an attractive one. Consequently, the narrative of Siegel and the Flamingo outlined above has remained a highly attractive one for the past fifty years.[47]

Part of the Flamingo narrative's power is the allure of its chief figure. For those who demand a "great man" explanation of historical change, the typical portrait of Siegel fits the bill perfectly; he is the lone genius who died for his dream but was vindicated by history. In a particularly poignant scene from *The Godfather II*, Mario Puzo's fictionalization of Meyer Lansky in the character of Hyman Roth memorialized the role of Siegel's cinematic alter ego, Moe Green, in creating Las Vegas: "He had an idea—to build a city out of a desert stop-over for GI's on the way to the West Coast . . . the city he invented was Las Vegas. This was a great man—a man of vision and guts. And there isn't even a plaque—or a signpost—or a statue of him in that town!"[48] From this movie and a variety of other sources the idea of Siegel as founder of the Flamingo and Las Vegas seeped into the public consciousness. At first deemed too shocking to speak of in public, this "truth," that a gangster had fathered one of the nation's most prosperous businesses, was eventually accepted as truth, if not gospel.

Just as Siegel reflects some of the darker qualities of the American dream, he personifies the image that Las Vegas casino operators have crafted for their desert Xanadu. He was flashy, sometimes beyond the point of bad taste, and he prided himself on his expensive wardrobe. Though he was generous, he could turn murderous with a capricious flash of anger. Casino resorts, too, can alternately favor their supplicants with fortune and then send them home penniless. A noveau riche second-generation American, he personified an industry set in a burgeoning city with a largely transplanted population. Siegel was regarded as one of the most feared members of the criminal underworld and an alleged Murder Inc. kingpin. Through film, fiction, and public record the gaming industry remains, despite years of state regulation and public scrutiny, unable to shake its early connections to gangster America. The mythic Siegel telescoped qualities that casinos hoped to project: he hosted a great Bacchanalian spectacle, but he was vicious when wronged. By adopting Siegel as creator, promoters chose the "hospitable, generous tough guy" as their totem; visitors could expect to have a great time in casinos, but if they violated the rules, written or unwritten, they could expect speedy and zealous justice.

The Californication of the casino resort

The association of casino resorts with Hollywood had begun before the Flamingo opened and would become one of the Strip's most salient selling points. The El Rancho Vegas and Last Frontier had slowly begun implementing entertainment policies designed to capitalize on their frequent famous guests from Los Angeles, and this only accelerated after the end of wartime travel restrictions. Most resorts maintained branch publicity and travel offices in Los Angeles and bought extensive advertising in Southern California newspapers. Even more revealingly, most resorts bought space in the phone books of Los Angeles and its environs; they obviously pursued the kind of drive-up visitor who would make a reservation without the help of a travel agent.

Much of the human capital of the early casino resorts, too, was drawn from Los Angeles. Many casino architects, from Tom Douglas (who followed his Flamingo work by expanding the El Rancho Vegas in the early 1950s) to Martin Stern Jr. (whose career, from the expansion of the Sahara in 1953 to consultation on 1995's MGM Grand, was one of the most influential in casino architecture) hailed from Los Angeles, and their designs brought a sense of Angeleno style to the resorts of the Strip. Some gambling operators, like Tony Cornero, who would begin building the Stardust, had fled from the antigambling efforts of Los Angeles mayor Fletcher Bowron and California governor Earl Warren in the early 1940s.

Rank-and-file employees also came from Los Angeles. Though there is no solid statistical support, a survey of the anecdotal evidence supports the idea that many of the men and women who worked in Strip resorts moved there from Los Angeles. Mort Saiger, whose oral history vividly recalls the early days of the Strip, moved from Los Angeles to Las Vegas and quickly found work at the Last Frontier.[49] Other Angelenos did the same, and they formed a large stratum of resort employees. Many Strip resorts also hired Los Angeles–based publicity directors, such as Al Freeman of the Sands and Dunes, to manage the Los Angeles media and from this base coordinate worldwide public relations coverage.

That a sizable chunk of resort guests came from Los Angeles is almost self-evident from the fact that the Strip blossomed along the Los Angeles Highway. It is therefore no surprise that Las Vegas was viewed by the early 1950s as a desert adjunct to the glamorous movie capital. Early in the decade, Lucius Beebe wrote in a book-length travel guide that the resort mirrored the:

> sports-coat and convertible-motor-car philosophy of life in Southern California. Its ranch-style architecture flows in terraced symmetry along U.S. 91 some 225 miles [sic] from Los Angeles. The guest lists of its super motels, which combine the functions of residence and casino, are generously recruited from top names in the film industry. Its nightclub headliners playing to capacity audiences in sports shirts along the Las Vegas Strip are the same who please the night-club audiences in hardly more formal attire along the County Strip in Hollywood.[50]

Beebe summarized Las Vegas as "very young, very affluent, and sometimes very brash," much like its metropole on the Pacific. The casino resorts of the Las Vegas Strip benefited enormously from association with glamorous Hollywood. Proximity to Los Angeles encouraged not only tourism from Southern California but also from around the nation. Those who visited Las Vegas primarily to gamble could also soak in the reflected starlight of Hollywood. Ironically, in the earlier years it was almost easier for Easterners and Midwesterners, who flew or took the train to Las Vegas, to get to the city than Angelenos who drove.

Perhaps the biggest hurdle that casino publicists faced was convincing Southern Californians to make the 300-mile trek across the Mojave. The Strip itself in the 1940s was a gravel road. Paving only extended to the city limits at San Francisco Avenue, after which motorists saw no asphalt until they reached Los Angeles.[51] That visitors made the trip despite less than ideal travel conditions speaks volumes about the effectiveness of Strip resorts in promoting themselves to Californians. One resident whose family frequently shuttled between Las Vegas and Los Angeles described the trip as taking "hours and hours" along a road that was "two lane all the way." If stuck behind a slow-moving truck, one could expect hours of slow movement in a car without air-conditioning. Train service was a more comfortable and convenient method of transportation for many in those years, as was air travel for more well-heeled visitors.[52]

As casino resorts became more sophisticated, they became natural extensions of the nation's film capital. Countless journalistic accounts of the Strip's resorts drew analogies between the casinos and Hollywood backlots, both for the social drama that unfolded in the pits and for the celebrities that one was bound to meet there. Film celebrities certainly had their share of high-profile weddings in casino resorts, and these weddings were doggedly promoted by the casinos. While visitors couldn't be assured of having a room next to Jimmy Durante, Danny Thomas, Joan Crawford, or any of the other celebrities who actively promoted Las Vegas, they might, if they gambled long enough, chance to see one of them. For this brush with greatness, a vacation in a casino resort seemed a small enough price.

Love for sale . . . or at least for rent

Casino resorts received much of their early buzz from the presence of women who worked and vacationed in the casino. In the Strip resorts, women were confined to a small number of occupations, including waitress, change girl, and showgirl. They were unofficially but firmly barred from dealing and other gaming positions. This stood in marked contrast to Reno, where women made up the bulk of the dealing corps and handled most daily patron-casino interactions. Most contemporary accounts depicted Reno women as mundane and unglamorous.[53] In Strip resorts, by contrast, women employees made their strongest impressions onstage, and they were usually depicted as exotic, desirable, and quite possibly attainable.[54] Sexy women were the fulcrum of Las Vegas's promotion; each cover of *Fabulous Las Vegas*, for example, featured a scantily clad woman posing in or near a casino.

This was partially because of the glamorous figure of the casino showgirl. From the days of the El Rancho Vegas, casino resorts featured their headline entertainers as centerpieces of an all-out floorshow. A line of dancing girls, and a comedian, magician, or specialty act preceded the star headliner. For these shows, producers wanted "girls" who were attractive but not necessarily trained dancers. The later semi-nude and nude extravaganzas, of course, demanded greater professionalism, but in the earliest days of casino entertainment, a friendly smile and positive attitude were more important, in the producers' eyes, than a miniscule dress size or dancing excellence.

Casinos had their own troupes of dancers with names like the "Flamingoettes," "Texas Copa Girls" (Sands), and "Desert Inn Beauties." The line of dancing girls opened and closed each show with kicking heels and, after the final show, mingled with casino patrons. Contrary to legend, the showgirls were not required nor even requested to sleep with high rollers. Jeanie Malone, a former Desert Inn Beauty, explained to a later writer that the showgirls "were not there for that purpose," but were intended to "decorate the casino."[55] The smiling "girls" of the floorshow were entertainers and not prostitutes, and to write them off as available playthings is irresponsible and inaccurate.

The women who worked as "girl dancers" were not, for the most part, professional dancers. Very few applicants for Copa Girl positions, for example, sought careers in dancing, and the majority were interested in more general "show business" careers or acting. In fact, most applicants frankly claimed that they wanted to be Copa Girls to advance their careers. A winner of a 1958 Copa Girl audition, for example, stated that she wanted to be a Copa Girl because she "didn't care to be married and I like the entertainment business." Another woman, buying into the ideology of the Strip, simply wrote, "excitement, and glamour." Most of these women, at the time of their applications, were working in fields typical to unmarried middle-class women, usually as secretaries or receptionists, although some were models and one was a "bank teller on roller skates."[56]

It is difficult to see these women, who by all accounts were bright, hardworking, and independent, as the pliable sexual raw material of rumor and legend. Still, by the late 1940s, casino resorts were inexorably identified in the public mind as a landscape of sexual possibility—no coincidence, since casino publicists relentlessly peppered the popular press, visitors, and anyone who got near with visions of off-duty showgirls lounging by the pool or fluttering about the craps tables. There was a curious parallel between the loosening of fiscal restraint and the lowering of sexual inhibitions. Tourists from Middle America left their Protestant work ethic at home when on vacation in freewheeling Las Vegas, and it is not surprising that they left their sexual restraint behind as well.

Part of the attraction of Las Vegas as a place without sexual restraint can be tied to larger trends in masculinity in the postwar period. During the same years that the casino resort grew in southern Nevada, men experienced a profound ambiguity about their roles as providers. In *The Hearts of Men,* Barbara Ehrenreich describes the tensions that accompanied the breadwinner ethic. Marriage in the 1950s was seen as the consummate proof of maturity; to be considered an emotionally healthy, socially adept man, one simply had to be married by his late twenties.[57] To rebel against the gray flannel world of corporate boardrooms and suburban bedrooms would have been tantamount to an admission of almost criminal deviance for many men. Yet, they still felt trapped by marriages and jobs they perceived as burdensome.

For these men, casino resorts, as described in newspapers, magazines, movies, and fiction, provided the perfect escape. Just as gambling away hard-earned dollars flouted Franklinesque thrifty virtues, so too did having a Las Vegas fling abnegate the sexual rigidity of postwar suburban married life. As Las Vegas developed as a bona fide convention town in the late 1950s, the possibilities for a married man to plausibly spend a week in Las Vegas away from his wife exploded. As gender roles tightened in the years after World War II but before the summer of love, the casino resort remained a potential refuge from marriage for many men.

From their very beginnings, casino resorts positioned themselves as destination resorts where visitors could win money and more for nothing. The Strip was promoted as a desert Xanadu of loose gambling action, virtually free food, world-class entertainment, and, not coincidentally, easy sex. Despite the individual realities of sexual adventure in Las Vegas, most visitors believed sexual promiscuity was the norm there.

Sexual expectations curiously followed the pattern of gambling expectations. The general tendency is for slot machine *losers* to internalize their losses as the result of individual bad choice rather than statistical certainty and slot machine *winners* to loudly brag about their jackpots, leading to the misleading anecdotal conclusion that everyone who plays slots wins big. A similar attitude carried over to sex. People seldom discussed spending an interminable night alone in a hotel room, broke and frustrated.

Those who engaged in or even imagined sexual adventures were far more voluble, and their embellished stories became accepted as the norm.

One early example of sexual expectations is as amusing as it is revealing. Local attorney Paul Ralli in his memoir *Nevada Lawyer*, written in 1948, summed up the expectations of many tourists in his anecdote about two men in their fifties, "Joe Blank" and "Bob Doakes." Ralli spotted Blank and Doakes at a dinner theater in one of the Strip hotels; the men were accompanied by two women in their early twenties. Ralli observed Blank and Doakes attempt to impress the women, but when he saw the pair two hours later in a cocktail room they were without their dinner companions. One man complained that the women were "chiselers" interested only in a free dinner, while the other rationalized that they were "probably a couple of Lesbians." Unfazed by their rejection, the men then discussed the relative charms of the telephone operator, the cigarette girl, and virtually every woman they had seen within the casino complex. Ralli assayed the men's chances as slim at best, but he did not think this would be reflected in their stories of Las Vegas:

> When they got back to their home town, however, it was probably something entirely different to relate. They will describe to their friends in colors of bright vermilion the orgies they had staged in Las Vegas that will make their listeners envious and acclaim and recognize them as the great Lotharios they are not.[58]

Ralli is perspicacious here. Despite their probable failure, the men *will* undoubtedly spread stories of the sexual availability of "Las Vegas women" and of the adventures that middle-aged men can have in the desert resort. Certainly nothing in the story of Blank and Doakes was unique to Las Vegas, but it is significant that virtually every contemporary account of Las Vegas identifies the city as a haven for promiscuity. As the word-of-mouth spread, the Vegas mystique only increased. Casino resorts reaped the benefits of this word-of-mouth windfall.

But not all men went home with only confabulated memories. Casino resorts gave sometimes not-so-tacit encouragement to a system of technically illegal prostitution (though legal in the state of Nevada, prostitution was outlawed in Clark County). As casino resorts catered progressively more to conventioneers, prostitutes became more common within them. While it is dangerous to generalize about quasi-legal activities that were never documented, a basic idea of the system of illegal prostitution in early casino resorts can be gleaned from oral histories and guide books. "Pit girls" were on call, at the demand of pit bosses, to satisfy high rollers while they were away from tables. In addition, prostitutes also plied the cocktail lounges of casino resorts. For those wishing to get away from the casino, massage parlors were a popular option[59] Brothels could also be found, although not in great number. The most notorious, Roxie's, located four miles outside of town, operated for years with full knowledge of Sheriff Glen Jones until its closure as a result of the *Las Vegas Sun*–bankrolled "Louis Tabet" sting operation.[60]

This general system mirrors in many ways the socioeconomic world of the Strip. For high rollers, the select pit girls were available, much like comped rooms and other luxuries. For less well-connected players, the cocktail lounge prostitutes provided a similar service within the casino resort. Finally, for those who either had little money or whose predilections, violent or otherwise, could not be satisfied by the "call girls" of the casino, streetwalkers represented the bottom of Las Vegas's prostitution hierarchy.

This system kept the actual casino operators' involvement with prostitution to a minimum. At the most, casino managers would introduce high rollers to "clean" prostitutes who would not attempt to rob or blackmail the player. Because prostitution was illegal, the casino could have a free hand in ejecting "undesirable" prostitutes from the premises. Of course, crusader reformers could sometimes upset the arrangement, as happened to Roxie's brothel, but just as nature abhors a vacuum, the tremendous sums to be made in prostitution ensured that the traffic in sex would continue. But this is not unique to the casino resort. Throughout human history, places where large numbers of unescorted men with disposable incomes congregate have usually invited the quick development of a flourishing prostitution industry. That prostitutes could be found in the lounges of the Strip means that casino resorts were in line with prevailing practices and expectations, not that they were somehow deviant.

The system of illegal prostitution that flourished within casino resorts served them quite well. It ensured that no one with enough money to spend went home disappointed. It allowed devout tourists to vacation and gamble without fear of openly abetting panderers and prostitutes. Although boosters were being disingenuous by claiming that prostitution had been stamped out in Las Vegas, they were also being shrewd. During the 1950s, "wide open" legalized prostitution was more a liability than an asset to a burgeoning resort industry because of sexual restraint. For casino resorts to sponsor prostitution openly would have been a public relations catastrophe. Some visitors may have wanted sex for money, but they did not demand it as a public right.

Whether lured by the possibility of boudoir encounters or lucky strikes at the tables, Southern Californians and, increasingly, those from around the country made the pilgrimage to the casino resorts of the Strip. Considering the dynamic growth of Los Angeles in the twentieth century, it is unsurprising that its satellite, Las Vegas, also grew. Indeed, Las Vegas owes its very existence to the construction of a southern rail route to Los Angeles. Once the skeleton of a hospitality and gambling industry developed in Las Vegas in response to the construction of the Hoover Dam in the 1930s, it was only natural that Angelenos would vacation in that city rather than Reno. Beginning in the 1940s, former illegal operators from cities like New York, Cleveland, Chicago, and Miami moved to Las Vegas, and Las Vegas began to draw visitors interested in gambling from throughout the United States. The influence of Hollywood and an influx of a national group of gambling operators, most often via Los Angeles, would soon cement Las Vegas's reputation as a national, rather than regional, vacation center. That many visitors to this new travel destination would be the very same suburban middle-class Americans who supported antigambling campaigns in their own areas is one of many ironies of the casino resort's development.

The success of casino resorts on the Strip in the late 1940s, as amazing as it seemed then, would soon be overshadowed by the explosive growth of the early 1950s. As the national antigambling movement gained momentum, the resorts of the Strip grew in size and popularity. When contained in resorts catering to middle-class suburbia on the Strip, gambling was permissible, and even fun. The pathbreakers of the 1940s, such as Thomas Hull, Bill Moore, and Billy Wilkerson, paved the way for the next group of arrivals, operators like Moe Dalitz, Carl Cohen, and Jack Entratter, who would perfect the design and operation of casino resorts on the Strip.

CHAPTER 3

A Fruitful Containment
Amid national antigambling fervor, the Strip becomes an American vacation ideal

As a case history of legalized gambling, Nevada speaks eloquently in the negative.
Senator Estes Kefauver, 1951

The "Howdy Pardner" and "Come as you are" approach has really paid off for Las Vegas. Fifty-two weekends a year the hotels are full and "No Vacancy" signs flash at every motel—which explains the lack of competitive rivalry between the resorts. There is business for all.
Ferris Scott in Las Vegas travel guide, 1957

The foes of gambling unwittingly nurtured the casino resort in its greenhouse on the nascent Las Vegas Strip. To the dismay of politicians who campaigned to stifle American gambling, the same middle-class suburbanites who supported antigambling initiatives in their home states increasingly chose to vacation and gamble in Strip casino resorts. In the late 1940s, the casino resorts of the Strip still catered primarily to tourists from Southern California, hopeful divorcées-in-waiting, and serious gamblers. The operators of these resorts had reason to fear that national sentiment against gambling could force their closure. But by the middle of the decade, antigambling action no longer loomed as a danger and the casino resorts of the Strip had been established as vacation spots with a broad base of national patronage. Surprisingly, the new national prominence of the casino resort as a vacation option did not happen in spite of the antigambling movement of the early 1950s; in fact, it was a direct consequence of that movement.

Though a local social and political backlash against gambling had been simmering since the war years, it was around 1950 that antigambling became a national force to be reckoned with. Earlier demonstrations against gambling were usually local, and they revolved around a few police or municipal officials whose corruption was particularly noisome. In Brooklyn, for example, a probe by King's County district attorney Miles McDonald raised the public outrage when it revealed that bookmaker Harry Gross paid more than $1 million annually in police protection. The police were so involved in his operations that, during a California vacation, Gross actually tapped a plainclothes detective to supervise his betting empire.[1] When reformers uncovered such an obvious betrayal of the public trust, police and politicians resigned in disgrace, the gamblers involved received jail sentences, and the coast was cleared for new operators to move in and corrupt the new political and police powers. With efforts at enforcement purely local, operators from nearby cities could extend their businesses to the "clean" city and easily fill the vacuum left by the previous reform.

Estes Kefauver's crusade against interstate criminal conspiracy is a case study in the law of unintended consequences. Though Kefauver sought first and foremost to uncover the truth about organized crime and to expose hidden criminal networks, in the final analysis the committee, and the publicity it generated, did a great deal to enshroud criminal syndicates in myth and to grossly distort their structure and sophistication. The campaign against organized crime that both inspired and drew strength from the Kefauver Committee's findings prompted many previously "wide open" jurisdictions like southern Florida, Covington, Kentucky, and Saratoga, New York, to more strictly enforce antigambling statutes, thus driving gambling professionals to Nevada, where they found a new security in the casino resorts of the Las Vegas Strip. Their added human capital bolstered these resorts, which were now guaranteed a virtual monopoly on casino-style gambling in North America, which led to the paradox of growing casino resort profits and popularity during the twentieth century's strongest campaign against gambling.

Antigambling anxiety in the McCarthy era

Scholars have characterized the early cold war as an "age of anxiety," and this anxiety extended to virtually every facet of postwar American life. Americans faced an escalating series of problems, each, it seemed, at crisis pitch. When not being assailed by communist conspiracies domestic and foreign, Americans had to worry about a variety of races (missile, space, bomber) that they were losing. Tentacles of subversion threatened home, school, church, and government. Nowhere was safe from the insidious influence of those who sought to infiltrate and corrupt freedom and democracy. It is no surprise that many Americans assumed that crime was not the product of a variety of social and economic factors structurally embedded within American society but rather the work of a sinister conspiracy. Lingering ethnic prejudices only fueled this conspiratorial mindset.

Indeed, postwar observers felt that they were in the midst of a massive wave of crime and official venality that surpassed Prohibition-era lawlessness. In some cases, allegations of governmental corruption were thinly disguised attacks on the New Deal, but even Democrats sensed ominous forces at work in the big cities. Conspiracy-minded newspaper reporters and semi-private local and state crime commissions eagerly looked for criminal syndicates with which to do battle. Anticorruption reformers quickly pointed out that gambling was a common thread tying together political and police corruption and general moral dissipation.

Although a puritanical minority has lashed out against vices like gambling in every generation, these vices have remained consistently popular. Gambling in the middle of the twentieth century was no exception, but at the time many observers believed that deviant outside elements should be held accountable for foisting gambling upon an unwilling American society. But in retrospect, it seems more likely that self-interest, rather than conspiracy, fueled the increasing wealth and power of underworld "gamblers." As gambling operators and ward politicians saw the necessary coincidence of interest between political protection and political patronage, the interlocking directorate of corrupt local politicos and illegal gambling operators solidified.[2] While it undeniably undermined clean and honest government, this corruption was purely local and not part of an international conspiracy to infiltrate the cities with gambling. But to Americans who couldn't make the connection between their own desire to gamble and the encroachment of "boss gamblers" upon the cities, conspiracy theories made sense.

As a result, the anticrime discourse shared the anxious zeitgeist that typifies the early cold war years. FBI director J. Edgar Hoover and U.S. attorney general Tom Clark, among others, insisted that crime rates were rapidly rising in the mid-1940s. Juvenile delinquency, aided by wartime dislocation and absent or divided parental concerns, reportedly rose precipitously. Making analogies to the period after World War I, experts such as Hoover cautioned Americans to beware of increased gang and organized criminal activity. Despite the avowals of several local police departments that there was no increase in such activity, an interested group of semi-private crime-fighters and journalists began to hunt for evidence that organized crime was on the rise.[3] Thus was born the postwar anticrime movement.

Just as federal anticommunist efforts represented only the most refined expression of a sometimes-inchoate national anxiety voiced with particular fervor by certain interested parties, so too did federal action against crime follow the general national mood. The public opinion that spurred government action against gambling was not formed by the dispassionate consideration of trends in criminal justice—it was inflamed by the investigations of journalists and crime commissions. Both of these groups had individuals who balanced, with varying degrees of sincerity, good intentions with self-serving ones.

Journalists wrote about criminal conspiracies out of a frank desire to boost circulation. Since the muckrakers of the Progressive era, the media had acquired an increasing role in American society and politics. These journalists may have been motivated by a desire to cleanse the body politic of corruption, but they also wanted to sell newspapers. Many would have agreed with Denver newsman Gene Lowall's assessment: "No matter how cheap a crime story may be, it is still better than any other type of story."[4] Such eagerness to report criminal activity, combined with a tendency toward sensationalism, ensured that the media would promote the most conspiracy-minded angle of the "postwar crime wave."[5]

These journalists worked with the cooperation of figures in and out of government. They were often fed leads by the various local crime commissions across the nation. Usually privately financed but staffed by former law enforcement officials, these groups constituted exercises in voluntarism that mirrored the kinds of industrial cooperation envisioned by Herbert Hoover. Indeed, the crime commission was an innovation of the Jazz Age. Appearing first in Chicago in 1919, they soon followed in Kansas City, Cleveland, Los Angeles, and Baltimore (among other cities), and a National Crime Commission, marshaled from the U.S. Steel office of Elbert Gary, was founded in 1925. These commissions collected information on illegal activities and court proceedings and issued recommendations to judicial and police authorities. When these recommendations went unheeded, crime commissions invariably turned to the newspapers. Perhaps because of the failure of virtually all attempts to muzzle bootlegging, the crime commission declined with the end of the decade. With the end of World War II and new vistas opening up with both criminal exploitation and journalistic verve, the crime commission experienced a revival in the 1940s.[6] The new crime commissions, while focusing on syndicate crime and political corruption in general, had a specific focus that the original commissions lacked—gambling.

A 1950 report by the Citizens Committee of Massachusetts exemplifies the work of these committees. The committee estimated that between $6.8 and $21.5 billion dollars was annually spent on racetrack and sports betting, numbers games, and slot machines. An additional $3 to $4 billion was spent on illegal off-track horse and dog race betting. The committee charged that rampant police corruption led, in some cases, to a breakdown of even token enforcement of antigambling statutes. Gambling operators had turned gambling into a nationally operated big business, in which "large-scale, illegal gambling activities [were] carried on by dangerous criminal elements who have adapted recognized systems of business organization." These syndicates were ubiquitous profiteers of vice: they controlled, "among other activities, bookmaking, slot machines, and organized gambling activities in their other forms." The committee was especially chagrined by the possibility that gambling retarded retail trade volumes and contributed to unemployment, and members noted that in-plant gambling "on an organized scale" existed in Massachusetts.[7]

The Chicago Crime Commission, headed after 1942 by Virgil W. Peterson, was the first among equals of postwar crime commissions. Peterson was a former FBI agent who had headed offices in Boston, St. Louis, and Milwaukee. While in the employ of the bureau, Peterson had not specialized in organized crime, but in Chicago he gained a reputation as a "walking encyclopedia" of both criminal syndicates and gambling. Lecturing in cities around the nation, Peterson would impress local journalists with his command of the "facts" of criminal syndicates; in short, he was able to name names. Peterson's efforts sparked a revitalization of the crime commission movement. Miami, California, New York, Dallas, Kansas City, St. Louis, and other cities had active commissions based on the Chicago model by 1950.[8]

Peterson and other figures in the crime commission movement adamantly linked gambling to organized crime. They argued that gambling profits funded other activities, such as prostitution and the narcotics traffic. In response to arguments that legal, state-regulated, taxed gambling would satisfy the need of the public for gambling while denying criminals the profits, Peterson and his protégés developed a series of rebuttals which revolved around the central tenet that once any citizen crossed the line and profited from illegal gambling, he or she was irrevocably tainted as an anti-social miscreant. Newspaper accounts and commission reports stressed the evils of the criminal, not the crime. Personal deficiencies, whether racial or psychological, were responsible for gambling crime, not structural demands within the American economy. Degeneracy was the *essence* of gambling criminals, a fact that no amount of "rehabilitation" could alter. Legalizing the crime of gambling would not end the criminal cycle; it would only give known criminals a foothold in legitimate business.

By defining gambling operators as ipso facto criminals, the ideology of the crime commissions and its apparent acceptance by most voters gave state governments and Congress little leeway to consider legalization schemes. The postwar campaign delayed the revival of public gambling for revenue purposes until 1964, when New Hampshire became the first state since Reconstruction to sponsor a lottery. In the absence of a coherent federal policy toward gambling, the state of Nevada continued in its "wide-open" status; despite run-ins with the Kefauver Committee and later Robert Kennedy's Justice Department, the federal threat to Nevada was always more illusory than substantive. It is unthinkable that southern congressmen, committed to states' rights as a defense against federal antisegregation efforts, would have supported federal encroachment upon Nevada's right to regulate commerce within its borders. Still, the furor directed against corrupting "boss gamblers" prevented other states from legalizing casino gaming for nearly a generation. This gave the casino resort ample time to develop, safe from competing gambling forms, in its desert hothouse on the Las Vegas Strip.

During this anxious period, efforts to legalize and tax gambling crumbled nationwide, allowing Nevada to maintain its monopoly on legal casino gambling. In November 1950, for example, proposals to legalize various forms of gambling, from lotteries to slot machines to "wide-open" state-regulated gambling, failed. Montana, Arizona, Massachusetts, and California all rejected pro-gambling initiatives. The Massachusetts example is particularly puzzling, because voters there quashed plans for a state-run lottery while endorsing a minimum old-age pension allowance of $75 a month that the lottery was supposed to fund. However, this turn against state-sanctioned gambling cannot be seen as a general tendency toward puritanism. Arizona, Arkansas, Oregon, and South Dakota all demurred on proposals to limit or ban the manufacture, sale, or consumption of alcoholic beverages.[9] Voters turned specifically against gambling because it had been identified as an explicit root cause of crime in a way that other vices had not. It was a pervasive source of American anxiety, all the more so because it was a common American pastime.

Estes makes his point, then craps out

The fullest elaboration of gambling as a pernicious national disgrace began in 1950 with the Special Committee to Investigate Organized Crime in Interstate Commerce, known popularly by the name of its colorful chair Estes Kefauver.[10] Out of the general anticrime clamor of the late 1940s emerged a call for national action against the national criminal syndicate that was believed to be running gambling operations all over the country. FBI inaction against organized crime created a void that the scattered efforts of local commissions could not fill, and many "concerned citizens" began to call for a national response to organized crime.

Kefauver proposed in January 1950 that the Judiciary Committee, on which he sat, formally investigate "interstate gambling and racketeering activities and . . . the manner in which the facilities of interstate commerce are made a vehicle of organized crime."[11] After a fair amount of political haggling and arm-twisting, the Senate delivered a temporary special committee to investigate crime to Kefauver. The committee's emphasis was to be on gambling and crime. Some of the chief procedural obscurantism had come from Pat McCarran, senior Democratic senator from Nevada and a formidable legislative presence.[12] Given the phraseology of Kefauver's request to open the committee and its a priori faith in the evils of gambling, McCarran's opposition was not surprising. The Truman administration, sensitive to charges of corruption that swamped the Pendergast machine in Missouri, was also leery of an investigation of gambling and crime. Through political logrolling and skillfull use of the media to pressure opponents, though, the freshman senator was able to carry the day, and he became the chairman of the committee.[13]

Kefauver's chairmanship and the committee's greatest public notoriety spanned nearly a year—from May 10, 1950 to May 1, 1951. The five committee members were Kefauver; Herbert O'Conor (D-MD), who succeeded Kefauver as committee chair in 1951, Lester Hunt (D-WY), Alexander Wiley (R-WI), and Charles Tobey (R-NH). Hearings were held in Washington as well as a number of cities throughout the United States. The committee's leap to fame, however, came with its nationally televised March hearings in New York City. With these broadcasts, the sight of "gangsters" bristling at the questions of committee counsel Rudolph Halley became familiar, as did the stock response of taciturn witnesses, "I refuse to answer on the ground that it may tend to incriminate or degrade me." The sight of suspected racketeers refusing to answer question after question, of course, incriminated these men in the court of public opinion.[14]

These hearings allowed the committee to make sweeping generalizations about the state of crime in interstate commerce. In its final report, the committee declared the existence of a *nationwide crime syndicate* in the United States, "despite the protestations of a strangely assorted company of criminals, self-serving politicians, plain blind fools, and others who may be misguided, that there is no such combine." This syndicate was paradoxically both "loosely organized" and "cohesive." The syndicate focused its operations chiefly on gambling in its several forms, including the race wire, slot machines, and illegal casinos. Behind this syndicate lurked a "shadowy, international criminal organization known as the *Mafia*." The Mafia's "origin and headquarters" were in Sicily, its major business was narcotics, and it was the final arbiter in disputes between rival criminals. This mafia sponsored a dramatic increase in *political corruption*. Such corruption stemmed from beat cops and detectives who took $10 to ignore small-time operations to sheriffs, mayors, and governors. Finally, the committee concluded that secure in their illegal profits, "known hoodlums" had begun the *infiltration of legitimate businesses.* Thus, by using "gangster methods," criminals branched out into legal industries, particularly in the alcoholic beverage retail trade.[15]

Arguments to legalize urban gambling and tax it were silenced, and the nation hunkered down for a "war" against the insidious conspiracy. The obsession with "hoodlums" infiltrating "legitimate business" reveals the antigambler mindset of the committee: it was not crime that was the problem, but criminals, even when they were not breaking the law; to legalize and tax gambling would only legitimize sociopaths. An exchange between Moe Sedway and Senator Tobey during the former's testimony in Las Vegas best typifies the committee's reasoning. Tobey derided the gambling business and Sedway did his best to defend it:

> TOBEY: You are growing rich, so to speak. . . . You don't contribute a thing in the way of production that makes real wealth. . . . Why do men play the game this way? What makes it attractive to them? What is the matter with men?
>
> SEDWAY: Just go into that type of business and you get into it and you stay in it.
>
> TOBEY: You say you knew Lucky Luciano? He is a moral pervert and the scum of the earth, Lucky Luciano, and he is playing the game over there still in Italy. [Gambling operators] may have money but that is all they have got.
>
> SEDWAY: We don't get as rich as you think. This is hard work. I work pretty hard in this business.
>
> TOBEY: But you get the rich end all the time. If you put the same talent you have got toward constructive things in life, producing something that makes real wealth and human happiness, men would arise and call you blessed.[16]

Tobey's indignation represented a dying strain of producerism in American culture, something that had all but disappeared in the postindustrial society of the late twentieth century. But he also echoed fears of corruption as an infection that needed to be contained, or, as he put it, "a cancer spot on the body politic." He expressed perfectly the anxiety of his constituents toward the dangers of unrestrained gambling, but he failed to recognize the emerging distinction between urban gambling and the suburbanized casino resorts. For this reason, Tobey comes across to current readers as a priggish moralist bent on denying others the fun of gambling rather than as a public servant deeply concerned about an urban activity that he viewed as a great social evil.

Because the postwar anticrime movement identified those who broke the gambling laws as inveterate criminal deviants, life was difficult for suspected syndicate members once they were publicly tarred with the Mafia brush. No matter what career they sought to pursue, they were still accused of using "underworld" methods and bringing a taint to legitimate society. The committee established that there was a Mafia by rather elliptical reasoning: if a witness denied that there was a Mafia, he was obviously a part of it, and, if he admitted to knowing men who were suspected of being in it, they were obviously "mobbed up" as well. In short, the committee interpreted its failure to find any "Mafia" members as proving conclusively the existence of that organization.

The Kefauver Committee, given its focus on "gamblers" as the evil conspirators behind organized crime, could hardly be expected to remain mute on the state of affairs in Nevada. The consensus in Nevada law enforcement was that "underworld" characters in Nevada gaming were not mobsters, but "gamblers." As Bill Moore maintained in the face of Charles Tobey's indignant protest, a felony conviction for a gambling violation in another state would not discount a potential Nevada licensee; after all, where was he to get experience, if not in an illegal operation? On this matter, members of the Kefauver Committee and proponents of Nevada gaming suffered an irreconcilable difference of opinion. Anticrime advocates howled at Nevada for coddling convicted felons, while Nevadans felt their own logic was unassailable. It was no coincidence that this difference in opinion allowed Nevada to sponsor an industry that brought in millions of dollars of investments and revenue.

In addition to the political pressure put on gambling by Kefauver and others, the late 1940s saw the elaboration of the social and medical discourse on problem gambling. In 1947, for instance, Gamblers Anonymous was organized by a "reformed gambler." The organization was consciously patterned on Alcoholics Anonymous and its birth highlights the new danger with which Americans viewed gambling.[17] Although many people still considered gamblers responsible for their losses, a growing number were more sympathetic to problem gamblers, particularly women. The housewife who plugged her grocery money into slot machines became a staple of antigambling literature. The prominent businessman who was brought to embezzlement by his weakness for a wager, a fixture of the literature since the antebellum period, appeared in a new guise: that of an honest man drawn into *organized* crime by gambling.

In short, the Kefauver Committee and other mid-century antigamblers did much to complicate the development of any national approach to gambling control. By retarding efforts in other states to legalize and regulate gambling, antigamblers unintentionally gave the casino resorts of the

Strip ample time to develop relatively free from competition. Thus, the Las Vegas Strip became a beacon of sorts for both suburbanites seeking to gamble safely and gaming operators needing new homes.

A wide-open town reaps the harvest

That the desperate tenor of antigambling campaigners could not halt the explosive growth of the Las Vegas Strip in the early 1950s might suggest that the growth of casino resorts was inevitable and that nothing, save an above-ground nuclear test gone horribly wrong, could stop it. But in fact, Kefauver and others set into motion events that would actually accelerate the growth of casino resorts on the Strip. Around the nation, local law enforcement agencies stepped up their efforts against gambling, and apparently, citizens, grew less eager to patronize certain kinds of illegal gambling. In 1951, federal laws banning the shipment of slot machines across state lines and requiring illegal bookmakers to register and pay a tax also discouraged gambling. At the end of that year, the *New York Times* reported that book-making activities had declined by 40 to 90 percent in most large cities. It further noted that "gambling syndicates' bosses" in general were operating at a greatly reduced scale.[22] American gambling appeared to be on the wane, at least outside of the casino resorts of the Las Vegas Strip.

The combined efforts of the Kefauver Committee, national antigambling action, and local initiatives drove slot machines and illegal gambling casinos out of most major cities and vacation spots. Idaho, which had legalized slot machines in 1947, banned them again in 1949 after widely publicized corruption seemed to reinforce Kefauver's claim that legalized gambling was unworkable.[23] Only in a few places, such as Hot Springs, Arkansas, did technically illegal but politically protected casinos survive into the 1960s. In most other formerly wide-open towns, such as Atlantic City and Miami Beach, the antigambling statutes began to be enforced with greater regularity. This served to remove both the physical gambling equipment as well as the human capital, experienced operators, from these jurisdictions. On the national level, Congress asserted itself by passing a bill, signed into law by President Truman in January 1951, that banned the transportation of slot machines across state lines. The bill also forbade the use of slot machines on federal land, which forced the removal of slots from officers' clubs on military bases.[24] Quick-witted operators easily circumvented the ban on interstate traffic by disassembling machines before loading them for shipment, but the bill symbolized the national desire to limit the availability of slot machines.

Local, state, and federal measures chilled urban gambling throughout most of the nation but did not imperil Nevada's legal casinos. This allowed

Kefauver does Vegas

Like an antipornography advocate drawn by revulsion to the most depraved hardcore porn, Estes Kefauver could not resist visiting the nation's capital of legalized gambling. The committee, during its epic road swing, stopped in Las Vegas for hearings on November 15, 1950, less than two weeks after its catastrophic (for Illinois Democrats, if triumphant for Kefauver) Chicago hearings. Given that the committee only scheduled one day of hearings followed by a press conference and was in Los Angeles for hearings by 10 the next morning, it is clear that the Las Vegas stopover was not a bona fide fact-finding mission. The Las Vegas hearings were almost a footnote to the rest of the committee's work, and the only message that the committee drew from the city was that legalized gambling was a major failure, a message that Kefauver and his fellow committee members accepted as self-evident before their airplane touched down in Las Vegas.

The committee questioned an interesting group of Las Vegans. The hearing began with the one-two punch of Bill Moore, of the Last Frontier and Nevada Tax Commission, and Clifford Jones, Lieutenant Governor and part owner of several casinos, including the Thunderbird, Golden Nugget, and Pioneer Club. Chief Counsel Halley led the questioning, which established to the committee's satisfaction that the Tax Commission and state government tolerated "a great many undesirable characters" who conducted gambling operations in the state.[18] Subsequent witnesses included Henry Phillips, chief operator of the Last Frontier's race commission room; Louis Wiener, attorney of the executor of Benjamin Siegel's estate; Lawrence Russell Greeson, Las Vegas chief of police; and Robert Kaltenborn, automobile parts store owner and real estate speculator.

The afternoon climaxed with the questioning of Wilbur Clark of the Desert Inn and then Moe Sedway of the Flamingo. Clark was queried about the investment of the "Cleveland group" (Dalitz et al.), while Sedway was questioned extensively about his criminal record and "associations" with Siegel, Frank Costello, Joe Adonis, and other reputed syndicate members. When questioning Sedway, Kefauver stated that Siegel had been killed "in connection with the wire service," but could not get Sedway to confirm or deny this.[19]

The committee's questioning attempted to establish that "hoodlums," backed by the national crime syndicate, had infiltrated the Las Vegas casino industry. Consistent with the committee's other work, the denials of Sedway and the others were interpreted as an admission of guilt: since they denied that the Mafia was in Las Vegas, the Mafia was obviously there. Yet the committee could offer no hard evidence to prove this assertion.

In keeping with the hearings, the committee's final judgment on Nevada gaming was harsh. The Third Interim Report, among its "general conclusions," stated without hesitation:

> The legalization of gambling would not terminate the widespread predatory activities of criminal gangs and syndicates. The history of legalized gambling in Nevada . . . gives no assurance that mobsters and racketeers can be converted into responsible businessmen through the simple process of obtaining State and local licenses for their gambling enterprises. Gambling, moreover, historically has been associated with cheating and corruption.[20]

This final report, in its further discussion of legal Strip casinos, married interstate gambling syndicates, casino operators, and Nevada Tax Commission, pointing out William Moore's dual role as member of the commission and part owner of the Last Frontier and other egregious conflicts of interest. The committee also decried the failure of Nevada authorities to deny licenses for past gambling convictions in other states.[21] Because of the negative portrait of Nevada gaming that emerged from the hearings, though, casino operators and state legislators endeavored to change the nature of Nevada gambling. Within four years of the committee hearings, a new, more stringent state regulatory regime was in place.

suburban middle-class voters to feel that they had done the urban poor and working classes a great service in prodding public servants into sweeping slot machines from taverns, craps games from the factories, and bookies from the schools. Congressmen could report to their constituents that they had taken vigorous federal action in the antigambling crusade while not trampling on states' rights. At the same time, suburbanites were secure in the knowledge that, should they wish to gamble, there existed an oasis outside distant Las Vegas that they had the financial resources and leisure time to frequent—a claim that those perceived to be the "victims" of urban gambling could not often make.

Zealous local crime commissions belied half-hearted national efforts at antigambling policy, though they too had the unintended consequence of fostering the casino industry in southern Nevada. Within the classic analysis of immigration patterns as the result of push and pull factors, the national gambling freeze of the early 1950s served as a tremendous push factor for "boss gamblers." Nevada, with a generation of legal casino gaming and the benefit of a sunny climate, no doubt would have attracted the interest of the gambling fraternity regardless of other developments. Still, the growing clamor against gamblers throughout the rest of the United States no doubt hastened many decisions to move to Nevada. In fact, dozens of gambling operators from throughout the United States brought their talents to Las Vegas casino resorts. In addition, countless gambling employees, their vocation now throttled by the law, resettled in Las Vegas where they might freely practice their trade.[25]

These "gamblers" were mostly drawn from the cohort of former bootleggers that had come of age during Prohibition and diversified into gambling. Eddie Levinson is emblematic of operators driven to Las Vegas by the national antigambling movement. Born in 1899, he grew up in Detroit and became a part of its thriving gambling subculture. He ran illegal gambling operations in his home city until the mid-1940s, slowed by occasional arrests, though most of the charges against him were dismissed. Levinson was a prominent member of the Detroit-area "gambling fraternity." He collaborated with Samuel Garfield, a Midwest betting and gambling operator and friend of Moe Dalitz.[26] Levinson's two brothers, Mike and Louis, ran illegal gambling operations in Covington, Kentucky, until a reform movement ended gambling there in 1960. In the late 1940s, Levinson began operations in south Florida, where he was arrested but not convicted in both 1950 and 1951 for gambling-related offenses in Miami. Conditions in Florida became untenable by 1952, and Levinson moved to Las Vegas, where he became a part owner of the Sands.[27] His greatest glory came with his development of the downtown Fremont Hotel, which successfully transplanted the Strip-style suburban casino resort into the urban framework of Fremont Street.

Like most of his fellow "gamblers," Levinson was Jewish, something that seemed to made him a more obvious target. Wallace Turner, in his book on Las Vegas, quoted an anonymous "high government official" in describing the Semitic predilection for gambling operations:

> There are all kinds in [gambling] like Irish and a few Negroes but the biggest group is Jewish. Beyond that, where the Italians get hold of a good gambling joint, they have somebody run it for them and that somebody is usually Jewish. . . . Meyer Lansky is a Jew, and he has

very, very close ties with the top hoods in the Cosa Nostra outfit. Bugsy Siegel was a Jew and he was hooked up real close with the Italian mob. Some of the places in Las Vegas today are really controlled by the Mafia . . . [but] the front men are almost always Jews.[28]

This was written in the early 1960s, when ethnic stereotyping could still be passed off as sociological analysis in certain circles, but the sentiments expressed betray the underlying social and ethnic prejudices that contributed to the antigambling movement.

Other writers could just as flagrantly apply a double standard, according to which crimes by some "Americans" were seen as less serious than those committed by "ethnics." Attorney Rufus King, in a 1969 book on gambling and organized crime, brushed over the a shady leaseback agreement entered into by Raymond Smith, owner of the Reno gambling hall Harolds Club, reporting that it "involved tax shenanigans rather than any infiltration by undesirable outsiders." On the same page, Dalitz and associates, by this time decades removed from their bootlegging Mayfield Road days, were described as "one of the toughest gangs in the country" and the Lansky brothers as part of a "savage coterie." Whereas William Harrah and Raymond Smith were deemed to be of "impeccable if modest background," Ben Siegel was dismissed as a "half-insane killer."[29] Levinson and others were often targeted because of their conspicuous ethnicity, and, once identified as "boss gamblers," they had little chance of "passing" in legitimate business circles. Only in Nevada was the "boss gambler" label not a stigma, but an asset.

Early in his committee's life, Estes Kefauver hoped that gambling and crime would crystallize as issues around which he could build a serious campaign for the presidency. For several reasons, that did not happen. By 1952, interest in gambling crime was waning, and by 1955 the gambling issue was essentially off the national agenda. Most consider the disappearance of crime as a national issue to be a result of the success of state and local authorities in containing illegal gambling. Unlike the issues of race and national defense, which dominated the national agenda in the 1950s, gambling crime control could be effectively administered on the local level. Indeed, it was. Crackdowns on illegal gambling operations markedly reduced the scale of illegal gambling.

Another explanation is that gambling crime had, by the mid-1950s, moved through the issue-attention cycle as theorized by Anthony Downs. Certainly, the sudden discovery of "boss gamblers" in America's cities mirrors the "alarmed discovery and euphoric enthusiasm" stage of Downs's process. The "realization of the cost of significant progress," that is, that Americans would have to give up gambling, contented citizens with the containment of gambling within Nevada and not to seek its complete extirpation from the Union. Having devised local solutions to local crime problems and unwilling to shoulder the burden of a national gaming moratorium, voters and politicians allowed the gambling and crime issue to slide into relative obscurity.[30] The lasting legacy of Kefauver and others who attempted to bring the issue of gambling and crime to national prominence was, ironically, the bolstering of Nevada's monopoly on casino gaming, which inestimably aided the elaboration of the casino resort on the Las Vegas Strip.

Zoomtown USA

Even as Kefauver and his supporters rousted gamblers from the poolrooms and plants of the East, Strip casino resorts made tremendous profits and buoyed the growth of the Las Vegas metropolitan area. The success of the first wave of casino development inspired newer, grander projects, which in turn spurred the renovation of existing properties and additional new construction. Contemporary boosters spoke of a seemingly infinite arc of new construction along the Strip in the early 1950s. The rising tide of wealth from Strip resorts buoyed gross state gaming revenue as it increased from just over $27 million in 1946 to nearly $120 million in 1956; flat gaming fees collected in the same period jumped from approximately a quarter million dollars to over $5 million. The population of the city of Las Vegas exploded from about 8,400 in 1940 to almost 50,000 in 1956, with almost all of the newcomers attached in some way to the resorts of the Strip. Perhaps the most telling sign of the new wealth of Southern Nevada was the increase in property tax valuations from about $10.5 million in 1945 to over $118 million in 1956.[31]

Some of this growth can be attributed to federal spending such as Nellis Air Force Base and the Nevada Atomic Test Site, but casinos were responsible for most of the increase. The composition of Clark County's labor force reveals how beholden the area's economy was to casino gaming. In 1940, the service sector, with 1,299 employees, was the county's largest; by 1958, it had maintained its primacy and expanded to include 13,900 workers. Statistics reinforced the boosters' claims that casino resorts brought wealth to Southern Nevada; these boosters felt justified in labeling Las Vegas first a boomtown, then, seizing on the atomic zeitgeist, a zoomtown.[32] When other jurisdictions considered the legalization of gambling beginning in the 1970s, it was this explosive growth that they sought to harness by creating casino resorts.

Detractors of casino gaming maintain that casino resorts are little more than sophisticated three-card monte stands; they parasitically drain money from a region's economy that would otherwise be absorbed into more legitimate entertainment sectors. But in Southern Nevada, casino gaming did more than cannibalize discretionary income; it constituted the driving force behind a profound reshaping of the region's economy. In keeping with a trend begun haltingly with the construction of the Hoover Dam, the economy of Southern Nevada in the early 1950s was reconstituted around tourism. By 1956, Southern Nevadans had built nearly 9,000 hotel and motel rooms to house their visitors; The casino and tourist industries combined maintained payrolls of almost $61 million in 1956. The total impact of this money on the rest of the region's economy is impossible to precisely tabulate, but it was no doubt gargantuan.[33]

The Strip's growth followed national trends. Between the end of World War II and 1960, the U.S. gross national product boomed from $200 billion to over $500 billion. Unemployment remained at or below 5 percent nationwide, and inflation held to about 3 percent a year.[34] Although segments of the American population, including the rural and urban poor, were left behind by this wave of prosperity, Americans in general had more discretionary income in the twenty years or so after World War II than at any previous time. More than anything, this fact made the time ripe for the creation of a new leisure industry. The average middle-class family would have had appreciably more money to spend on luxury services like a gambling vacation. It was natural that the newly affluent middle class would choose to vacation in a resort that resembled the orderly life of the suburbs while allowing a modicum of hedonistic release.

The resorts that welcomed tourists to the Strip in the 1950s were larger and gaudier than earlier houses. New casinos like the Sahara, Sands, Riviera, Royal Nevada, and Dunes vied for the title of "newest with the mostest." Despite a downturn in new construction, a string of casino failures and near-misses, and a tightening of the market after a 1955 building boom, casino operators and local boosters continued to convey optimism for Las Vegas's future.[35] In a telling transformation, the New Frontier, a space age vacation paradise, replaced the Last Frontier, with its Old West theme and historical village. The original wave of casino resort-building on the Strip, bringing new capital, people, and ideas into Las Vegas, begged for the comforting presence of nostalgic theming, and, tying the new gambling industry to the trusty (though mythic) frontier past assuaged anxieties that the new was not necessarily good. But by the mid-1950s, the new had become familiar and the atomic age was a very present reality at the test site to the city's north. The new confidence in the casino resort reflected a national optimism that no challenge, including that of space, was insuperable.[36]

Perhaps the most convincing sign of the casino resort's rise to dominance was its appearance outside of its Strip birthplace. The Fremont

By the early 1950s when the Dunes was planned, casino design was more or less set: a central casino/restaurant/theater building with wings of motel buildings that could be cheaply expanded. The actual Dunes looked a great deal like this, with the addition of a giant cartoonish sultan that towered over the entrance, a early attempt to make a rather pedestrian building seem fantastic. Courtesy UNLV Special Collections.

Hotel, which cost $6 million to build, was the first non-Strip casino resort. Its hotel towered fifteen stories and was the tallest building in Nevada when it opened in May 1956. Instead of a voluminous parking lot, the Fremont boasted a multilevel parking garage. Its height and garage were structural adaptations of the casino resort to the higher land prices and more congested space of downtown. The major functions of the casino resort remained intact, however. The Fremont had a glitzy casino, gourmet restaurants, and a showroom.[37]

Structurally integrated casino hotel complexes such as the Fremont and the Showboat on Boulder Highway applied the lessons of the Strip to new locales. Even downtown casinos, loath to let patrons leave for other properties with lodgings, began to add hotels and parking facilities.[38] The era of smalltime urban gambling halls was waning as integrated, mall-like casino resorts pulled most tourists south to the Strip and even began to gradually encroach upon the downtown. The replacement of traditional gambling halls with casino resorts on Fremont Street, the city's downtown center, shows the dominance of the casino resort paradigm.

The boom of the mid-1950s affected the future of the casino resort in two ways. Most obviously, the superlative mood that successive "newest with the mostest" casinos created spurred tourism and further development. On the other hand, the market was effectively overbuilt. The worst fears of casino operators, namely, that increased competition would bring doom for all, never materialized. The boom of growth never really turned to bust; rather, it progressed to a plateau of level, if not spectacular, growth. As a result, casinos were forced to develop more efficient and effective cash controls and operating procedures. Abundance, not scarcity, paradoxically forced casino operators to restructure and set the pattern for casino design and operation into the next century.

Watching the watchmen: Creating Nevada's gaming regulations

Concomitant with the physical expansion of the casino industry outside of Las Vegas came a dramatic redefinition of the purpose and scope of the state of Nevada's regulatory regime. This sudden increase in Nevada's regulatory apparatus was more than a knee-jerk reaction to the increase in casino revenue. It signaled an entirely new conception of the gaming industry as an important one to Nevada, and as one to be actively promoted rather than grudgingly tolerated. The casino resort had become a valuable asset to the state and one that consequently warranted protection.

Casino resorts needed a protection that only state regulation could provide for several reasons. As businesses with inventories composed almost entirely of cash, they presented innumerable opportunities for theft at all levels. Indeed, it was long an accepted way of doing business that everyone, from the dealer to the casino president, got a "cut" of the casino revenue en route to the count room. The biggest loser to this kind of shrinkage was the state; with smaller reported earnings, casinos paid less in revenue taxes. Since it was in the best interest of most casino employees to not only ignore but even to actively take part in skimming, only a strong regulatory presence could effectively play watchdog.

The other major asset that needed regulatory protection was the reputation of the industry, and this was the foot that the state stuck into the door of the casino industry. Allegations of organized criminal influence might have somewhat chilled business but casino operators positively dreaded any kind of cheating scandal. As businesses that lived and prospered through good press, casino resorts were particularly vulnerable to any sort of bad press, particularly stories that led prospective tourists to doubt that they would get a square deal. Therefore, in the early 1950s, when industry leaders began to accept the need for more regulation, it was chiefly cheating scandals that they believed would be the target.

But the only way to ensure that casinos were honest was to follow the money, and following the money would invariably lead investigators to any silent underworld investors. To receive the seal of state regulatory approval, casinos had to be, at least on paper, free from the influence of organized crime, something that led to even more convoluted financing and skimming arrangements that continued to confound regulators into the 1980s. But in 1955, most casino operators, experiencing a jubilee year of profit and growth, felt that the best way to safeguard their wealth was to permit and even facilitate a more stringent regulatory presence.

Before the reorganization of Nevada's regulatory structure, the Tax Commission had possessed the chief responsibility for both collecting revenue from casinos and licensing them on the state level. From 1931 to 1945, there had been no state effort in licensing or regulation. Rather, counties licensed and collected fees from each gambling hall. These fees were assigned on a per-table, per-machine basis and were payable quarterly in advance. In 1945, a new law required that casinos pay a quarterly state license fee tied to gross gaming revenue. Initially, the fee was 1 percent of revenue over $3,000. This licensing system was slightly amended in 1949, when new legislation eliminated the $3,000 exemption, raised the rate to 2 percent and assessed an additional annual state license fee based on the number of games operated by an establishment.[39]

This system served decently enough for the small gambling halls it was designed to oversee, but it was clearly inadequate for the new resorts. The Tax Commission, for one, was responsible for the collection of all state taxes and was not suited to deal with the specific problems of regulation on the scale needed by the new casino resorts. The casino resorts of the Strip, operating around the clock, collected revenues that were simply unimaginable to those who had framed the original gambling oversight. The potential for underreporting gambling income—skimming—was great, with few mechanisms to ensure that operators correctly reported their gambling win and paid their allotted taxes. This system would obviously need major overhauling, but two menacing developments in the early 1950s crystallized the need for change.

The first threat was federal. Even after the Kefauver Committee disbanded, its report on Nevada threatened trouble for the state. In 1951, Senator Pat McCarran and other Nevadans lobbied vigorously to defeat a Kefauver-inspired bill that would have heavily taxed gambling establishments. Even after that bill's demise, Nevadans remained wary of Kefauver's political ambition. Alan Bible, McCarran's successor in the Senate, feared that Kefauver would attempt to push a federal tax on gambling through Congress. Such a tax would have devastated the casino industry and the entire state of Nevada. If Nevada were to avoid federal scrutiny, many, including Governor Charles Russell, felt that it had to tighten its gambling controls.

The second threat was local. Goings-on at the Thunderbird brought the issue of gaming regulation to a head in 1954. The Thunderbird, a popular casino with locals, was initially believed to be "clean." Clifford Jones, the lieutenant governor of the state, held an 11 percent interest in the casino, and it was a favored haunt of politicians throughout the early 1950s. But in 1953, rumors began to circulate that "gangsters" from out of state secretly financed and controlled the Thunderbird. Publisher Hank Greenspun's *Las Vegas Sun* sponsored an investigation in which an undercover detective posed as "Louis Tabet," a thug from the East with a police record seeking a gaming license, and he recorded conversations with a number of local officials. The *Sun*'s investigative team discovered a good deal of corruption. Sheriff Glenn Jones, County Commissioner Rodney Colton, Lieutenant Governor Jones, and his law partner Louis Wiener were among those discovered to have financial arrangements with alleged organized crime figures. This threatened the reputation of casino resorts as "clean" forms of gambling, and it forced action from the institution's legislative protectors in the Nevada state legislature.

The Nevada public found the Kefauver hearings, the Tabet investigation, and other unsavory revelations about organized crime elements in the state to be compelling reasons to reform the system of gambling oversight. The legislature in 1955 created the Nevada Gaming Control Board (GCB) within the Tax Commission. The purpose for the change was to "inaugurate a policy to eliminate the undesirables in Nevada gaming and to provide regulations for the licensing and operation of gaming." The Gaming Control Board consisted of three full-time members appointed by the governor, and a staff of auditors, investigators, and office personnel charged with researching license applicants and policing casinos to ensure compliance with gaming legislation.[40] In order to finance the expanded staff, license fees were raised.

Under the new regulatory structure, ownership of a license was specifically identified as a privilege that the Gaming Control Board could revoke at any time. Only with this power, it was believed, would the board have the "muscle" to keep organized crime out of Nevada gaming. The board's power was established with a case involving the Thunderbird. After hearings that lasted well into 1955, the Tax Commission revoked the Thunderbird's license because of the illicit investment by Meyer Lansky. A court-ordered injunction prevented the closure of the casino until the matter was resolved, which would not be for two years. When the court finally did rule, it reversed the revocation of the Thunderbird's license as "without substantial evidentiary support" saving thousands of jobs and preventing reams of bad publicity, but it upheld the right of the executive branch (Gaming Control Board) to "fix the standards by which suitability is to be determined." With the threat of immediate, noninjunctive suspension of licenses, the Gaming Control Board would have the power to maintain industry standards, set and policed by itself.

This system suited the casino resorts of the Strip admirably, if not perfectly. By later standards (particularly New Jersey's gaming law), the Nevada regulations of 1955 seem remarkably reactive. They gave the new Gaming Control Board the right to investigate and penalize flagrant violators of the code, but didn't follow the system through to its obvious conclusion—to involve state officials in the daily operations of the casino resort, which would ensure that revenues were reported accurately. But it gave Nevadans a sense that they had done something to keep "undesirables" out of the industry, regulators the theoretical power to press sanctions against offenders, and casino resorts a seal of state sponsorship and protection. Most important, operators could continue to skim revenues, both to lower their gaming taxes and to pay dividends to investors who were not licensed.

Nevada's regulatory regime grew and adjusted with the expanding casino resorts. In 1959, at the request of Governor Grant Sawyer, the legislature reconfigured the state's regulatory apparatus. Recognizing that the scope of gaming regulation was overburdening the Tax Commission, the legislature created the Nevada Gaming Commission. The Gaming Commission assumed the licensing and taxing functions that the Tax Commission had formerly exercised, whereas investigation and enforcement remained the province of the Gaming Control Board, which was now placed directly under the aegis of the Gaming Commission.[41] Thus, gambling regulation, which had originally been the province of an arm of the general tax-collecting agency, became a separate arm of the executive branch of Nevada. More than anything, this development indicates the tremendous importance of gaming to Nevada's economy.

The Gaming Commission consisted of five members appointed by the governor to four-year terms. No more than three could share the same political party, nor could any member have a direct financial interest in gaming. The commission adopted regulations governing the gaming industry, issued and revoked licenses, imposed fines and penalties for infractions of gaming regulations, and collected all state gaming fees.[42] The Gaming Control Board continued to consist of three governor-appointed members. GCB members were prohibited from political activity and from having any stake, direct or indirect, in gaming. Qualification for nomination to the Gaming Control Board included "experience in accountancy, administration, investigation, law enforcement, law, or gaming." This board enforced the regulations of the commission and made recommendations to the commission about the issuance of licenses. Serving under the three members of the GCB were a full-time professional staff that included an Audit Division, Investigative Division, and Enforcement Division.[43]

This new regulatory structure indicated the increased size of Nevada gaming, as well as its expanding economic importance. The ultimate establishment of a strong regulatory presence provided more than good publicity for the casino industry. It gave the industry standards of accountability and therefore a layer of insulation from charges of corruption, as well as an unparalleled participation of the state in an ostensibly private industry. Within ten years of the final disposition of the Thunderbird case, major national hotel corporations would be casino owners, a shift that even the most prescient would be hard pressed to imagine during the heyday of the antigambling scare. And the system of regulation that Nevadans hammered out in the mid-1950s would in turn serve as the model for the stricter New Jersey model, which would be the regime of choice for legal casino gaming across the nation a half century later.

"Klondike in the desert:" Promoting the new Xanadu

After weathering the storm of the mid-century antigambling wave, Nevada's casino resorts became permanent fixtures on the American landscape. With illegal gambling operations around the nation fast falling victim to the wrath of reformers, the palaces of the Strip beckoned as oases where gambling was legal and removed from the problems of city gambling. Casino resorts now had a national reason for being—to provide gambling and entertainment to the middle-class suburbanites who had deemed urban gambling unsound. By the early 1950s, it became appropriate to speak of the casino resort's appeal as a durable national phenomenon, as newspapers and magazines across the United States began to speak of casino resorts as places for fun, safe adventure.

The Kefauver Committee represented the high-water mark of the mid-century antigambling movement. Since the people of Nevada did not turn against casino gaming then it seemed likely that they would not in the future, all things remaining equal. The absence of a national gambling policy agenda and the impossibility of federal antigambling enforcement, combined with Nevada's increasing reliance on the gaming industry, made it clear to astute observers that casino resorts would not disappear. Too many people simply had too much to lose.

The new permanence of the casino resort in Las Vegas is seen in the spate of new openings and expansions of the decade's middle years. The nine stories of the Riviera, which opened in 1955 as the Strip's first "high rise," proclaimed that resorts were civic beacons, not dens of infamy to be hidden in the sagebrush. Casino operators, many of whom had been initially intrigued by short-term possibilities in Nevada, began increasingly to plan for the future. Moe Dalitz, whose investment in the Desert Inn began in 1950, permanently settled in Las Vegas in 1954. He would become a chief real estate developer of the city and eventually earn the honorific title of "Mr. Las Vegas." Others, too, began to see casino resorts as permanent institutions. Even as national media outlets described Las Vegas as a neon Klondike where one could strike it rich and return home, the men and women who owned and worked in casino resorts began to shift from strictly extractive policies—get as much as possible and get out at the first sign of trouble—to genuine community building.

The idea that the national antigambling campaign boosted the growth of Las Vegas is made fairly obvious by a comparative reading of accounts of urban gambling and Strip vacations. Stories about urban gambling spun around political corruption, ancillary criminal activities, and problem gambling. But these three factors, which had been associated with American gambling from its origins, were nowhere to be found in writings about the Strip. Journalists penned gape-mouthed testimonials to the fantastic world of casino resorts, in which nonstop gambling, sunshine, premier entertainment, good food, and even the possibility of sex were virtually free for the taking. Thus, they popularized the gambling available on the Strip. The appearance of articles supporting Strip gambling in the selfsame newspapers that campaigned against local gambling syndicates reassured tourists that their trips to casino resorts would be fun, innocuous, and free from the problems that made gambling dangerous in their hometowns.

Strip casino publicity directors actively courted favorable press. The Las Vegas News Bureau churned out massive amounts of material, but the PR directors of individual resorts, men such as Harvey Diederich, Bert Perry, Gene Murphy, and Al Freeman, worked particularly hard to cultivate the press. In this, they were hardly atypical of any business, particularly tourist and entertainment ones. But in relying so heavily on favorable press agentry, Strip resorts made use of a press corps that, increasingly during the postwar years, wrote glowingly about Sunbelt cities that had, seemingly, left the social problems of the Northeast behind with their snow shovels.[44] It didn't hurt that casinos bought regular quantities of advertising space. Writers assigned to cover the casino beat experienced a range of complimentaries, which only further put them in the mood to sing the praises of the zoomtown resorts. The results were a sometimes-embarrassing enthusiasm for the Strip that often outdistanced even the most ebullient public relations director.

Throughout the 1950s, Gladwin Hill wrote a series of articles for the *New York Times* travel section on the splendors of Las Vegas casinos for tourists. His 1953 article "Klondike in the Desert," is typical of the series and of pro-casino journalism in general. It was printed conveniently at the start of the summer tourist season, and explicitly places the reader in media res among the gambling action on the Strip. Actually visiting Nevada, it seems, will almost be a formality. In a caption, Las Vegas is described as a "neon-lighted paradise passionately and legally dedicated to gambling around the clock." Hill's description of the casino as a magical place peopled around the clock by interesting and sometimes exotic tourists and characters was certainly intended to fuel the curiosity of potential visitors. He described a landscape where one was free to "wander in" to play, talk, or gawk. Uniformed employees, presided over by "Sphinx-like floor managers, eyes ever peeled for subtle skullduggeries," were present to serve tourists. The effect, according to Hill, transcended the ethereal:

> Lights, mirrors, and the restrained, rhythmic movements of gamblers and attendants merge in a sort of slow-motion ballet, punctuated by the methodical operations of white-coated bartenders on the sidelines. Thick carpeting and acoustic paneling muffle the welter of sounds into a low-key chorus—murmurs of elation, sighs of despair, the clanking thud of slot machines, the unending drone of the stickmen.... Grizzled frontier characters—either bona fide "desert rats" or holidaying Hollywood Western players—hunch at the tables beside glamour girls in strapless gowns, sport-shirted vacationers, and rumpled trippers.[45]

Hill painted a portrait of an ordered, safe environment that promised relaxation and pleasure, as compelling a depiction of the "green felt garden" as can be imagined. The dangers of urban gambling were clearly eradicated by the new, nonurban, gambling experience, full of opportunity for the visitor. Although winning was not guaranteed, an enjoyable vacation was. Hill's articles in general stressed the "other attractions" of Las Vegas, its universal appeal, and its accessibility to virtually anyone. Within "Klondike," Hill stressed the predominance of the "family trade" and strongly implied, as did most accounts, that ultrarich super-gamblers' losses subsidized the cheap accommodations and entertainment of Las Vegas for the average visitor.

The work of Hill and other journalists eased the acceptance of Nevada gaming and the casino resort by a majority of the American people, particularly the broad middle class that occupied the nation's growing suburbs and had money to spend on a gambling vacation. In the middle 1950s, several writers made it clear that casino resorts were not a necessary evil, but a positive social good. Because of the resorts' positive influence, Las Vegas, rather than being peopled by con artists and shysters, boasted a stable, thriving populace that middle-class Americans anywhere would welcome as suburban neighbors. These friendly on-the-square natives would help tourists find a variety of honest pleasures. In his 1956 book *How to Enjoy Your Western Vacation*, Kent Ruth promoted Las Vegas as a tourist site that featured far more than gambling. Ruth detailed several nearby attractions, including Hoover Dam and the Lake Mead National Recreation Area, Valley of Fire State Park, and the Death Valley National Monument. Ruth also felt obliged to assuage skittish tourists by asserting that Las Vegas boasted, in addition to honest Western hospitality, "a score and a half churches and one of the lowest juvenile delinquency rates in the nation."[46] By vacationing at casino resorts, then, visitors were sponsoring a healthy, energetic, even God-fearing city. Ruth, Hill, and dozens of other writers made casino resorts safe for mainstream tourists by arguing that although it was different and exotic, it was unambiguously a safe and relaxing place for middle-class Americans to vacation.

Reading the "objective" journalistic accounts and unabashedly boosterish texts, one is struck by the suspension of the ordinary that took place in the resorts of the Strip. Walking around a casino resort, one might bump into anyone, including a host of Hollywood and entertainment stars, both performing on stage and relaxing at poolside. The reality actually outstripped the usual "celebrity sightings" genre. On any given weekend, wealthy and influential Americans could indeed be found in casino resorts. When they did vacation there, they did so openly and often with public fanfare, further establishing the reputation of casino resorts as places that were acceptable for "normal" Americans. A partial list of "important people" staying at the Sands on a September weekend in 1960 is instructive. It included the president of Bethlehem Steel, a vice president of programming for CBS, the chief of detectives for San Diego, the mayor of Chicago, the president of the *Wall Street Journal*, several record and movie executives, actor Howard Keel, and a division chief of International News Photos.[47] Obviously, these high-profile men (most accompanied by their wives) found nothing untoward about visiting a casino resort, and it is easy to imagine that their employees and neighbors felt the same way.

An interesting map sheds light on who was visiting casino resorts on the Strip. A promotional pamphlet of the late 1950s folded out to a map-sized depiction of Las Vegas at the center of a number of regional attractions, including national parks such as Yosemite and Sequoia in California and Zion and Bryce in Utah; natural wonders such as the Grand Canyon, Death Valley, and the Salton Sea; the Nevada Test Site; and, most tellingly, Knott's Berry Farm, Disneyland, and Marineland in Southern California.[48] Promoters of casino resorts evidently pursued the same middle-class American visitors as these paragons of postwar family vacations. Casino resorts themselves, as exciting as they might be, were safe for upstanding citizens.

The reputation of casino resorts as lawless underworld jungles has been exaggerated as much as their reputation as places where "family values"

Gambling at Marriage

Although casino resorts were havens from marriage vows and domesticity for many, in the 1950s they cemented a reputation as great places to be married (and, if the marriage did not work out, great places in which to await a divorce). This was again one of the paradoxes of Las Vegas; some visitors came there to escape marriage, either temporarily or permanently, whereas others viewed it as the ideal place to exchange vows. In 1954, for example, there were nearly seven times as many weddings as divorces in Las Vegas. Nevada's liberal marriage statues did not require blood tests or waiting periods.[49] Highlighting the importance that weddings would have for Las Vegas tourism for decades, a 1969 guidebook featured an entire chapter on "Marriage."[50]

Resorts actively courted the wedding trade from the 1940s. One of the earliest casino wedding chapels, the Little Church of the West opened in 1942 and has been in operation since (although it has moved twice). For celebrity couples, casinos would furnish a complementary photographer, food, and rooms, and even handle the press releases. Those who were not so famous also enjoyed the benefits of casino-catered weddings, and in some cases "Vegas weddings" within casino resorts have become family traditions—often outlasting the resorts themselves.

were suspended. Even in its headiest boom years in the early 1950s, the Strip was as ordered an environment as the shopping malls and subdivisions that developers were building throughout the nation. Significantly, it drew its clientele from many of the same patrons. As would be patently obvious with the Strip's courting of the convention trade, which began in the late 1950s and has only intensified, casino operators targeted an affluent client base. Their most cherished visitors were not seasoned veteran gamblers and habitués of the demimonde, but rather financially secure, debt-paying customers who appreciated a fun, but organized, vacation. The day-rate motels of downtown Las Vegas had their guests, to be sure, but the money-shot casino patrons, who bet with enthusiasm and accepted their losses before leaving town to spread the good word, almost always chose to vacation on the Strip.

The casino operators and their employees on the Las Vegas Strip certainly worked hard in pursuit of success, but it is apparent that a number of trends in American life worked to their benefit. Perhaps the greatest liabilities for Las Vegas's previous development, its remoteness, lack of industry, and small population, now became its greatest assets, as these factors made it the perfect host for casinos. Most American observers in the 1950s would have agreed completely with the notion of Las Vegas Strip casino resorts as an experiment in the containment of gambling. Voting with their feet, they said that though gambling was ruinous in the major cities, when confined to an isolated desert outpost it was actually desirable. The nearly unanimous clamor against gambling in citizens' own regions and the equally vociferous celebration of casino resorts as gambling havens was an early manifestation of the "not in my backyard" politics of the 1970s and beyond. Voters allowed their fears of the moral contagion of gambling to outlaw it near their homes. At the same time, and with no fear of hypocrisy, they patronized the thriving casino resorts of the Strip. Geographic distance not only did not interfere with tourists' plans to visit casino resorts on the Strip but also it actually assuaged their consciences and made them more eager to go.

This distance may have saved the Strip from the wrath of Kefauver in the early 1950s. Still, had the citizens of Nevada been less committed to retaining their "peculiar institution," the Strip resorts may well have been shuttered. Casino operators survived the crisis, partially by pressuring the state of Nevada to increase its regulatory presence and acknowledge its inextricable ties to the casino industry. As early as 1951, it was clear that gambling was woven "warp and woof" into the fabric of Nevada, but by 1955 at the latest it was just as obvious that it could not be untangled from that fabric. The casino resort, too, would retain vestiges of its suburban Southern Nevada origin far from the Mojave.

CHAPTER 4

Organizing Luck
In business to stay, operators routinize
management and seek new customers

There are more "socially prominent" hoodlums per square foot in Las Vegas than in any other community in the world. To fully document the sinister deeds of all these thugs, panderers, thieves, hopheads, and murderers would require a shelf of volumes the size of the Encyclopaedia Britannica. *They hail from every section of the country, and all of them are men of enormous wealth, power, connection, ego, appetite, temper, and ignorance.*
Ed Reid and Ovid Demaris on casino operators, 1963

A casino is a complex of services that can exist only in one specific environment: that in which gaming is legal and both its operation and patronage are socially acceptable. Its jewels are its reputation for fair play and ability to pay. Its reason for being is to furnish, for a fee, such facilities and personnel as may be needed for play. . . . It has a duty to create and maintain an atmosphere conducive to decorum and propriety. It has a responsibility to assure all players that they will be completely protected from sharp practices from within or without . . . that appropriate payment is guaranteed and . . . will be supervised by trained personnel.
Charles J. Hirsch, casino accountant, 1960

When erstwhile illegal gambling operators initially set up on the Strip, many of them assumed that the wide-open tolerance of gambling would not last forever. The gala openings and mellifluous press agentry of the early casino resorts disguised a boomtown mentality, as operators sought to extract as much money as possible as quickly as possible from the legal

Delegates to a meeting of General Electric managers before the show at the Sands' Copa Room, March 1966. Casino resorts actively courted convention groups, and the groups found nothing untoward in holding their meetings on the Strip. Courtesy UNLV Special Collections (Sands Collection, 40/3).

casino industry. As national sentiment against gambling crested in the early 1950s, many operators had good reason to believe that their run of luck in Nevada could soon end. But by the boom year of 1955, three developments proved the skeptics wrong. First, the national fervor against gambling and "boss gamblers" waned as more pressing issues such as race relations and the cold war, foreign and domestic, dominated the national discourse. Second, the gaming industry, as even its least enthusiastic supporters admitted, emerged as the central underpinning of Nevada's economy. The 1955 expansion of the state's regulatory regime signaled both the importance of gambling to Nevada and its permanence there. Third, a rising national prosperity, which created a suburban nation from Long Island to Palos Verdes Estates, produced a special class of consumers for these resorts: a responsible suburban citizen seeking sunshine and adventure in a safe setting.

Thus, in the years that followed, casino operators began planning for the long term. The "high rise" hotel towers of the Riviera and Fremont superceded older motel bungalows. As new casinos opened and old ones expanded, the skyline of the Strip assumed a pronounced vertical aspect. These new towers reflected casino operators' new confidence in Nevada's "experiment" with legal casino gaming, flaunting what had previously been written in one-story buildings: Southern Nevada's destiny lay with gambling. Having stared down national vituperation and local scandal, casino operators now believed that nothing could stop the dice from rolling in their desert Xanadus.

Lounge lizards and floorshow follies

Casino resorts, true to their nature as complete tourist destinations, always focused much of their appeal on entertainment. Throughout much of the 1950s, the national media reported "headliner wars" on the Strip, as casinos outbid each other for such luminaries as Nat "King" Cole, Frank Sinatra, Liberace, Betty Hutton, and Milton Berle. In 1955, the total bill for entertainment in all Strip casino resorts was reportedly $175,000 a week, and headliners averaged $35,000 for a week's work. For the privilege of seeing such superstars, guests were charged no cover and held to no drink minimum—but they had to pass through the casino to get to the show. As one reporter put it, entertainment could be had "for the price of a bottle of beer—if you're a man of resolution."[1] Casino resorts banked on the idea that most show patrons were not men or women of particular resolution.

Casino resort entertainment was split into lounge and theater divisions. Casino lounges featured virtually nonstop entertainment. The Sands' Silver Queen Bar, for example, hosted acts each night from 5 P.M. until 6 A.M. Lounge acts were usually small instrumental or vocal combos. Some featured entertainers who would eventually evolve into headliners, whereas others were simply journeyman entertainers who excelled within the lounge dynamic. Lounge shows were almost always free to the public and usually had no drink minimum. Casino visitors simply regarded continuous, high-quality, free entertainment as an entitlement and a necessary amenity. Casino lounges were uniformly loss leaders that sold few drinks in proportion to their entertainment expense, but they served the needed function of luring interested patrons into the casino, where their losses would more than pay for the entertainment.

Major shows were usually the province of the dinner theater and from the start featured several acts presented within a single framework. They, too, were not run for profit, but as a special perquisite for hotel guests and casino patrons and, again, as a way to lure people into the casino. They usually provided a broad range of acts that would hopefully appeal to even the most finicky guest. Entertainment directors became well versed in the science and art of putting together fresh shows monthly or bi-weekly, and they constantly improvised new combinations of song, music, comedy, and dancing. The Copa Room's October 1955 show "Autumn in New York," produced by Jack Entratter, starred singer Vic Damone but also showcased the comedy of Jack Carter, leavened with Antonio Morelli's orchestra and the dancing line of the Beachcombers with Natalie. Other shows playing that month included the Ritz Brothers at the Flamingo (backed by Teddy Phillips and his Orchestra, and "National Champion Square Dancers") Guy Lombardo and his Royal Canadians (with an "All Star Revue") at the Desert Inn, and Marlene Dietrich (backed by the Saharem dancers et al.) at the Sahara.[2] Big names, combined with regular musical and dancing talents, were fused into high-budget, low-cost shows.

Casino entertainment changed in 1958, when Stardust entertainment director Frank Sennes, a former Midwestern and Southern Californian nightclub operator, teamed with Moe Dalitz to bring the *Lido de Paris* revue from France to the Stardust, which Dalitz's syndicate had just begun to manage. Directed by Strip entertainment icon Donn Arden, the *Lido* was the Strip's first "Parisian floorshow" spectacular.[3] The concept, a production show with dancers but no star headliners, would become a staple of the Strip. The Lido de Paris was quickly followed by the Tropicana's *Folies Bergère*, which cemented the reputation of gala revues as surefire entertainment options. Entertainment director Lou Walters (father of newswoman Barbara Walters) imported the *Folies Bergère* directly from Paris, France. Walters's version of the *Folies* opened in the Fountain Theater and featured French and American talent. The *Folies* were wildly popular and gave the Tropicana one of its marketing catchphrases, "Home of the Most Beautiful Women in the World."[4] Other shows like the *Casino de Paris*, *Hallelujah Hollywood*, and *Jubilee* would continue in the same vein for years.

In most of these shows, presented as artistic French dance celebrations, the dancers went topless. Initially, impresarios had a difficult time finding American dancers who would appear topless and due to difficulties like these Arden brought the *Lido* directly from France. Given the relatively staid mores of most Strip tourists, ii was feared that the topless show might be too risqué, even for a casino audience. But casino guests, male and female, loved the shows. Dancer Kim Krantz (who did not work topless) believed that shows like the Lido "liberated" women: "I felt [topless revues] were kind of a neat thing for American women . . . for our guests that felt that maybe they were too small or they were too big, you know."[5] But more than nudity, it was the extravagance of the shows that drew audiences: ornate costumes, oversized feather headdresses, and intricate production numbers. Even though semi-nude shows quickly proved their worth at filling seats, some entertainment directors, like the Sands's Jack Entratter, refused to permit their showgirls to dance topless.

Shows like this defined casino resort entertainment for a generation; gala topless French-themed extravaganzas became a sine qua non of a Strip vacation. Though they were expensive to produce, and looked far more lavish visually than earlier floorshows, these shows actually allowed casino resorts to stabilize entertainment costs. As much as it might cost to install (over $5 million by the early 1960s), these gala revues could be depended upon for a high entertainment value for several years. With no high-profile headliners to woo from other casinos, gala revues were, in the long run, cheaper to stage than the constant merry-go-round of big-name stars. The revues were usually reliably spectacular and satisfied guests' demands for entertainment without overstimulating them. Casinos could still sign headliners for special engagements, but they were free from the need to have a marquee name signed to perform every week of the year.

So the coming of the stage revue spectacular, although it added another dimension to casino entertainment, did not completely dethrone the star headliner. In the 1960s, when the revue had been firmly established, it shared prominence with traditional headliners. A 1966 Dunes press release hailed the Strip as the "entertainment capitol [sic] of the world," and listed the shows regularly available: direct-from-Paris extravaganzas like *Casino de Paris, Folies Bergère*, and *Lido '66*; Betty Grable in *Hello Dolly*, as well as lesser-known shows like the Desert Inn's "native *Hello America* revue," the Hacienda's *Hank Henry laugh show, Life Begins at Minksy's*, and *C'est La Femme*. But headliners were also an important part of the mix, as the release further detailed the stars appearing more or less regularly on the Strip, a list that ranged from Johnny Carson to Andy Williams, along with Strip staples Sinatra, Martin, Davis, Goulet and Newton and a host of others. On the Strip, and particularly at the Dunes, entertainment icons "participate in that kind of frolicking which has made Las Vegas a veritable Disneyland for adults."[6] All that vacationers had to do to participate in the fun, of course, was to make a reservation at a Strip resort—the niceties of show reservations would naturally fall into place as a cornucopia of staged delights was opened to them.

Whether a show headlined by a major star, a revue spectacular, or a lounge act, entertainment within the casino resort had a singular purpose—to bring patrons into the casino. Acts that boosted the casino's table "drop" were enthusiastically held over, whereas those who didn't, no matter how many tickets they sold, were not. If a major headliner gambled back most of his or her paycheck (as many did), so much the better. But the entertainment directors of 1950s casino resorts could have doubtless taught MTV a few things about using entertainment to stoke consumption.

Get more done . . . then have more fun

The carefree glitz of shows like the *Folies* disguised a growing crunch in the Southern Nevada casino industry. There were signs of a tightening market as early as 1955, and casino operators became more nervous as the Royal Nevada casino failed outright in early 1958 after three years of struggle and did not reopen, the first Strip casino resort bomb so spectacularly. The casino had been under a cloud, having been unprofitable since its opening, but its bad luck went beyond leaky tables; the casino was accused in late 1957 by the Gaming Control Board of cheating, an extraordinary charge given the negative publicity that it engendered.

In the standard rhetoric of the Strip, cheating by the house was a thing of illegal clip joints. The pleasure palaces of the Strip were so profitable, publicists and journalists crowed, that no house would risk public censure by cheating. But in fact, house "protection" of games often extended to activities that, if the player had done them, might be termed cheating. A former dealer recalled:

> Everybody dealt single deck [blackjack] and you had to know how to manipulate cards. You had to know how to count cards to protect the deck. Not necessarily to steal from a customer, but you learned how to deal and count cards while you dealt so that the deck favored the house. You didn't shuffle up if the deck favored the house. If the deck favored the player, you'd break the deck and shuffle up. Simple stuff like this, but you had to know how to cheat in order to protect the game. . . . You had to learn how to deal seconds, how to sneak a peek, how to roll the deck, how to do a straight and crooked shuffle, how bets are capped, how they're dragged, how they're pressed, how you get past posted. These are all things you had to know or you couldn't get a job as a dealer.[7]

But more important than having the manual dexterity to perform these feats was the adroitness needed to avoid detection by players and state agents, something that a Royal Nevada clerk apparently lacked, having been caught peeking at cards in the shoe. The Tax Commission did not suspend the casino's license immediately, but rather gave the casino time to recoup its investors' money.[8] Still, the casino, facing the triple burden of the cheating charge, sieve-like gaming tables, and anxious creditors, finally rolled its last dice in early 1958.

The Royal Nevada was the rule rather than the exception, as several other resorts struggled after the 1955 boom. The solution appeared to be consolidation, if not of ownership, than of management. The Flamingo group, for example, acquired a contract to manage the Riviera, the Desert Inn syndicate acquired the management of the Stardust, and the Sands entered into a lease arrangement with the Dunes in September 1955. The Dunes had opened months earlier and encountered fiscal setbacks so severe that part-owner Al Gottesman felt obliged to issue a defiant press release that August denying that the casino had "gone broke" and threatening libel action against newspapers that had reported so. Rather, he explained that he and other Dunes investors had always intended to develop the resort as a "major hotel property," ends that could be best met by leasing the entire property to the Sands group, which would assume complete control over all operational aspects.[9]

These leasing arrangements signaled a trend toward greater consolidation on the Strip. By 1958, *Newsweek* magazine could report that the day of the "little gambler" in Las Vegas was over, as smaller properties were acquired by stronger ones. Tax commissioner William Deutsch was quoted as saying that this consolidation was inevitable: "If a man operates a small casino honestly, he'll get caught by a big winner. If he cheats, the state will catch him eventually. . . . The smaller places cannot afford to give away drinks and entertainment as inducements for customers, as the larger outfits can. . . . The days of the little gambler are numbered."[10] Thus, the dynamics of the business dictated a natural oligopoly of ownership and management syndicates that could offset losses at one property with wins at another.

Interestingly, the Royal Nevada was not simply acquired by a different management group and reopened. Perhaps so great was the taint of a cheating charge that the casino, if not demolished and plowed with salt, was to be doomed to obscurity. So the Royal Nevada lost its identity and was effectively cannibalized by its next-door neighbor, the Stardust, as its casino and public spaces were remodeled as convention space and its hotel rooms and pool simply added to the Stardust's own. This peculiar form of corporate annexation gave the Desert Inn syndicate a solid block of the central Strip and indicated that the market for new properties was finite. With a tightened market, consolidation and retrenchment, rather than giddy expansion, became the order of the day. In the late 1950s, the Strip was at a plateau; the middle-decade boom had brought a new class of leisure traveler to the resorts of the Strip, but there had been no expansion of the Strip's target market since then. If they could not find a new market, Strip casino owners would have to battle for increasingly smaller pieces of a static pie. The solution, many resort operators found, was to expand into the convention business.

Just as its construction as a national leisure destination had facilitated the boom of the early 1950s, the Strip's evolution into a convention destination in the latter part of the decade signaled its expansion into a new market. Casino resorts that were filled with vacationers on the weekends were not nearly as profitable as those also packed with conventioneers during the week. Thus, in the late 1950s, individual resort operators worked together to establish Las Vegas as a convention town and turn their casino resorts into convention resorts. Their work culminated in 1959 with the opening of a publicly funded convention center near the Strip.

Conventions became vital to individual casino resorts. Casino sales and marketing executives spent a great deal of their time chasing conventions. These convention groups were not necessarily large, but they were steady. In 1965 the Sands, for example, held blocks of rooms for groups like the American Association of Junior Colleges, which only took up ten rooms, to the National Automobile Dealers Convention, which took 350 rooms plus an overflow of fifteen rooms at the nearby Castaways. Throughout that year, the Sands averaged five convention groups a month, with each group reserving between 50 and 300 rooms.[11] This even flow of conventioneers enabled the Sands and other casinos to keep their rooms full throughout the year, something that strictly vacation-oriented resorts could not do.

Convention bookings assumed a paramount role for casino operators, who tirelessly promoted their casinos' convention facilities. In a promotional brochure dating from the 1960s, the Stardust billed itself as "the world's largest resort-hotel," which had "what it takes for a successful business meeting. To get work done . . . to have some fun." To better explain how this useful dichotomy could be achieved by booking a convention at the Stardust, the brochure devoted a total of ten pages to pictures, diagrams, and descriptions of its convention facilities (of which the Stardust had plenty following the 1959 conversion of the Royal Nevada's casino into the Stardust Auditorium), followed by two-page summaries of the Stardust's restaurants, entertainment, golf, swimming, accommodations, shopping, and the lures of "The Great Outdoors" in Southern Nevada.[12] Thus, convention planners could assure their constituents that a group meeting at the Stardust would draw on the latest edge of convention technology and, after hours, offer relaxing entertainment options.

Conspicuously absent was any reference to the Stardust's casino, the one thing that would have distinguished it from a convention hotel in Anaheim, Miami, or any other city. The only hint that games of chance might be found anywhere near the convention floor was found on a full-color drawing/map of the property, which afforded a small dot to identify the "casino." Even this insignificant dot was crowded out by the surrounding International Room East and Café Continental. That the brochure devoted a full page, with a color illustration, to a stirring description of a Greyhound bus terminal to be erected on the hotel's grounds but barely acknowledged that it even had a casino seems disingenuous, and it was a slick promotional technique, one that continues to be a cornerstone of Strip marketing today. Groups undoubtedly had to register at least token objections to meeting in what was in many respects a glorified gambling hall, and marketing pieces like the Stardust's let advocates demonstrate that the casino, far from being an integral part of the complex, was simply another diversion, probably of less import than the on-site haberdashery or swimming pools. But this was, of course, all done with the tacit understanding that conventioneers were expected to gamble, at least perfunctorily, and preferably enthusiastically.

Group sales extended beyond business conventions. Casino executives also pursued junkets of those who not only had money but also influence in their hometowns. In early 1963, for example, the Sands contemplated flying in a group of forty-five "young businessmen" from Dallas on a chartered plane. Publicist Al Freeman calculated that the total cost to the Sands for the charter flight and a reception would be around $20,000, yet the potential gambling gross from the Texans would be "not even $5,000." While he admitted that the potential income from the junket itself was not favorable, he also noted that "this is the new, young blood of wealthy families—potential good customers for the Sands . . . in a few years to come."[13] He therefore recommended the group be feted by the Sands. Other executives followed similar policies in using convention and group sales to promote growth at their properties. The importance of group and convention sales to casino resorts would only grow in the years to come, and convention facilities would become yet another integral part of a viable casino resort.

An enigmatic tangle: Casino ownership

Within the folklore of the twentieth-century gambling demimonde, the dream of every two-bit hustler and card sharp was to own a "piece of the action" in the form of his or her own gambling house. Some authors, such as *New York Times* reporter Wallace Turner, believed that all those who owned or invested in casino resorts were mega-gamblers who had saved enough scratch to open their own "joint." But when one looks at the real skills needed it becomes clear that being a prolific gambler offers little guarantee of success in the realm of casino ownership. In fact, casino owners were drawn from a variety of strata in American society. The actual owners of casinos, usually members of syndicates, were not that far removed from the middle-class suburbanites that filled their hotels.

Many writers on casinos during the precorporate era, including Turner, described casino owners as gamblers. In a sense, they were correct; many of the early casino operators did indeed gamble on horses and in casinos. But most were not professional gamblers who made their living from their gambling winnings. Rather, they derived their incomes from bootlegging, illegal gambling *operations*, and other illicit industries. To square their known legal, taxed earnings with their actual income, many of those in the

The Las Vegas Convention Center

Individual resorts couldn't hold conventions larger than a certain size, so casino operators joined forces to promote a civic convention hall which opened in 1959. The Las Vegas Convention Center's centerpiece was a domed, UFO-like main rotunda. The dome was indicative of the progressivist styling of the city. Keeping with this, the Convention Center was actively billed as an air-conditioned, soundproofed, fully modern facility:

> Designed with all the lessons in mind learned from the convention facilities in the world's older convention cities, the Las Vegas Convention Center is so modern . . . so completely ample . . . for every possible kind of meeting, sales gathering, display show, and convention . . . THAT IT WILL ALWAYS BE NEW!

Capitalizing on the latest advances in climate control, broadcasting and communications, lighting, telephony, and electrical engineering, the Convention Center was seen as a full-service facility that would meet all the needs of any business group.[15] Not coincidentally, most of these business groups would be composed of the same suburban Americans who were lured to Las Vegas by the promotional fervor of Strip casino operators and their mouthpieces.

As reflected in their dualistic slogan, "Get more done, then have more fun," the Las Vegas Convention Center trumpeted the entertainment options readily available in Las Vegas. Its first promotional pamphlet stressed that over 10,000 hotel and motel rooms were within minutes of the center. Nearly half of them were in "resort hotels," that is, casino resorts. Conventioneers were promised that they could see a galaxy of stars during their stay in town: Frank Sinatra, Jimmy Durante, Joe E. Lewis, Red Skelton, Jack Benny, Betty Hutton, and Eddie Fisher were specifically cited as Strip regulars. The pamphlet also celebrated Las Vegas as "a wonderland of year 'round sunshine and pleasant weather," and within reach of natural attractions like Mount Charleston and the Valley of Fire. Lake Mead, three golf courses, and thirty-two heated pools were additional outdoor lures. Two of the many endorsements listed in the pamphlet demonstrated that Las Vegas as a productive, safe, and enjoyable place for a convention:

> In all our years of conventions never have we accomplished so much and still enjoyed ourselves so much. Las Vegas is the

convention spot that every convention director dreams of . . . truly the convention city. (Chrysler Dealers)

Las Vegas ought to be proud of the fact that those charged with the responsibility of enforcing the laws of every jurisdiction in the United States not only accomplished the important serious purpose of their business meetings in our recent convention, but were provided in their leisure hours with the type of entertainment that can be secured nowhere else in the world. (National Association of County and Prosecuting Attorneys)[16]

This was the birth of the casino resort as a convention center. Conspicuous by its absence was any overt reference to gambling. The chief entertainment option of casino resorts could be implied rather than stated directly.

underworld economy told the press (and the Internal Revenue Service) that they got their money from gambling. Only in this way could a Frank Costello, for example, reconcile his prodigious personal fortune with his modest holdings in legitimate business. Without doubt, the label of "gambler," which stuck with casino operators even after their gambling interests became both legal and taxable in the state of Nevada, was a dodge. Though it was somewhat disingenuous, the label remained; when gambling opponents fulminated against "gamblers," they meant gambling operators, not the people who wagered.

"Boss gamblers" included all types; there seem to have been few prerequisites for owning a piece of a casino. A 1955 *Harper's* article listed "solid" hotel men, former hoodlums from New York, an ex-brewer from Pennsylvania, a Texas theater owner, former operators of Los Angeles gambling ships, Hollywood personalities like George Raft, and "gamblers" from Cleveland as among the Strip's owners.[17] Of course, these visible "gamblers" were usually fronts for the syndicates that actually owned the casino, but they still give a good idea of the plasticity of casino ownership—anyone, it seemed, could own a piece of the action.

Despite their idiosyncrasies, the histories of most Strip casino hotels built in the 1940s and 1950s, as they are conventionally told, have a striking monotony. Like a *VH1: Behind the Music* marathon, they relate essentially the same story with incidental differences of character and circumstance.

They usually feature a Runyonesque-type Hero, a former bootlegger or illegal gambling operator who wants to finally "go straight." Hero leaves California, Chicago, or Florida for Las Vegas, where he dabbles in ownership of small downtown gambling halls. One night, he has an epiphany: he will build a larger, more luxurious casino far away from town. He tours the country and manages to scrape together funds to begin construction, but, alas, there are cost overruns, and his dream is beached like an improbable inland whale on the Nevada sands. At this point, Hidden Interests, perhaps former bootleggers or those still connected with organized crime, step forward and offer Hero funds to complete the project in exchange for control of the finished casino. Hero reluctantly agrees. The casino is finished and is a huge success, but Hero, the alienated creative genius, never truly enjoys it. In the final act, Hero is bought out (Clark), dies of natural causes (Cornero), or is murdered (Siegel). The Hidden Interests, whose real partners are only hinted at, chuckle and count their money.

This archetype has more to do with justifying corporate ownership of an institution that gloried individual risk than a real explanation of the casino resort. Las Vegas casino resorts, from their inception, held to no single pattern of ownership or investment. The most ballyhooed genus of casino owner/investor is, of course, the alleged former bootlegger/crime syndicate member. One popular view of the history of Las Vegas, propounded in book form by David Johnston, is that the state of Nevada invited "Mafia" members into Las Vegas to build the casino industry. Later, with its duplicity matched only by its rapacity, the state swept them out and replaced them with respectable corporate owners once the industry was safely established.[18]

Antigambling writers have scrupulously tracked down hidden mob interests in countless casinos and explained away those with no known connection to organized crime as bagmen for some unknown criminal entity. But saying that a casino was "mobbed up" doesn't explain who owned casino resorts, how one invested in them, and what this meant for the institution's development. Because of the quasi-legal nature of gambling in most of the United States, most owners and investors held their cards close to their vests, leaving few records. Still, there are patterns discernable in early casino resort ownership. Unsurprisingly, for such risky investments, collective ownership was the norm, and mainstream investment was slow in coming.

Syndicates and corporations share the wealth

By the early 1950s, even a shabby casino on the Strip cost at least $5 million to build. That kind of money was simply out of the hands of even the

William Harrah: Industry Icon?

While sole ownership of a resort was never really an alternative on the Strip, it played an important role in the mythology of the casino resort. Some casinos had a member of the ownership syndicate who acted as impresario, such as Wilbur Clark in the Desert Inn or Jack Entratter at the Sands; these men didn't really own the casino but, for public relations purposes, they took a high-profile role as "operator." But though they might appear exercise great authority (or not, in Clark's case), they still answered to the syndicate.

Nonresort gambling halls, on the other hands, were often owned by individuals and families. Harold's Club in Reno, for example, was owned by the Smith family, and downtown Las Vegas gambling halls constantly changed hands. But one man stands out as an exceptional sole owner—William Harrah.

Harrah's Reno operations were landmarks in the casino world for their efficient management and effective marketing. Harrah parlayed a succession of gambling halls in downtown Reno beginning in the 1940s into a sizable northern Nevada casino empire. Combining a solid understanding of the gambling business with opportunism that bordered on the predatory, he was able to stake a place for himself in the competitive Reno gambling market. He was not above industrial espionage to press an advantage.[19] But Bill Harrah was able to account for every quarter that passed through his gambling halls and his operations were successful; therefore, he was an industry lion.[20]

Because of the success of Harrah in northern Nevada, though, some industry observers felt that he should serve as the model for all casino ownership. Wallace Turner even titled a chapter in his antigambling expose, "If They Were All Like Harrah . . . " Part of Harrah's appeal, no doubt, was his ability to trace his ancestry in the United States to WASP stock that predated the Revolutionary War. Harrah's public relations vice president Mark Curtis chose telling words to eulogize his boss: "This man was not from Chicago or Detroit, he had no tarnished image. He was from the West. Neither Harrah nor his people were born into gaming."[21] Harrah certainly had engaged in an illegal gambling operation that he bought from his father, and his business practices were frequently cutthroat. He spent most of his fortune on a 1,400-car collection of classic automobiles; his public service was subsumed primarily by a vague support for the John Birch Society. Operators with "tarnished images" gave millions of dollars to charities in Nevada and throughout the country. Yet for many observers, Harrah stood out favorably, in stark contrast to operators of Jewish and Italian extraction with "tarnished" images.

biggest-shot gamblers, and most investors from the legitimate business world balked at flinging their fortunes on the risky proposition of a gambling casino. Since single ownership was impractical and publicly traded corporate ownership legally unworkable in the Nevada gaming industry until the late 1960s, the syndicate emerged as the most common form of casino ownership. In the early 1950s, no casino syndicate received more press, positive and negative, than the Desert Inn's. The Desert Inn can be considered the archetypal syndicate-owned casino of the period. During his committee's hearings in Las Vegas, Senator Kefauver and his compatriots evinced a fascination with the workings of the syndicate; they questioned Wilbur Clark extensively but learned little, thanks to Clark's apparently vague understanding of his own casino.

As it was legally organized circa 1962, the ownership group of the Desert Inn comprised seventeen individuals. Wilbur Clark owned the largest share of the enterprise with over 17 percent. Moe Dalitz, Morris Kleinman, Ruby Kolod, and Sam Tucker each held over 13 percent. At 7.1 percent, Thomas McGinty was the smallest investor of note; all other members held 1 percent or less of the whole. Although each of the above men, except Clark, had come to prominence in Cleveland via the Mayfield Road Gang, none currently resided there. Kleinman, McGinty, and Tucker had retired to South Florida, and the other major figures in the syndicate gave the Desert Inn Hotel as their address of record.[22]

The Desert Inn syndicate was typical of other syndicates in that it had three approximate levels. Onionlike, the syndicate had successively deeper layers of investors. On the surface, Wilbur Clark, the happy gambler who had never been convicted of a crime, had his name in lights and was the "front" for the second layer of actual owner-operators, which included Dalitz and other "Mayfield Road" figures. These men often had previous gambling convictions or were suspected of affiliation with organized crime, but they were "clean" enough to obtain gaming licenses. Behind this group of official investors was an even more shadowy group of investors who for a host of reasons could not or would get receive official licenses.[23] Meyer Lansky and Frank Costello were two of the most notorious examples of this third layer of syndicate ownership, though they were certainly not alone. These undercover investors did not, for the most part, interfere with the day-to-day operations of "their" casino and were usually content to receive their "cut" of casino profits via skimming operations.

But these syndicates were not usually the free-wheeling combines of happy-go-lucky gamblers, shady investors, and gruff mobsters that have become legend. Rather, they were pedestrian, even soulless, business partnerships. Ernest Havemann, considering the state of legalized casino gaming circa 1955, wished for a more personal touch:

As for the house, who is the house? Usually a syndicate, a corporation. The hired hands are almost as disinterested as the shills. Even the boss, if there is one, seldom knows how the house is doing at the moment. . . . I liked it better in the old days when the house was likely to be someone no more formidable or impersonal than old Harry B____, a fat and worrisome businessman who ran a crap game on the side in a little Illinois town where I spent a good deal of time.[24]

While the syndicates that controlled most casino resorts had their share of colorful characters, it is interesting that, as early as 1955, some observers were decrying corporate gambling as bland and lacking in real risk. Fifty years later, people would make the same charges against the "new era" of corporate casinos, harking back to the Elysian fields of the 1960s and 1970s.

Whether or not one considers ownership syndicates "corporations," (indeed, to some ears calling the Desert Inn ownership group a "corporation" sounds like a shameless sanitization), there was a substantial corporate presence on the Strip as early as 1951. Contrary to the popularly accepted version of casino history, publicly traded corporations *did* operate casinos before Nevada's gaming laws were amended in 1967. The Del E. Webb Corporation incrementally increased its involvement in the industry over two decades, emerging as a major force in the casino world. In 1946, Webb assumed construction of the Flamingo with Siegel's banishment of Wilkerson, and, as a noted Sunbelt contractor, naturally maintained an interest in this growing region. In 1951, Webb partner L.C. Jacobson secured financing for Al Winter and Milton Prell's Sahara project for which Webb also served as contractor. Jacobson himself had a 20 percent stake in the casino. Del Webb also partnered with the Sahara group in building downtown's Mint casino before, in 1961, the Del E. Webb Corporation acquired the Sahara group's Las Vegas interests (chiefly the Sahara, Mint, and real estate).[25]

Jacobson and Webb mitigated the impossibility of a publicly traded corporation owning a licensed Nevada casino through an ingenious feat of corporate prestidigitation. They created a wholly owned subsidiary, the Sahara-Nevada Corporation, to own the gaming properties, retaining Winter and Prell as chairman of the board and president, respectively. An owned subsidiary of the publicly traded Del E. Webb Corporation, SNC could not secure licensing, and so Webb set up the Consolidated Casino Corporation, owned by Jacobson, Prell, and Winter, to operate the casinos. This managing company paid a rental fee to Sahara-Nevada that just happened to match its gaming receipts.[26]

To current readers chastened by the meltdown of Enron in late 2001, this scheme seems to present obvious problems. Jacobson, the de facto boss of Consolidated, theoretically was expected to maximize the profits for that company and also protect the interests of stockholders in Del E. Webb, Consolidated's landlord, in which he was a partner. Obviously, these two roles were hardly complimentary. It is easy to imagine a number of schemes that could be used to defraud Del Webb or siphon profits from Consolidated. But Nevada regulators welcomed the presence of the "clean" Webb Corporation in the gaming industry, and Del Webb indeed became a leading gaming company, owning and operating casinos ranging from the Sahara Tahoe to Atlantic City's Claridge. Though it liquidated its casino interests in the 1980s to concentrate on real estate development (i.e., the Sun City communities), Del Webb proved early on that publicly traded corporations could successfully compete in the casino industry.[27]

Del Webb's early role as a corporate operator of casinos later became obscured by later mythmaking that imagined a titanic struggle of clean corporations against mob domination. In the 1980s, a Del Webb group presentation stated without irony, "Legend has it that at J. Edgar Hoover's suggestion, in an effort to clean up Nevada's act, Howard Hughes bought all the land in Las Vegas and Del Webb built on it."[28] Just as later hotel corporations did not purchase casinos merely to improve the public image of Nevada, Del Webb became involved in gaming to profit from it. Jacobson's incredible profits from his original stake in the Sahara gave the Webb corporation entrée into the industry, and the group slowly built up management structures to maximize revenues from its casino holdings. But at the time, Webb was not acting as an antimob crusader. Rather, the company was just another collective group bending the gaming regulations to operate casino resorts profitably in Nevada.

That the Webb group made such profits from casino resorts begs the question of why other corporations didn't jump into the business after the 1955 boom. While some hotel corporations made half-hearted attempts to acquire resorts in the late 1950s and early 1960s, the true transition to corporate ownership did not take place until the 1970s. Partially, this was because of the archaic licensing requirements that barred publicly traded corporations from owning casinos outright—it is easy to imagine that stockholders might have balked at arrangements like that "between" Del Webb and Consolidated Casino that, if they did not break the law, certainly skirted it. But mainstream corporations also hesitated because of the inherent risks involved in gaming and because they did not have specialized managers who could effectively supervise a casino.

But the transition from syndicate and semi-corporate ownership to full-fledged corporate ownership is more accurately described as large organizations (with access to more capital) pushing out smaller organizations than as an ethical or managerial great leap forward. The smaller combines of the 1950s were adequate to the scale and legal bounds of the Nevada gaming industry of the time, and they permitted the development of casino resorts that made admirable profits for their owners and investors. That these investors were often connected to the criminal underworld does not eclipse the work of their syndicates in building casino resorts on the Strip.

Holding points in paradise

No matter what paragons of business sense their owners might have been, casinos were volatile investments, and mainstream businesses not only shied away from owning casinos but they also frequently demurred from investing in them because of the risk involved. The Kefauver Committee and antigambling muckrakers of the early 1950s painted the Nevada casino industry not as a place where reformed mobsters had "gone legit" but rather as a den of underworld intrigue. Certainly, the Kefauver Committee's pronouncement that the Nevada gaming industry was in fact a beachhead for the infiltration of legitimate society by gangsters gave pause to potential outside investors. Kefauver "shed no tears over the fact that experiments being conducted at the new atomic bomb testing range near Las Vegas are rattling the windows of the gambling dives and making the sharpers nervous,"[29] as his abhorrence of gambling led him to believe that legal gaming casinos represented a greater public health hazard than atmospheric nuclear weapons testing. Kefauver asserted that "big-time gambling" as conducted in casinos was amoral and "more often crooked than not," a point not backed with proof since he believed it self-evident.[30] Many businesspeople who might have found vacationing among gangsters dangerous and exciting would not have sought the same "gangsters" as business partners. So, for the most part, investment in the casino industry remained the preserve of the nation's fiscal margins.

Because of the dearth of investment from mainstream financial institutions, prospective casino operators relied heavily upon individually recruited investors to get their casinos built. These investors were a diverse group, but they had in common a willingness to risk money on an unproven industry. Not surprisingly, many of them had checkered backgrounds. Often, they had profits from illegal gambling ventures or other illicit activities that could not be funneled back into the legitimate economy. Because oftentimes these investors had been involved in criminal syndicates together, antigambling investors assumed that their joint presence in Nevada's nascent gaming industry was a sure sign of "Mafia" infiltration. This was a gross oversimplification, as the criminal underworld's penetration into casino resorts was more often the story of competing individual investors than group conspiracy.

Although he cannot be said to represent the rank and file of individual investors, Meyer Lansky can be taken as an example of an extremely successful one. There is some doubt as to whether his entire ownership interests in Las Vegas casinos were his own or whether he was a front for other, even more secret, investors. Having emigrated with his family from Russian-Poland to Brooklyn as a child, Lansky evinced an early curiosity in Gotham's underworld. With Prohibition, Lansky moved into "vice" full-time, though he also held legitimate business interests. By the time Prohibition had ended he was undeniably a member of New York's criminal underworld. Much has been made of his reputation as "accountant for the mob," a reputation probably borne out by his extensive involvement in a string of underground and offshore enterprises. By the 1950s, his reported investments in gambling alone were international in scope. They included the Arrowhead Inn and Piping Rock Casino in Saratoga Springs, New York; the Colonial Inn and Lucayan Beach Hotel in South Florida; the Gran Casino Nacional, Nacional Hotel, and Riviera Hotel in Cuba; the Beverly Club outside of New Orleans; the Dodge Park Kennel Club in Council Bluff, Iowa; and the Flamingo, Fremont, and El Cortez in Las Vegas.[31] All of the operations, with the exception of those in Las Vegas and Cuba, were at least technically illegal. With Fidel Castro's cessation of Cuban gaming and the impact of national antigambling forces on local illegal operations nationwide, it is clear that only Las Vegas, into the 1960s, remained as a safe place for such investment.

Other investors had less grand portfolios, but the essential pattern was the same. They usually had profits from illegal gambling, prostitution, or loan-sharking and needed a place to invest it. In the 1940s, such men might have plowed their money back into the local underworld, running a floating illegal craps game or a more elaborate carpet joint. But the national clamor against gambling and corruption of the early 1950s ended many of these opportunities. If such investors declined involvement in the burgeoning narcotics trade, one investment opportunity seemed logical: Las Vegas casino gaming.

As the casino industry of Southern Nevada grew in the 1950s, quasi-legitimate investment in it increased. This included corporate sources of capital that were official businesses yet outside the world of mainstream finance. The most notorious source of investment for casinos in the late 1950s and 1960s was the Teamsters Central States Pension Fund. In their book-length denunciation of Las Vegas, antigambling investigators Ed Reid and Ovid Demaris featured a chapter with the picturesque title, "Hoffa's Fountain of Pension Juice." Mixed metaphors aside, many critics of Nevada gaming focused on the Teamster investments as proof of the casino resort's inherent criminality. Such critics argued that if the Teamsters invested in them, casinos must be bad. Similarly, investing in casinos was seen as the final proof of the Teamsters' corruption. This circular logic does not aid a historical analysis of casino ownership.

At Hoffa's direction, the trustees of the Central States Pension Fund assembled an idiosyncratic portfolio. As opposed to other corporate pensions, which invested heavily in common stocks in the early 1960s, the CSPF largely avoided stocks. In contrast to other funds, which had an average of slightly more than 3 percent of their holdings in mortgages, over two-thirds of CSPF assets were invested in real estate mortgages.[32] The trustees embraced risky investments usually eschewed by conservative lenders, such as shopping centers, hotels, and motels. Most analysts regarded hotels and motels as particularly bad risks for two reasons: the danger of being surpassed by new highways and travel patterns, and the ever-present threat of newer, more glamorous facilities. Yet by 1963, hotels and motels constituted over 60 percent of CSPF investments.[33]

Within real estate, CSPF investments centered in Florida and Nevada, two of the least stable real estate markets of the early 1960s. CSPF policy seemed to be the assumption of risks that more conservative investors avoided. Most institutions, because of the risk inherent in such investments, would charge higher interest rates. Yet under Hoffa's direction, the CSPF levied a modest 5 to 7 percent interest charge on even the riskiest investments. For personal or political reasons (i.e., payoffs and gifts to cronies or potential allies), Hoffa let customer service—keeping the borrowers happy—outweigh purely fiscal concerns.[34] The loans offered to Las Vegas projects are entirely in tune with the rest of the CSPF portfolio. That the Teamsters did not levy usurious interest rates on casino borrowers with no other options is completely in conformity with their other investments.

Following a 1959 loan that made possible the construction of Las Vegas's Sunrise Hospital, the fund continued its association with the Desert Inn syndicate. The Desert Inn, Stardust and Fremont, all Desert Inn syndicate-associated properties, were among the first wave of CSPF loans to Las Vegas. Later loans financed the construction or renovation of casino resorts such as the Dunes, Landmark, Aladdin, Circus Circus, and Caesars Palace.[35]

Although these loans were of incalculable value to the development of casino resorts in the 1960s, their soundness as investments on behalf of the Teamsters' rank and file can be questioned. Indeed, the Department of Labor sought action in 1978 against former CSPF trustees for mismanagement of fund assets.[36] But the Central States Pension Fund loans met a structural need for casino resorts, which needed capital and could find few lenders. The Pension Fund was made available to them. Whether the reasons were for personal or political payoff may never be truly known. The popular notion that "Jimmy Hoffa's Pension Juice" built the gaming industry, however, is erroneous. The first pension loan was floated in 1959, when most of the Strip's casino resorts had already been built. Teamster loans did indeed help several existing casinos finance expansion projects, and they helped others (most notably Caesars Palace) get off the ground in the 1960s, but to speak of the mob, via Jimmy Hoffa, creating the casino resort is inaccurate.

Perhaps the Teamster loans' greatest value was their legitimizing power. This is ironic, considering the circumstances under which they were made, the people involved, and the furor that surrounded them. But they can be conceptualized as a point midway between Tony Cornero's basement printing press stock issues that started the Stardust's financing and the large-scale corporate investment that would begin in the late 1960s. Although antigambling authors viewed the loans as proof positive of the mob's dominion in Las Vegas, they were a public investment open to scrutiny that clued financial pundits to the possibilities in the gaming industry.

The Valley Bank of Nevada, which opened as the Bank of Las Vegas in 1955, served as another popular source of casino capital in the late 1950s and 1960s. The bank was headed by E. Parry Thomas, a Utah Mormon who had speculated in Las Vegas real estate for years before heading up the Bank of Las Vegas. Developers who deplored the failure of mainstream investors to enter the Las Vegas market had been clamoring for a "bank of their own," and Thomas's Bank of Las Vegas fit that need nicely. Thomas convinced his former employer, Walter Cosgriff of the Continental Bank of Salt Lake City, to capitalize the new bank.[37]

The Bank of Las Vegas immediately funded several casino projects, beginning with a loan to the Sahara for a 1955 renovation.[38] This can be seen as a conservative entrée into an untraditional business; the Sahara, while not fully owned by the Del Webb company at the time, did count several Webb principals among its major investors. It was thus a casino, but a casino with a substantial investment from a mainstream business. Subsequent Bank of Las Vegas projects included the construction or expansion of resorts like the Desert Inn, Sands, Dunes, Hacienda, Stardust, Riviera, and Thunderbird. The bank emerged as the only lending institution to regularly loan money to casinos. Thomas, along with his chief partner, Jerry Mack, built the Bank of Las Vegas into a powerful institution, merging it in 1968 with the Valley Bank of Reno. The bank, which was initially capitalized in 1954 at $250,000, had $400 million in equity when the Bank of America acquired it in 1992. Certainly, Thomas's policies of lending to casinos had paid off.

Even as the Valley bank represented the legitimization of casino capital, links to more traditional channels remained. In the late 1950s, Thomas began an association with Morris Shenker, a lawyer and political figure who represented Jimmy Hoffa and had many links to reputed organized crime figures. Shenker's influence at the American National Insurance Company of Texas induced that firm to direct many major loans to Shenker through the Bank of Las Vegas. Thomas's most famous quote, that he worked "for the Mormons until noon, and from noon on for my Jewish friends," reflects the lingering dichotomy between the "straight" world of Mormon and WASP finance and the "crooked" investments with predominantly Jewish gamblers.[39] The Bank of Las Vegas, with one foot in each world, was a commercial bank that engaged in lending practices similar to financial institutions in any growing city.

Even in the 1950s, patterns of casino ownership and investment were shifting. The standard interpretation of casino history, that the "mob" owned most houses until Howard Hughes and corporate investors arrived in the late 1960s, belies the complex changes that had swept through the industry in the previous decade. Certain operators had more than a passing familiarity with organized crime in the East and Midwest, but this was a requisite part of their illegal gambling operations there. Because of a dearth of "legitimate" investors, even homegrown casino operations, such as the Thunderbird, often turned to "mobsters" for investment capital. The failure of mainstream lenders to embrace the risks of casino investment in turn guaranteed underworld lenders a sizable share of the casino market, which in turn further alienated potential mainstream investors. Despite the fulmination of antigambling writers, such investment in Las Vegas was more about fiscal opportunism and diversification than a national criminal conspiracy to sap and foul America's moral economy. When large-scale, publicly traded corporations moved into casino resort ownership in the 1970s, the change would be one of scale rather than style or substance.

Bureaucratizing chance

In the 1950s, there were no formal professional schools to churn out fresh-faced young casino executives. Indeed, virtually anyone who was qualified to run a casino resort on the Las Vegas Strip was, technically, a criminal. It would be a mistake to conflate having a police record with a general tendency toward thuggishness or moral lassitude. The quotation from *Green Felt Jungle* at this chapter's start reflects such a narrow view of casino ownership and operations. Its juxtaposition with the buttoned-down prose of Hirsch, whose experience in gambling accounting predated World War II, should reveal its fundamental ignorance.

A multimillion dollar operation run by a convicted felon was sure to raise eyebrows, particularly during the heyday of the postwar anticrime and antigambling scare. Perhaps the chief irreconcilable difference between the Kefauver Committee and Nevadans, in fact, was the acceptance of those with criminal records in Nevada gaming. William Moore, speaking as a casino owner and member of the Tax Commission, agreed that the state's policy was, "because gambling is legal in the State of Nevada . . . anybody who has been convicted for gambling in other States is not . . . disqualified," for a license.[40] While convictions for other criminal acts or known associations with organized crime figures could disqualify potential license holders, merely participating in illegal gambling could not. To this, anticrime outsiders shook their heads in disgust.

Nevada authorities were right to allow experienced personnel into the industry; running a casino was never an easy job. The chief problem of casino management was following the money that moved through the premises. Theft was a constant concern of casino managers. The freewheeling atmosphere of the casino floor certainly did not discourage employees and patrons from trying to wet their beaks in the casino's till. The preeminent test of a casino manager was his or her ability to establish and maintain rigorous cash accounting on the casino floor. To this end, casinos developed management structures that sought, like all management teams, to maximize profits and minimize losses.

The most indomitable foe of reliable casino cost accounting was not theft by patrons through artifice or cunning but embezzlement by employees, a practice known colloquially as *skimming*. Skimming could take place at any point in the money's path through the casino, from the first moment cash was exchanged for chips or coin. In many casinos, the entire working hierarchy, from dealers to the casino president, took home "a little extra." When large-scale skimming took place, the top managers or owners of a casino left some funds officially uncounted in order to hide taxable revenue or to deliver furtive dividends to sub rosa investors. In such a case, skimming became a problem for those investors or owners who were not in on the skim. More important, the state, which lost tax revenue, was the biggest loser in skimming.

Though illegal and unethical, skimming was actually rational, and was in fact structurally unavoidable. Many sub rosa investors in casino resorts could not get licenses because of their criminal records. The fiscal structure of the Nevada casino industry demanded that capital to finance casino resorts come from those with criminal pasts, but the growing regulatory structure of Nevada gaming attempted to keep these same men out of the state. Casino operators obviously could not mail illicit investors their fair share of corporate dividends, and instead skimmed cash to pay the dividends of hidden investors.

Robert Lacey, a Meyer Lansky biographer, described these skims as paying investors "a couple of thousand dollars per point per month" in addition to a larger payment after the tabulation of the casino's annual profit. Although investors could have their skimmed dividends sent to them by courier, most preferred to visit the casino in person to collect. Then they could "stay in their own hotel—comped, caviared, and champagned like pashas—and would gamble on credit which they did not pay for, up to the amount of their share." Those who did not come to Las Vegas might be given casino debts to collect or organize junkets of players who gambled on credit and paid off their debt directly to the investor.[41] In this way, operators transferred dividends to silent investors. The structural realities of casino finance and investment in the precorporate era, not insidious criminal conspiracies, caused skimming. Most casinos had to run profitably with skimming, not in spite of it.

If a skimming operation were conducted with the approval of a casino's leadership, state regulators could do little to stop the concealment of revenues. Skimming most directly hurt the state in the form of lost taxable revenue; individual casino investors and employees actually profited from skimming and they could not be expected to stop it. The only way to truly prevent skimming would be to involve state officials in the daily operations of the casino. This would subject casinos, in effect, to the continuous presence of a state auditor. When New Jersey legislators drafted legislation establishing casino gaming in Atlantic City in 1977, this was exactly the approach they took. But in Nevada, for most of the history of the casino resort, state regulators were unable, before the fact, to prevent skimming. Thus, it became *the* problem of gaming control and a stumbling block to effective, honest casino management.

Casino managers faced the problems of any large enterprise, coupled with a host of others unique to a business built on chance. In addition to coordinating hundreds of employees, casino managers had to consider an inventory that was almost completely made up of currency. That much of the currency was in small denominations and coins made accounting for it even more trying. But it is important to remember that, by the 1950s, casinos were run as businesses, and they had a great deal in common with mainstream American businesses.

Some hold the notion that before the advent of corporate ownership in the late 1960s, casino cash controls consisted of men in shiny suits stuffing bills into paper bags. This is demonstrably false. Although publicly traded corporations brought casino resorts into national marketing and hotel management networks in the 1970s, corporations did little to alter the internal management structures of casinos, and these institutions had, since the 1950s, shared accounting and operational procedures with the mainstream of American business. As institutions whose primary medium of exchange is cash and coin, profitable casinos demanded a rigorous accounting of currency. In addition to gambling specialists who could manage the action on the casino floor, casinos required trained accountants to track the wealth produced by the games. The success of the lavish resort casinos that sprawled along the Strip hinged on the ability of managers to determine where money was going. Without cash controls, cheating, theft, and embezzlement would have brought down even the most popular and moneymaking casino operation. It might have surprised many vacationing suburbanites, but the management of Strip "pleasure palaces" was as regulated—and prosaic—as any insurance agency or manufacturing plant.

Bookkeeper in a gambling joint: Charles Hirsch and Professional Casino Management

In the popular imagination, the casinos of Nevada, though certainly profitable since the 1940s, surrendered to professional accounting and management only with the coming of "corporate control" in the 1970s. The usual glib rehash of the 1950s casino scene imparts, intentionally or not, that all casinos managers were frog-throated mob torpedoes who relied on guile and terror to keep the money flowing. In this telling, any serious consideration of the development of professional casino management is unimportant, because it was only the "corporations" that brought professional management to the business and rescued it from its shameful mob roots.

But this interpretation unfortunately neglects the men and women who actually developed the accounting and management techniques that keep casinos running in the black to this day. Dismissing the fiscal foundations of the gaming industry as the province of "mob money" doesn't at all clarify how casino operators successfully operated businesses built on risk. To do so, they by necessity relied on meticulous auditors. It was the development of professional casino management in the 1950s that was to demonstrate the stable profitability of Nevada's legal gaming industry, enabling the evolution of corporate casino ownership. Professional accounting and management produced corporate control for Nevada casinos, not the reverse.

Still, "precorporate" casino professionals have remained more or less invisible in popular historiography. The relative inscrutability of early casino management, though, has been more the product of intellectual laziness than a true lack of documentation. After all, to truly consider the roots of professional casino management before the 1970s would force scholars to questions many popularly held assumptions about gaming history. For if

Working On The Casino Floor

Dealers for many years constituted the blue-collar aristocracy of the casino resort. Dealing was a position that demanded high levels of skill and manual dexterity. Consequently, good dealers were well compensated. According to Friedman, the combined salary and tips for many dealers was greater than the salary of many casino executives. Thus, adroit dealers offered a promotion to boxperson or floorperson actually contemplated pay cuts for joining the managerial elite.[42] In addition, most dealers worked a relatively easy forty-minute on, twenty-minute off schedule, which both guarded them from the enervation of a highly stressful job and reduced the opportunities for dealer/patron confederacy in embezzlement schemes.

Other employees in the pits at any given moment might include security officers, either as runners for cash, coins, or chips, or as deterrents to patron and employee chicanery. From the earliest days, casinos relied upon large forces of uniformed and undercover officers to monitor the gaming areas. Cocktail waitresses also plied the pits, supplying players with complementary drinks. It is ironic that one arm of the casino filled patrons with free alcohol while the other attempted to keep order among the sometimes unruly intoxicated patrons on the casino floor.

Slot areas had their own management hierarchy. At its summit the slot manager directed the policy of the slots department. The slot manager's responsibilities included the selection and installation of slot machines as well as the design of the slot area, including power sources, control systems, aisle widths, and change booth locations. Below the slot manager were several slot floorpersons who were responsible for particular banks of machines on a shift basis. This floorperson was the first line of defense for any problems that arose in his or her slot zone and also verified currency jackpot payouts.[43]

Front-line slot employees included cashiers, changepersons, and mechanics. Slot cashiers staffed booths that contained the operating bankroll for designated slot zones. The cashier facilitated transactions between his or her slot zone, the main casino cage, and changepersons. Changepersons paid off machine jackpots larger than the machine's coin reserve and "sold" change to patrons. Women typically made change and the job was colloquially that of "change girl." Finally, slot mechanics kept the machines in working order.[44]

In general, slot operations emphasized friendly customer relations. Unlike the confrontational pits, the slot zones were viewed as a relaxed, stress-free haven. Casino manager John Drew of the El Cortez and Stardust remarked:

> The slot department is the one area in the casino that permits your employees to mix with the customers without a physical barrier [a gaming table or keno counter] separating them. Cheerful, pleasant people can give you an advantage more crushing than that of the percentage on the reel strip. Your employees should feel it is their duty to root for the customer against the machine. Gambling is supposed to be entertainment.[45]

Obviously, those unfamiliar with the intricacies of the table games of the pits felt much more at ease in slot zones. Interestingly, the "relaxed" slot areas were primarily the province of female employees, whereas the intense pits used mostly male workers and managers. Thus, slot machines were consciously used to create a less hostile gaming atmosphere for neophyte gamblers.

Currency and coin ceaselessly percolated through the slot zones. The ideal casino patron "bought" change at a change booth and put her coins into the casino's slot machines. Thus, the casino did not garner a net increase in coin, but currency. Coins rode through the casino on an endless carousel of fate; their path usually led from:

1) The main casino cage
2) to slot booth
3) to changeperson
4) to a customer, who put them back into a machine
5) to slot machine drop
6) to count room
10) back to the main cage[47]

Even if customers hit a coin jackpot, they usually converted their coins back into currency at a coin redemption booth before leaving the casino. Thus, once coins found themselves in the maelstrom of a slot zone they could conceivably remain there indefinitely.

early casinos shared management techniques with today's industry, might there be other parallels as well? That early casinos were fundamentally similar to modern ones, not only in accounting but also in marketing, operations, and structure, is a notion that, if fully explored, would effectively set most of the popular writing about casinos on its head.

Nevertheless, Nevada's casino industry indisputably utilized professional, college-trained, managers quite early. Nowhere is the early professionalization of casino management seen more clearly than in the career of Charles J. Hirsch. Born in 1912 in New York City, Hirsch earned a degree in accounting from Pace University and in 1938 moved to Las Vegas, where he worked as an accountant for the Apache Hotel and did independent accounting work. With the advent of World War II, Hirsch entered the armed forces and rose to the rank of captain while auditing contract terminations. After the war, he returned to Las Vegas and, following a brief stint in two local accountancy offices, took a job with the Golden Nugget, then an unremarkable downtown casino. His tenure spanned from 1950 to 1970, twenty of the most formative years in the development of the casino resort. By the early 1960s, he had risen to the position of chief accounting officer, controller, and assistant secretary. In 1970, he went to work for Howard Hughes's organization at the Sands as controller.[48]

Hirsch's press-oriented biography sheet claimed that he "pioneered in casino systematization," and the detailed records to be found in his collection substantiate this assertion. Extant records enumerate the drop, net recovery, and percentage of profit for roulette, blackjack, and craps for the period 1952 to 1966. Hirsch also tracked profits in the poker room from 1958, the year that it opened. Hirsch's bookkeeping was meticulously detailed. By the mid-1960s he supervised an office of seventeen employees, nine of whom worked solely on accounting and audit functions. Hirsch and this staff produced both daily operational reports and a monthly financial report. As Hirsch described it:

> the preparation of the daily operating control is only a small part of an audit function which culminates in the financial report produced on the seventh of each month.
>
> This is a respectable document in itself. It consists of twenty-two pages of financial information with year-to-date, prior month, current month, and current year-to-date comparisons. It includes a net variation in fixed assets analysis and an analytical presentation of current income tax liability.
>
> These financial statements are drawn from general ledger accounts so organized that all supporting schedules for federal income tax purposes are maintained on a current basis and for twelve years our FITRs [federal income tax returns] have been filed on the fifteenth day of January.[49]

These financial statements provided more than interesting reading for casino executives—they formed the backbone of casino audit procedures, which in turn permit in-house and state audits. These regular audits formed a necessary precondition for mainstream investment in the industry as well as state regulation of the industry. The power to track winnings and losing effectively being, more or less, the power to detect skimming, cheating, and fiscal irregularities.

On a daily basis, casino managers wrestled in particular with three categories: the Drop, Win, and Hold. The "Drop" was the money (placed in "drop" boxes) with which customers purchased chips at gaming tables. Drop effectively measured the business a casino conducted during a shift—how many chips players "bought" at the tables. The amount of money dropped at a table, minus the amount of chips missing from a table at the end of a shift, was that table's "Win" for the shift. When the cumulative wins of the casino's tables were added, this produced the casino's total shift win. The "Hold" percentage of an individual table was the fraction of money dropped that the casino retained. In a nutshell, casino managers struggled to increase the Drop and Win of their casinos by keeping the Hold percentage as high as possible—something that they could do only with the assistance of "casino systemization" as pioneered by Hirsch.

By recording table game statistics, accountants could track the efficiency of certain games, tables, and even dealers. They maintained a fiscal surveillance that often pointed managers to "leaky" tables. For an interested newspaper reporter, Hirsch skillfully demonstrated the skill of management in using Drop and expected Win numbers to maximize efficiency:

> Hirsch showed me a graph of red and green lines, a chart of the play at one dice table. The red line was the day shift, the green line the night shift. The red line went along decently, getting back a little for the house. The green line didn't. The green line looked like the graph of a soup kitchen. All out-go.
>
> "Now," said Hirsch. "Was it psychological? A difference between night play and day play? Or were we being taken? We changed the shifts. See the graph change? The red and green lines are similar for a month. Then the bottom drops out of the red line—the shift formerly represented by a green line. Somebody had been scared by the shift change, and then recovered. So we knew there was a defective employee."[50]

Casino managers left little to chance. They were fully aware of the parameters within which "square" play operated. When a consistent disparity between drop and win could not be explained away by luck, they usually found the source of the "variation" in the win. Through skill, casino managers hoped to triumph over all those who attempted to tilt the wheel of fortune in their direction through deception. "We get a lot of people who think we are easy marks," Hirsch told *Newsweek* in 1961. "But it's impossible to outsmart us—we're professionals."[51]

The accountant's pride in his professionalism was more than gum-flapping badinage. The organization that used his accounting skills was as sophisticated as any industrial model then available, thus his assertion that "industry" had adopted *his* "functional controls." Since casinos were doubly vulnerable—to the vicissitudes of the dice and to the deception of dishonest employees and customers—it stands to reason that they developed stringent control mechanisms.

The rigorous cost accounting of casinos made them examples for other businesses to follow. Hirsch was fond of telling his listeners that there was little fundamental difference between "the administration of a casino and that of the more usual industrial enterprise." Both enterprises existed to make money, and, in both, there was, for managers, "the duty to earn profits for owners and stockholders." Hirsch often argued that "*industry* has finally accepted the validity of *casino* functional controls."

As skillful as he was in the accounting room, Hirsch aspired to be more. His formative years in Las Vegas—the years immediately after World War II, witnessed the bloom of the hardy flower of Las Vegas boosterism. Visiting writers like Katherine Best and Katherine Hillier produced glowing tracts like *Las Vegas: Playtown, USA*. Local attorney Paul Ralli, another exemplar of the booster writer, wrote two books in which he described the growing town through the eyes of a divorce lawyer and public citizen. So it makes sense that Hirsch, the behind-the-scenes casino accountant, also took upon himself the booster's prerogative to "set the record straight" about his hometown.

Thus, the private protector of the house's riches also adopted the role of public defender of the faith. Hirsch, a slight, slender man with a mischievous grin, acquitted himself as not only an excellent accountant and statistician but also a sought-after raconteur for both auditors and general audiences. He declaimed chiefly upon the bourgeois normalcy of Las Vegas and the travails of quality control in the gaming industry. He received invitations to address American Society for Quality Control (ASQC) chapters from every section of the nation; a partial list of invitations includes: Omaha/Lincoln, Nebraska; Kansas City; Richmond, Indiana; Kankakee/Joliet, Illinois; Huntsville, Alabama; Seattle; Utica, New York; and Orange Empire (Anaheim, California). Hirsch also was a desired speaker on the service organization circuit. Groups as disparate as the Long Beach Rotary Club, Oakland Paint and Varnish Association, Sacramento American Institute of Industrial Engineering, and assorted other Kiwanis and Rotary Clubs requested his presence as an after-dinner speaker.

Hirsch had appeal as a middle-American everyman. Born in New York but a Westerner since his twenties, he could transcend narrow regionalisms. He shared armed forces service with many men who had just reached middle age in the late 1950s. Like many of them, he had made the move from an Eastern city to a Sunbelt suburb. Hirsch was a senior warden of Las Vegas's Christ Church Episcopal, as well as a leader in the Boy Scouts. One glowing newspaper account of a Hirsch appearance in St. Louis remarked that Hirsch "takes his work seriously but knows when to cut it back with a fine edge of humor."[52] In his tweed jacket and bow tie, Hirsch undoubtedly looked to members of local businessmen's lodges like a fellow (business) traveler. "He did a real good job of 'good-willing,'" the Kansas City Rotary Club reported in describing a typical Hirsch appearance at which he distributed "freebies" in the form of used dice and cards to the audience.[53]

Hirsch sought tirelessly to "spread the good word" about his adopted hometown, Las Vegas, and the gaming industry. When speaking before the statisticians and accountants of the ASQC, his self-deprecating claim to still be a "bookkeeper in a gambling joint" was belied by his thorough analysis of every aspect of the daily operation of a casino. Hirsch's various orations covered three main themes: the general reputability of Las Vegas and the legal gaming industry, the difficulties of auditing the cash flow of a casino, and quality control within the casino.

Hirsch used humor and semantic argumentation to spread a more positive image of his hometown. The *Winston-Salem Journal* captured Hirsch's technique in a 1971 account of Hirsch's appearance before the Central North Carolina Section of the American Society for Quality Control:

> Hirsch comes from Las Vegas, and he says that most of us have Las Vegas all wrong.
>
> This, he said, happens because "more good-natured nonsense has been written about Las Vegas than has been written about any other city in the country except Washington, D.C."
>
> He hastily added that this is about the only thing his hometown has in common with our nation's capital, because:
>
> "We are not noted for giving people a lot of money."
>
> All this talk about gangsters and the Mafia?
>
> Hirsch sighed his misunderstood businessman's sigh and said, "Our business is about as mysterious as living in Hershey, Pa., and eating Hershey bars.
>
> "You've heard of Monaco? I don't think anyone ever called Princess Grace a gangstress."
>
> Running a gambling joint, he said, "is just a business."[54]

Hirsch used two contrasting images to underscore the purity of Nevada gaming. First, he described the nation's purported glamour capital in disingenuously unglamorous terms, implying that the casino's dealers and executives were cut from the same cloth as the chocolate makers of Hershey. Next, he introduced a contrasting linkage of Las Vegas gambling with Monaco and Princess Grace. For the people of central North Carolina, Princess Grace was doubtless above reproach, and any gambling conducted under her watch was incorruptible. Therefore, though the pits and count rooms of Las Vegas were manned by men and women who would be equally at home in Hershey (or Greensboro, by extension), they conducted themselves with the class—and probity—befitting Monte Carlo.

Hirsch's defense of Las Vegas was apparently effective; press reports of his speeches were unstintingly positive. It is impossible to dismiss his pooh-poohing of "gangsters and the Mafia" as simple deception. After all, he never denied the presence of "gangsters" in Nevada gambling. Instead, he emphasized that the gaming industry was "just a business." It was his job, and that of other managers, to ensure the efficient running of the casino and the maximization of profits for investors. That a portion of these investors, unable to be licensed, received their dividends via skimmed proceeds, is undoubtedly important, but it is no reason to call into doubt the "legitimacy" of casino operations or the efficacy of functional controls. So Hirsch was right in insisting that, in spite of the cloud of disreputability that still obscured it, gambling was "just a business."

And it is in his discussions of gambling as a business that Hirsch's speeches yield their greatest value. Hirsch spoke frequently about the "nightmares" engendered by a "liquid inventory" of cash. He paralleled the problems of the casino with those of any business, arguing that if one substituted agents, managers, and salesmen for the terms floormen, boxmen, and dealers, one could easily see the "control requirements" of the pit. As in any business, the "net effectiveness of individual employees" directly impacted the profitability of the operation. Instead of a markup on retail stock, casinos had a hold percentage that allowed profits. Diligent managers had to constantly monitor the win and drop to maintain a profitable operation. "Individual performances must be gauged against acceptable standards of deviation," Hirsch wrote. "Prompt recognition is essential in the investigation of assignable causes as differentiated from the chance causes of variation which abound in gaming." In other words, Hirsch and his peers had to find cheaters quickly in order to remain in business.[55]

Hirsch also described the pervasive governmental presence within the casino. The Nevada casino industry, he noted, was "publicly controlled to a degree that in any other industry would constitute an invasion of privacy." Gaming Control Board agents were free at any time to take "custodial samplings," that is, to impound cards, dice, and slot machines. All employees were required to annually renew their police clearances. Ownership of a casino was tightly monitored. Any interest in excess of 1 percent was "the subject of federal, state, and local reports, quarterly and annually," with changes in stock ownership reported monthly. Hirsch reported that his casino had 2,000 stockholders "scattered from here to Spain," and he left to the listeners' imaginations the "methods necessary to conform with the state and federal licensing requirements." Hirsch believed this regulation made casino gaming a boon to Nevada and a public good. He proudly stated that, unique to any industry, casino licenses were issued with "public policy as the only criterion."[56]

Finally, Hirsch stressed the importance of quality control to the profitable operation of a casino. As a "high-volume, fast turnover, low markup" business, a casino needed to rely on a razor-edge of probability. Any defects in cards or dice could be turned to the advantage of an observant customer or double-dealing employee, so strict controls were instituted. Hirsch convincingly used slide displays of cards and dice to enumerate the details of their manufacture and attempts made to manipulate them by cheaters. Each die was checked upon delivery to ensure its flatness and symmetry to one ten-thousandth of an inch. Playing cards were subject to a similarly stringent accuracy. Nothing was wasted, however; decks that did not pass muster were repackaged and given to patrons as souvenirs.[57] Some of them, no doubt, Hirsch passed out on his "good-willing" tours. Emblematic of the astute managers of early casino resorts, he found ways to turn even the dross of his business into profit.

Though not as colorful as the breed of casino managers seen in Martin Scorcese's *Casino*, the men who ran Las Vegas casino resorts in the 1950s kept the wheels turning and dice rolling. Their casinos dazzled vacationers with lavish entertainment and epicurean gourmet rooms, but every diversion was carefully measured against the bottom line—casino drop. Behind the scenes of the casino, a ballet of accountancy as intricate as any production number tracked earnings and ensured the redistribution—legal and extralegal—of casino profits. Although many of the owners and managers of these casinos had experience in illegal gambling operations, many of them were not very different from the vacationing suburbanites who made the casino business so profitable.

CHAPTER 5

Wiseguy Empire
The "golden age of cool" paves the way for even larger empires

We're not setting out to make Hamlet *or* Gone with the Wind. *The idea is to hang out together, find fun with broads, and have a great time. We gotta make pictures that people enjoy. Entertainment, period. We gotta have laughs.*
Frank Sinatra to Sammy Davis, Jr.
on the filming of *Ocean's Eleven*, 1960

The tone of his voice was menacing and I asked, "Are you threatening me?" He replied, "No . . . just don't fuck with me. . . . And you can tell that to your fucking Board and that fucking Commission, too."

Repeatedly, during the conversation I suggested to Mr. Sinatra that he hang up and call back when he was not so emotionally overwrought.

This suggestion only seemed to make him angrier. He noted that he has other enterprises from which he makes his living, that Cal Neva is only incidental to his welfare but is important to the livelihoods of many "little people."

I suggested it might be better for all concerned if he concentrated on his enterprises elsewhere and departed the Nevada gambling scene.

He replied, "I might just do that . . . and when I do, I'm going to tell the world what a bunch of fucking idiots run things in this state."
Gaming Control Board Chairman Edward Olsen's account of a
telephone conversation between himself and Sinatra, August 1963

By the mid-1960s, the tendency begun in the early 1950s to make each new casino the "newest with the mostest" markedly transformed casino resorts.

The Las Vegas Strip matured as a convention and leisure destination resort, a development that mirrored individual resorts' transitions to convention hotels. Resorts sought to maximize their own piece of this expanding pie by building more rooms, adding more slot machines, and expanding their facilities. To do this, they needed more capital than the traditional underworld sources could supply. In essence, the very success of Strip resorts began to irrevocably drive up construction and operating costs. Within a decade, casino resorts would be much larger and, more often than not, would be owned by publicly traded national hospitality corporations. Victims of their own profitability, the friendly adventure that had been casinos' greatest appeal would be replaced by more cost effective—but also less personable—marketing and operating systems. The resulting casino resorts, while they retained the functions of earlier Strip pioneers, were strikingly different in structure.

Just before casino resorts outgrew their original mold, though, they enjoyed a golden age on the Strip. The first half of the 1960s is, for the casino resort, best understood as the Copa era, years when the Sands' Copa Lounge was perhaps the nation's premier entertainment venue. In that room, the onstage frivolity of the Rat Pack, the era's archetypal headliners, wooed visitors from across the United States. As in other suburban spaces, racial segregation crumbled on the Strip in this period. Visitation climbed continually higher but, for a few years, the resorts of the Strip remained intimate enough that one might watch the hijinks of Sinatra, Martin, and Davis literally at arms length. Though some grumbled about organized crime infiltration into the gaming industry, it seemed, to most observers, that the institution of the casino resort had solved the problem of urban gambling in a way that still permitted vacationing suburbanites the privilege of gambling.

The combination of "boss gamblers," underworld financiers, and big-money celebrities who had created the casino resort as a unique tourist destination enjoyed a final, shining moment during the Copa era. Within a decade, motel bungalows would be replaced by hotel towers, lounges and dinner theaters by showrooms, and boss gamblers by gaming executives. The empire of the wise guy, even as it produced its apotheosis in Caesars Palace, would soon be integrated into a new corporate order. But the years of its triumph were heady ones for those who worked in and visited the resorts of the Strip, and they reverberate to this day in casino design, operation, and regulation.

The Cool Consensus and the Copa Era

The most identifiable image of the Strip's swinging heyday is undoubtedly the Rat Pack performing in the Sands' Copa Lounge. A multiethnic collec-

By the late 1960s, the Strip was still a series of insular resorts. From the bottom to top, Dunes, Caesars, Flamingo, Flamingo Capri, Castaways, Sands, Frontier, Desert Inn, Stardust, Riviera, Sahara. Downtown Las Vegas is visible in the distance. Note that all casinos still have parking lots—the transition to larger hotels, which needed multilevel garages, was just beginning. Courtesy UNLV Special Collections.

tion of entertainers with a frankly hedonistic ethos, the Rat Pack would seem out of step with the culture of the homogenous conformity of most Strip patrons' suburban communities. But just as the anything-goes insouciance of the Strip complemented the tense orthodoxy of the suburbs, the Rat Pack represented the flip side of sober, monogamous suburban life. Devotion to work and family was replaced with an allegiance to self-gratification that permitted any number of peccadilloes.

But there was a more serious side to the Rat Pack. Its collective members stood as a liberal consensus model of American society in which hard work and talent would give all members access to wealth and opportunity— especially in the wonderland of casino resorts. The Rat Packer represented the millions of Americans who, secure in the knowledge that they were surrounded by fellow members of the broad middle class, vacationed and caroused freely on the Strip. Casinos, of course, were not egalitarian—they made serious distinctions between low- and high-caliber players, and within them relative deprivation is experienced more intensely than anywhere else. But because vacationing stenographers and salesmen chanced to sit across the bar from regional vice presidents and other fiscal gentry, casino resorts gave the appearance of a rough democracy. Few institutions reflected the consensus of the Strip better than the Rat Pack.

The Rat Pack that graced the Strip formed around Frank Sinatra in the late 1950s. At this time, the Rat Pack consisted of five full-time members: Sinatra, singer Dean Martin, entertainer Sammy Davis, Jr., comedian Joey Bishop, and actor Peter Lawford. In addition, a galaxy of occasional joiners swelled the Pack's ranks. The Rat Pack's chief contribution to American life was a candid espousal of an unapologetically libertine lifestyle. Rat Packers unabashedly chased women, drank liquor, and generally thumbed their noses at established social mores. Sinatra and the Rat Pack provided important alternate images of masculinity during a period of social and cultural flux.[1] They were not the careerist organization men of sociological despair, or even the rugged individualists cut from the cloth of John Wayne. Rather, they were self-centered, silly, and almost stupidly immature. In a sense, they told men that it was perfectly fine to drink, gamble, and philander—a message that no doubt helped casino resorts.

But hidden behind this insouciance was a more serious commentary on postwar American social realities. A multiethnic, biracial coalition, the Rat Pack projected a consensus vision of America. Drawing on the talents of the children of "new" immigrants and a black man, the Rat Pack reflected an inclusive model of America. Bishop and Davis, whose religion and race a generation earlier would have restricted their participation as equals, were showcased in the Rat Pack as important, though clearly subsidiary, members.

Davis's role in the Rat Pack offers particularly interesting insights into the construction of race within the group. Although hailed as a talented, even genius, performer, he was frequently made the butt of racial jokes. In one oft-repeated bit, Martin would pick up Davis and thank the NAACP for the "award," thus playing on both Davis's race and diminutive stature. Davis's subordinate, though valued, status in the Rat Pack would be unacceptable in a later generation, but it was then a bright alternative to Jim Crow. Davis may not have been the leader of the Rat Pack, but he was an equal, and his essential rights as such were never questioned. Davis himself commented that with the Rat Pack, "We were like a team. . . . We traveled as a group, and people couldn't get over it." Davis's controversial marriage to Swedish actress Mai Britt in November 1960 drew the ire of many American racists. But Sinatra was unambiguously supportive of Davis, serving as best man.[2]

The Rat Pack's flexible social mores mirrored a tendency toward liberal politics. Davis worked tirelessly on behalf of civil rights, and Sinatra was, until his snub by Kennedy, an energetic liberal. As a member of the original Holmby Hills Rat Pack, he stood with a prominent group of Hollywood liberals and espoused several progressive causes in the 1950s. But the liberalism of the Rat Pack did not survive the 1960s. By the end of the decade, the political landscape had shifted so profoundly that Sinatra and Davis, previously well to the left of the middle, were now conservative defenders of the status quo. Demands for immediate racial equality superceded the gradualist integration that the Rat Pack represented. Davis, who had once been considered troublesome by the white power structure for his attempts to foster integration, was now considered an Uncle Tom by more militant African Americans. By 1972, both men were stumping for Nixon. Like many other members of the generation shaped by the Great Depression and World War II, the men of the Rat Pack made the shift from hopeful liberalism to cynical conservatism.

But the Rat Pack best represented America at play. The hedonistic indifference of Frank and the boys projected precisely the image that casino owners embraced. The Rat Pack made their brand of carousing synonymous with casinos like the Sands. Actor Victor Buono, who collaborated with the Rat Pack in *Ocean's Eleven, Four for Texas,* and *Robin and the Seven Hoods,* described the drinking, dancing, and womanizing of those film's sets as resembling a "Vegas nightclub." Sinatra and Martin, Buono continued, "turned every place they went into a Vegas club."[3] The kind of favorable publicity that the Rat Pack created for the resorts of the Strip could not be bought.

As top-flight entertainers, the Rat Pack brought many fans to Sands—a matter of no small interest to them, because both Martin and Sinatra ostensibly had points in the casino.[4] For decades, Sinatra was considered the preeminent entertainment "draw" by casinos from Caesars Palace to Foxwoods. Even at the height of his career during the Copa years, he could not touch rock-and-roll acts in records sales or box office, but casino entertainment was never about making profits at the box office—it has always been above all a marketing tool to lure players into the casino. And Sinatra fans, to the delight of casino bosses, liked to gamble.

In the early 1960s, Sinatra, Martin, Davis, and Bishop were established talents who appealed to a middle-aged, white, suburban audience—exactly the clientele that Strip casinos pursued. But the Rat Pack also symbolized another side of Las Vegas: its connections to organized crime. Sinatra's associations with alleged organized crime figures are legendary. The presence of Sam Giancana at Sinatra's Cal-Neva lodge and Sinatra's subsequent intransigence toward the Gaming Control Board eventually cost the singer his casino license and his stake in the Sands. A traumatic rupture with the Kennedy clan marked the end of Sinatra's public political dalliances. The same associations that gave Sinatra mystique in the 1950s ruined his political and business aspirations in the 1960s.

The relationship between the Strip and the Rat Pack had its most definitive statement in *Ocean's Eleven*. Sinatra, Martin, and others were not shy about admitting that the purpose of filming the movie was not to produce a cinematic gem, but to party. Much of the film was shot at the Sands, where the Rat Pack played two shows a night. Originally conceived of as a "summit conference of cool" to mirror the proposed Eisenhower-Khruschev summit in Paris, the film helped the Sands sell out its hotel and fill its Copa Lounge beyond capacity. The Rat Packers performed their two shows, partied the night away, and during what remained of the day filmed the movie.

Sands publicity maven Al Freeman used Hollywood hype to promote the casino and the movie. Some prominently announced guests in the audience at the Copa during the summer of 1960 included Bob Hope, Milton Berle, Harry James, Red Skelton, Shirley MacLaine, Danny Thomas, and others. MacLaine, a fringe member of the Pack, even had a minor role in *Ocean's Eleven* as a "tipsy girl," and Skelton had a cameo as a casino customer. The Sands strenuously publicized the movie's filming, announcing that Jack Entratter had combined the movie's production with the Rat Pack's stage act "to give you the biggest show we've ever seen." Visitors were promised the chance to see any number of stars in attendance besides the billed headliners: "Don't be surprised if Frank Sinatra, Dean Martin, Sammy Davis, Peter Lawford, and our good Philly friend Joey Bishop will be the person greeting you at the door and helping you find a table. That's the kind of place the lounge is—at the Sands."[5] Even before it was released, the movie was used to bolster visitation to Strip casino resorts.

Ocean's Eleven is an entertaining if casually acted diversion. The plot hinges on the plan of racketeer Spyros Acebos (Akim Tamiroff) to simultaneously rob five casino resorts, the Sands, Sahara, Flamingo, Riviera, and Desert Inn, at midnight on New Year's Eve. The week before Christmas, Danny Ocean (Sinatra), a former sergeant in the 82nd Airborne, summons ten of his former cohorts to Las Vegas to pull off the robbery. Through a series of vignettes, these former GIs reveal that they have not shared in the rising tide of general postwar affluence. Despite flawless planning and execution, the eleven are unable to enjoy the spoils of the robbery and the film ends with the famous five walking in front of the Sands's marquee bearing their names.

The casting of Sinatra and others as World War II veterans is significant. They represented the underside of the "greatest generation" who had not settled down into suburban family life. For men of that generation, the freewheeling eleven represented what they might have become had not they been saddled with families and responsibilities. The film portrayed the conspirators not as deviant members of the underworld, but as basically good men who had caught a few rough breaks. Thus, the audience was invited to sympathize with them. Although the robbery ultimately failed, viewers could admire the military precision of the conspirators as well as their stoic response to defeat. The final scene, in which the Rat Packers walk down the Strip as Davis bursts into song, captures the coolness of Sinatra and others; they will undoubtedly live to fight another day.[6] This cool reaction to defeat perfectly mirrored a high roller's proper response to his or her losses on the casino floor.

For those who, like the film's characters, had not gotten their due from life, the resorts of the Strip promised redemption. "Well, we're not all champions, " Acebos rationalized before the robbery, "But we *will* be. This time, we can't miss."[7] In the mythos of the casino world, though, being a "champion" was not about actually winning money at the tables—it meant having the dispassionate fortitude to bet—and lose—one's gambling stipend cheerfully. The idea, of course, that one "bought" the casino experience rather than won money had been the credo of the Strip since the 1940s.

The presence of racketeers in the film reflected the perception and reality of Las Vegas as a town with mob ties, with telling departures. Sinatra's proud Italian heritage resulted in the mobsters being given non-Italian surnames. Spyros Acebos is presumably Greek and another "connected" figure, Duke Santos, Latino. They are not menacing figures; Acebos in particular on several occasions is shown to be Ocean's dupe. Santos is a crafty operator who has "gone legit" and gets results through cunning rather than brute force, though he still has "connections." The film's casino operators are portrayed not as mafia henchmen but stumbling executives with distinctly un-Italian names such as Brice, Gillette, Freeman, and McCoy. Though they have "partners to answer to," these partners are distant and threaten only the executives; even that is implied rather than stated.[8]

The casinos of *Ocean's Eleven* were adult playgrounds where gambling and drinking were twenty-four hour pleasures, and patrons were loose with more than their spare change. The film reflected a relaxed attitude toward what was later called casual sex. In one exchange, a casino manager cautions a TV producer to be careful in selecting patrons to put on air. "Do me a favor," he drolly states, "If you're gonna interview people, pick elderly couples. Some of the others don't always belong together."[9] Within this milieu, presumably, what was not permitted in the bedrooms of suburbia was easily permissible. The freewheeling fun of the Strip was, for many, a welcome counterpoint to the staidness of middle-class American culture. For fans of the Rat Pack, the Copa years were the Golden Age of Strip casinos, in which presidents in the making and entertainment superstars mingled freely with former bootleggers and vacationing suburbanites.

The end of Jim Crow on the Strip

Contemporary viewers of the original *Ocean's Eleven* might find Sammy Davis Jr.'s role a bit odd. Within the storyline, it isn't that unusual that one of Ocean's crew was fallen from top baseball prospect to garbage truck driver; all the men have had reverses. But the other ten men either pose as hotel guests or are employed within the casino as dealers or other customer contact positions. But within the storyline, Davis's character could have done neither of these things; he was a black man, and as of 1960 African Americans were barred from casino resorts as guests and relegated to the most menial jobs as employees.

The discussion of segregation on the Strip is in many ways larger than the story of civil rights in Las Vegas, and reveals much about the impact of race on the development of the casino resort. Since the 1950s, high-profile entertainers had challenged the Strip's de facto segregation. Nat King Cole, Sammy Davis, Jr., Lena Horne, and Eartha Kitt were the most prominent African Americans who appeared in Strip showrooms during the 1950s. As was the case throughout the South, black entertainers were typically not allowed to patronize the establishments where they worked; they were usually barred from the casino and other public areas as well as the hotel. Thus, members of Duke Ellington's Orchestra could thrill audiences twice a night yet be forced to room on Las Vegas's predominantly black Westside.

Within the casino resorts, Jim Crow was not absolute, as it could be negotiated by those with fame and influence. Star performers might be permitted to stay in the hotel but banned from the casino and restaurants. Alternately, stars might be given free run of the casino resort, while rank-and-file orchestra members were consigned to arriving through the service entrance. Sometimes, the results bordered on the comic. Black singer Herb Jeffries, though given a room in the casino in which he performed, was told that his accompanist, Dick Hazard, would not be afforded the same privilege. Jeffries put on an indignant front and told the casino's owner that if Hazzard was forced to stay on the Westside, the singer would join him. When Jeffries introduced Hazzard, the joke was on the owner: Hazzard was a white man.[10]

As was the case throughout much of the United States, the narrative of the Strip's desegregation involves a complex shuffle of local actors and national pressures. In 1960, Las Vegas NAACP president Dr. James McMillan announced plans to picket Strip casino resorts if they did not immediately repudiate Jim Crow. Over the ensuing weeks, he became the center of a firestorm of controversy. Although Mayor Oran Gragson and representatives of the casino industry remonstrated with McMillan to call off the planned pickets, he refused. Casino operators feared the bad publicity that a boycott would bring about. At the same time, McMillan worried about the commitment of several local clergymen to the effort and feared that the protest itself would draw few supports and end in embarrassing failure. Shortly before the scheduled start of picketing, though, representatives of the casino industry, reportedly at the behest of Moe Dalitz, contacted McMillan and told him that Jim Crow's career in Las Vegas was over. The casinos accepted McMillan's demands for an end to discrimination.[11]

Local leaders held a high-profile meeting at the Moulin Rouge to announce the agreement. Governor Grant Sawyer and a host of politicians also attended, as did the media. Although it was later believed that at the Moulin Rouge an agreement was signed to formally end segregation, McMillan maintains that nothing was actually put into writing and that the politicians who claimed credit for the victory had been ineffectual at best. McMillan declared that Oscar Crozier, who owned a small club on the Westside, and a "handful of powerful hotel owners," had actually settled it for frankly commercial reasons:

> The hotels had settled because it was good business to settle. They knew that some southerners wouldn't want to gamble at an integrated casino, but they also knew that they needed to make sure that the convention business stayed, and that white people would not boycott Las Vegas. Money moves the world. When these fellows realized that they weren't going to lose money, that they might even make more, they were suddenly colorblind.[12]

For the casino owners, economic self-interest would beat out racial anxiety every time. Because of the casino resorts' connections to the national travel and convention market, they were particularly susceptible to the bad publicity of the NAACP's planned picket.

The resort owners' sudden reversal on this issue was, as McMillan said, strictly a business decision. In the 1950s, they had believed that white Americans would feel uncomfortable staying at a resort with black guests or shooting craps with a black dealer. In 1960, they were convinced that many white Americans wouldn't really mind, and that black Americans might make good customers. The Moulin Rouge Agreement symbolically marked the casino resorts of the Strip as places where all Americans with money to gamble were welcome. The casino resort was now a truly democratic institution that took the money of all gamblers without regard to race, religion, sex, or creed.

This was, of course, entirely in step with events throughout suburban America. Segregation was never an inherent part of the structure of casino resorts, and its institutional support was always tenuous. Many white casino employees agonized over the exclusion of black friends from resorts. But for years whites' dislike of segregation was tempered by the belief that it was mandatory, even imposed by law. Mort Saiger, for example, bitterly recalled the exclusion of blacks from the Last Frontier:

> I was so hurt that I couldn't see straight because this is the way I was treated in Poland, as a Jew, so I just ached. . . . [When the Will Mastin Trio was appearing] I had to bring sandwiches for them to eat [outside]. They couldn't even eat in the kitchen. Now that was criminal. Thank God that the law has changed.[13]

As much as he detested segregation, Saiger insisted that it was a "a state policy . . . the city's policy," and even "the law of the land at that time." Segregation within casino resorts was, in fact, an unofficial series of agreements to limit access that was not written into law, but its universality gave it the appearance of official dogma.

Throughout the nation, suburban developers often echoed Saiger's sentiments, and they often took the line that integration would devastate them economically and end in violence toward integrating black families. But when pushed to the brink, suburban developers removed restrictive covenants and quietly developed plans for integration of neighborhoods. The Pennsylvania Levittown, for example, integrated in 1960, just as Strip resorts did. Because of larger social and economic trends in American society, suburban populations often remained segregated by race, but the presence of men and women of color signified that the end of strict segregation had arrived.

On the Strip, predictably, operators put a decidedly commercial spin on the end of Jim Crow, as they extended their marketing to previously excluded audiences with little hesitation. As early as 1965, the Sands was hosting the "Ebony Fashion Fair," an exhibition of top designers featuring African-American models. The show became a heavily-attended and well-publicized annual event that filled the resort's Grand Ballroom.[14] Interestingly, since the advent of international marketing in the 1970s, casinos have become exemplars of multicultural tolerance, as casino hosts fawningly attempt to curry favor with high rollers of every race and nationality. Thus, in the final analysis, James McMillan was vindicated; when it came to increasing their casino win, operators were indeed "colorblind."

Why play cowboy when you can play emperor?

Even as Sinatra and company captured the essence of the Strip casino resort on film and stage, the Strip was changing. The early 1960s saw the completion of a paradigm shift in casino theming, as the new casino re-sorts all eschewed Western and desert themes for more universal ones. Be-ginning with the Flamingo in 1946, certain casinos had consciously deemphasized the Western element of Las Vegas, but not until the 1960s did a new era in the creation of lavish casinos begin. Caesars Palace stood as the most obvious exemplar of this new model. This change in casino theming obscured a deeper structural transformation as casino resorts be-came convention hotels with casinos attached, rather than casinos with nightclubs and motels tacked on.

Caesars Palace had a single genius and driving force, something rare in a business dominated by groupthink: Jay Sarno, formerly the operator of the Cabana chain of motor hotels, and a visionary the likes of which the indus-try has rarely seen. The casino purported to treat all of its guests to the lux-ury of the caesars of Rome, hence the word "Caesars" being plural rather than possessive. Sarno had borrowed Teamster Central States Pension Fund money for other Cabana hotel projects, and the fund's trustees floated him a generous loan in 1961 to rent land and construct the $25 mil-lion complex, at the time the most expensive in Nevada history. When it opened in August 1966, Caesars Palace consisted of the obligatory casino as well as 680 rooms in a fourteen-story hotel tower, the 980-seat Circus Maximus Theater, a coffee shop whimsically called the Noshorium, and the Bacchanal restaurant.[15] For all its expense, it was remarkably similar to older resorts in general design—bigger than the Riviera, the Strip's first midsize hotel tower, but not by that much. The theater was a little larger than most but, otherwise, Caesars Palace was not that original—except, of course, for its abundant theming.

If it followed traditional structures in its layout, Caesars Palace demon-strated the inadequacy of existing models in its ownership. The difficulties that Caesars Palace encountered in securing capital highlight the cash flow problems that plagued the industry during the 1960s. Nearly sixty in-vestors comprised the ownership pool of Caesars Palace, and a former in-surance executive, Nate Jacobson of Florida, was tapped as president of the casino while Sarno served as executive director. Midway through construc-tion, the Gaming Commission told Jacobson to raise an additional $350,000 to increase the casino's operating capital to $1.04 million. Sarno and Jacobson were able to find additional backers, but Jacobson decried the tight credit afforded the casino industry, declaring that, "financing was a tremendous problem with the tight money market. Conservative lending institutions are not interested in Las Vegas because of its image. Most won't even write insurance here." The Palace's expected operating costs of over $40,000 a day were nearly prohibitive. Clearly, this kind of money stretched the limits of traditional "mob" channels; underworld figures simply did not have enough money to satisfy demand. Still, the profits to be gained were dazzling; even before it opened, Caesars Palace was projected to gross $23 million a year. Assuming a daily operating budget of $40,000, the total of roughly $14.5 million annual operating costs leaves a substantial profit margin.[16]

Though its operators promoted it as a fantasyland pastiche of ancient Rome far removed from everyday life, Caesars Palace drew a great deal of its business from the convention trade; it boasted 25,000 feet of meeting space. As such, it was clearly part of the new breed of convention hotel/ vacation spots that casinos had become. The Stardust, for example, had added its convention space after acquiring the Royal Nevada property, and other resorts had begun to add convention rooms. But Caesars Palace was designed from the start as a convention hotel. Weekenders, newlyweds, and vacationers continued to fill many of the rooms, but convention business provided a constant, steady stream of visitors with disposable income and free evening hours to spend at the tables. For contemporary observers, Caesars Palace represented the latest in casino design in that its operators had planned for the convention business.

But today's student of the industry looks back to Caesars not for its now unremarkable convention space, but for its theme. Caesars Palace far surpassed the generalized Western traditional, Caribbean modern, and desert exotic themes of earlier casino resorts with its thoroughgoing classical Roman theming. Italian marble was imported by the ton, and Romanesque fountains and statues dotted the premises. In Caesars Palace, guests could forget their busy lives and relax near fountains and gardens of imperial Roman splendor.[17] It became a world famous casino, hotel, and resort attraction.

Despite its attractions, a unique theme alone could not guarantee a casino success; the most important elements of a casino resort remained the interconnected hotel, restaurants, entertainment venues, and casino. When these elements were not present, no matter how overstated the theme, the casino did not stand a chance in competing against full-fledged casino resorts, no matter how prosaic. Sarno learned this lesson with his next Strip venture, Circus Circus, which he designed and opened as a casino without a hotel. It was a gigantic themed entertainment experience, with elephants, clowns, acrobats, and high-wire artists performing in and around the casino, a "circus for adults" in which they, not children, were catered to. Sarno oriented the casino toward the high-roller market, even charging admission, something deservedly anathema on the Strip. The casino predictably struggled from its 1968 opening. Sarno did add a hotel tower in 1972, but he sold the property two years later to William Bennett and William Pennington, who added more hotel rooms, scotched the ad-

missions charge, and turned the casino into one of Nevada's most successful. Pennington and Bennett's company, Circus Circus Enterprises, is today
industry giant Mandalay Resort Group.

The new ownership turned Circus Circus into the family attraction that
Sarno had parodied. A promotional flier for the directly adjacent Westward
Ho motel suggested that Circus Circus was the ideal family destination:

> Astonishing! Amazing! Beyond Imagination! World's largest gam-
> ing and entertainment center. A $15,000,000 "BIG TOP" with the
> world's foremost high-wire and trapeze acts in death-defying
> stunts. Girls! Girls! Elephants, 14 bars and restaurants, shows,
> clowns, prizes galore. World's largest privately-owned water foun-
> tain display. Breathtaking excitement 24 hours a day, spectacular
> games of chance! Food, entertainment, and fun for the entire fam-
> ily! SPECIAL NURSERY CENTER FOR YOUR CHILDREN. Come
> One . . . Come all![18]

This kind of family-oriented advertising indicates another attempt to stake
out a new market for the casino resort experience. Earlier casinos, including the Desert Inn and Dunes, had featured child-care facilities, but they
had not attempted to actively integrate children's activities into the vacation experience. Appeals to the old remained, though, with the supplica-
tion to "Girls! Girls!" amidst the family fun spiel.

As revolutionary as they seemed at the time and as prescient as they appear in the narrow lens of casino history, Sarno's ideas conformed with a
general movement in postwar American culture towards theming.[19] The
Las Vegas Strip was from its beginnings a place where themed environments predominated. But the theming of most casinos was suggestive
rather than immersive. Vacationers at the Flamingo or Riviera could not
suspend their disbelief and imagine that they were actually in a Caribbean
resort. Rather, both resorts made selective use of motifs to suggest the
tropics. As one reporter put it: "Handsome, yes; inviting, yes. But little in-
congruities keep alerting you to where you are."[20] The sights and sound of
legal public gambling within the casino itself were enough of a novelty that
casino themes needed no real elaboration. Strip resorts vied for superla-
tives (largest pool, most rooms, most beautiful showgirls) rather than individual exoticism.

The trend toward bigger and more lavish casinos reached its apotheosis
with the Stardust and Tropicana. By the end of the 1950s, the casino resort
had reached its optimal size under its structural restrictions—casinos built
with capital that could be raised simply could not be any larger. Once the
limits of size had been reached, casino operators needed new strategies to
maximize their turnover. Therefore, they began to turn increasingly to

"gimmicks." As early as 1953, Oscar Lewis recognized that high turnover was a key to success in Las Vegas and that casinos "must offer attractions of one sort or another" to operate profitably. For most casinos of the 1950s, being the "newest with the mostest" or having a coveted headliner was the "attraction." Casino marketing and promotion was sophisticated, but theming was not an important part of selling the casino experience. The Stardust, Riviera, and Tropicana, to name a few, were not devoid of themes, but it is difficult to say exactly what their themes represented outside of vacation luxury.

Caesars Palace and Circus Circus represented a novel use of themes as marketing tools. In Caesars Palace, the physical plant did not merely suggest classical Rome; it was meant to transport the patron *to* classical Rome, after a fashion. Upping the ante even further, Circus Circus transformed the heretofore-sacrosanct casino proper into the ground level of an actual circus. The gambling experience itself was no longer the center of attention, but the themed atmosphere itself. The heightened theming that began with Caesars Palace intended to replace a trip to Rome with one to Las Vegas. This, of course, required a willfully ironic excursion. Classical Rome hardly featured a Chinese restaurant, much less blackjack and slot machines. This trend would reach a sublimely extravagant culmination with 1990s projects like New York-New York; Luxor; Paris, and the Venetian. The themed endeavor eventually became so extreme that these resort's promoters could claim, without humor or irony, that a visit to their property should replace a trip to the actual destination.

Scholars from Robert Venturi to Mark Gottdiener have written on the significance of Las Vegas as a themed atmosphere.[21] But seldom has the underpinnings of the historical development of casino theming received any but the most cursory consideration. In fact, the elaborate casino themes of Las Vegas grew out of very tangible fiscal considerations. By the 1960s, when Caesars Palace appeared, the casino market had reached a plateau. While gaming-related employment had increased over 13 percent from 1965 to 1966 with the new casino openings, Clark County's gaming revenue climbed only 9.8 percent that year.[22] Competition was becoming more pitched. In order to draw new patrons, a new casino needed something more enticing than a casino, retail shopping, gourmet restaurants, or opulent swimming pools. The turn to hyper-theming was intended to lure new patrons to the Strip, and to Caesars Palace specifically.

However, the use of extended theming would remain confined to Caesars Palace and Circus Circus for the time being. The International and MGM Grand, Kirk Kerkorian's megacasino resorts, didn't use themes as powerful as those of Sarno's resorts; the International had a vaguely "international" theme, and the MGM Grand made only limited use of Hollywood imagery. Imitating most other casinos built in the 1970s and 1980s, these resorts evoked distant locales without attempting to imitate them. Even the Grandissimo, a project that Sarno planned but unfortunately didn't build, lacked the cartoonish overstatement of Circus Circus. It was not until 1989 and Steve Wynn's construction of the Mirage that flamboyantly themed casinos reemerged. At this time, as in the mid-1960s, casino operators sought to expand the market. The continued operation of under-themed and "traditional" Western themed casinos most everywhere besides the Las Vegas Strip proves that theming is but one variant on the casino resort. This is why hyper-theming is far less present outside Las Vegas, the nation's most mature and crowded casino market.[23]

The Black Book: Containment continued

Even as the Rat Pack partied on stage and business boomed, all was not sanguine for the Strip's casino operators in the early 1960s. For the first time since Kefauver's abortive attempt to tax gambling in 1951, the threat of concerted federal action against Nevada's casino industry loomed, as Attorney General Robert Kennedy sought unsuccessfully to close down the "bank of the underworld." The state of Nevada, even before Kennedy's attempts to attack the casino industry, had begun to intensify its efforts to limit the presence of "undesirables" in the casino industry. The regulatory regime, strengthened in 1959, reacted to public perceptions that Mafia figures secretly controlled Strip casino resorts by more strictly enforcing licensing requirements. Regulators even moved to regulate the patrons' side of the gaming tables by drafting a list of persons whose mere presence in a Nevada casino was deemed deleterious to the industry's reputation. The state's increasing need for the revenues generated by casino resorts was seen as ample justification to give state regulators the unparalleled power to restrict even prospective patrons from casino resorts.

In 1960, the Gaming Control Board compiled and distributed an eleven-page document known as the "Black Book" to all casino license holders. For students of postwar anticommunism, the term no doubt recalls the black-listing of suspected communists and communist sympathizers in the late 1940s and 1950s.[24] Each of the eleven pages included the photograph, arrest history, city of residence, description of activities in Las Vegas, and FBI file number of an individual. The eleven and their cities of reputed residence were: John Louis Battaglia, Los Angeles; Marshal Caifano (John Marshall), Chicago; Carl James Civella, Kansas City: Nicholas Civella, Kansas City: Michael Coppola, Miami; Louis Tom Dragna, Los Angeles: Robert L. Garcia, Southern California: Sam Giancana, Chicago: Motel Grzebienacy, Kansas City; Murray Llewellyn Humphries, Chicago; Joe Sica, Los Angeles.[25] Casino license holders were charged with keeping these eleven men out of their casinos. The absence of any figures from New York's underworld is curious, as the Kefauver and McClellan Committees had concluded that the "mobsters" the list was directed against were part of a national criminal conspiracy headquartered in New York.

Officially, the Black Book served to safeguard the reputation of Nevada gaming and uphold the good name of the Silver State. A statement that accompanied the Black Book noted: "The notoriety resulting from known hoodlums visiting Nevada gaming establishments tends to discredit not only the gaming industry but the entire state as well." Casino owners were asked to "prevent the presence in any licensed establishment of . . . 'persons of notorious or unsavory reputation' including the above individuals [listed in the Black Book]."[26] It was feared that even as paying customers, these individuals would bring the appearance of mob corruption to Nevada gaming.

The Black Book is better understood as a form of containment than control. Those suspected of mob ties but already licensed were not barred from Nevada gaming. Those "grandfathered" included several successful casino operators, including the bulk of the Desert Inn syndicate. The cynical interpretation is that regulators allowed those who had significant investments in the state to remain while barring the door to those with less financial power. If the Black Book represented an effort to strictly control Nevada gaming by driving out all those suspected of mob ties, it appears to have been an exercise in hypocrisy. But the Black Book's real purpose was to prevent those who would discredit gaming from becoming involved in it. By 1960, most of the former illegal operators had spent nearly a decade in Las Vegas and had become part of the industry establishment. Whatever their past or present associations, these figures formed an essential part of the casino industry. Regulators did not want to roll back suspected organized crime from the state, which would have had significant fiscal and social costs, but, instead, they settled on a policy of containment.

With the Black Book, the state of Nevada dramatically restated its supreme power over the gaming industry. With the state's future resting squarely on the shoulders of the casino industry, the state had to foster an image of Nevada gaming as an industry with its house in order. Even though the list was only eleven names long, its mere promulgation suggested that the state had the right to regulate not only the owners and operators but even the patrons of casino resorts.

At first blush as a document that carried the full faith and credit of the Nevada regulatory apparatus behind it, the Black Book, in June 1960, actually had rather spurious legal precedent. There was confusion as to whether the Black Book would stand up to judicial challenges and what methods the Gaming Control Board would take to ensure casinos' compliance with the exclusion list. Two prominent figures in the Black Book issued early public challenges to the notion that the state could bar individuals from casinos.

A month after the Black Book's issue, Louis Tom Dragna, accompanied by two attorneys with noted reputations in the field of civil rights, William B. Beirne and A. L. Wirin, registered as a guest at the Dunes. Although he was allowed to circulate on the Strip unmolested, Dragna subsequently filed an injunctive claim in federal court to have the Black Book declared illegal.[27] Another "excluded person" challenged the Black Book in October when John Marshall, who had legally changed his name from Marshall Caifano, under which he was listed in the Book, arrived in Las Vegas. Marshall mocked and intimidated regulators throughout his stay in Las Vegas as he made the rounds of the Strip, including jaunts at the Desert Inn, Flamingo, Stardust, Sands, Riviera, and Sahara, while staying at the Tropicana.

Marshall's itinerary reveals the abundance of entertainment options available in Las Vegas, regardless of the hour. Marshall started his Friday evening at the Stardust, where he watched singer Roberta Linn perform her lounge act. Under the watchful eyes of Control Board agents, part-owner Wilbur Clark fecklessly joined Marshall's table for the performance. After finishing her act, Linn also joined Marshall. After remaining at the Stardust for an hour, the pair then went to the Desert Inn and finally to the Sands, where they enjoyed drinks in a lounge and, finally, breakfast. Marshall's night on the town ended after 5 A.M. On Saturday night, Marshall and Linn followed the same general itinerary but stayed out even later. Sunday evening, Marshall started with dinner in the Flamingo's Candlelight Room, followed by appearances at the Desert Inn and Riviera. At the Tropicana, Miss Linn joined him for a drink, and the pair enjoyed an early-morning Chinese dinner at the Sands. The night ended relatively early, and Marshall was back in his room by 4:30 A.M.[28]

Though Marshall was theoretically persona non grata, several casino executives and owners, like the less-than-insightful Clark, publicly fraternized with Marshall. The gauntlet thus thrown down, the Gaming Control Board was dared to act. The board instituted quick, extralegal reprisals against the casinos hosting Marshall. Without a legal method of enforcing the Black Book, Global Control Board chair Ray Abbaticchio impounded and inspected cards, dice, and gambling equipment to harass casinos harboring Marshall.[39] Executives at these casinos found themselves between the Scylla of Gaming Control Board card and dice confiscation and the Charybdis of Marshall's threats to sue any casino that ejected him, an unenviable position. Finally, executives at the Desert Inn succeeded in expelling

Marshall, who promptly flew to Los Angeles and initiated lawsuits against Nevada governor Grant Sawyer, gaming regulators, and the Desert Inn.[30]

Marshall, who retained the same attorneys as Dragna, combined with Dragna in arguing that the Black Book denied them their rights to due process as guaranteed by the Fourteenth Amendment, a federally guaranteed freedom. Nevada's attorneys argued that gambling in casinos was not a national right but a local one. Challenges to decisions to bar individuals from casinos should thus be addressed to state courts, not federal ones. The federal trial court sided with Nevada, but the U.S. Ninth Circuit Court of Appeals reversed the lower court's decision. The appeals court, after hearing the cases of Marshall and Dragna, ruled in *Marshall v. Sawyer* that the state's classification of those in the Black Book was reasonable and thus not a violation of the Fourteenth Amendment. The state was cautioned, however, to conduct hearings to place future undesirables in the Black Book, a request which the state heeded. Marshall's lawyers argued the case up to the Supreme Court, which refused to review it in 1967, thus ending any doubts that the state could ban those with "notorious or unsavory" reputations from casinos.[31]

Viewed solely within the continuum of casino history, the decision is a federal confirmation of Nevada's right to police its gaming industry. But within the context of civil rights, the case touches on several important points. Though the federal court ultimately allowed Nevada to maintain the Black Book, it did so only after deciding that the regulators' case against those in the Black Book was justified. The appeals court thus held out the possibility that states would not have the right to restrict local commerce without such justifications. Within Nevada, the ruling effectively authorized the maintenance of the Black Book and smoothed the way for its subsequent routinization.

The development of the Black Book in the early 1960s has its echoes in casino regulation to this day. On the federal level, it affirmed the right of state gaming authorities to bar prospective patrons and to force casinos to honor that ban. Established in Nevada, this legal precedent would follow casino resorts elsewhere. In New Jersey, state authorities, prepared a black book of their own before the first casino opened and other states followed suit. Just as it could deny the privilege of owning a casino, the state could retract a citizen's privilege to gamble in one—a concept that further identified the casino resort as a special island of entertainment that could be entered only by those not prohibited by state authorities.

One of the most widely reported applications of the Black Book under Abbaticchio's replacement, Edward Olsen, essentially drove Frank Sinatra out of Nevada gaming as an owner. In July 1963, Sam Giancana, alleged Chicago underworld boss, vacationed at the Cal-Neva Lodge, a small casino hotel on Lake Tahoe in which Sinatra was the chief stockholder. Giancana, it was alleged, was treated with warm hospitality, being served food and drinks and having the Cal-Neva's automobiles at his service. Giancana was infamous for his alleged position at the top of Chicago's mob underworld, and his open residence at the Cal-Neva was unconscionable for Olsen.[32]

On September 13, 1963, Olsen filed a formal complaint against Sinatra, citing four specific grievances, the most serious of which was Sinatra's chumminess with Giancana at the Cal-Neva. Sinatra was forced to defend himself before the Nevada Gaming Commission or forfeit his license. After some back and forth between Sinatra and Olsen, including the conversation excerpted at the beginning of this chapter, Sinatra, infuriated that the Gaming Control Board had subjected him to the same standards as other owners, made the decision to surrender his ownership interests in the industry.[33] The message was clear: association with reputed mobsters was no longer considered amusing; it was a breach of the state's gaming regulations, and it was to be punished. Sinatra's case, because of his high profile as an entertainer and notorious associations with alleged organized crime figures, was a bellwether for the Black Book. If the wealthy and powerful Sinatra could not defy the Black Book, it was thought that few could.

Significantly, the right of state regulators to bar citizens, even those who have not violated gaming regulations or, for that matter been convicted of any offense, from casino resorts has become an accepted part of the regulatory regime wherever casino resorts have been adopted. Though they have since become common throughout the United States, casino resorts are still considered special space, into which entrance is a privilege and not a right. This says a great deal about the importance state regulators place on keeping casino resorts "safe" from "undesirables," and it also highlights the continuing status of casino resorts as disconnected, self-contained gambling and entertainment venues.

Since this time, court rulings have upheld the principle of the Black Book in Nevada and other jurisdictions. This has served to make abundantly clear that casino resorts are, indeed privileged space. Often, one needs an expensive license and must undergo an extensive background investigation to own a casino or just to work in one. For the privilege of running or working in the casino business, a prospective owner or employee must prove to the state that he or she is free from mob ties and financial difficulties. Given the past problems the industry has had with organized crime infiltration, this is perfectly understandable. But states take an extra step toward defining casinos as particularly worthy of protection when they decide that, for the common citizen, visiting a casino is not a right, but a revocable privilege. The legal status of casino resorts as privileged space is a direct consequence of their development on the Strip. They evolved to be both self-contained (and therefore able to exercise a stronger degree of control over their guests) and vitally important to the state (and therefore required to remain free from even the possibility of mob influence). The Black Book confirms that casino resorts are markedly different kinds of gambling and entertainment businesses.

Requiem for a bootlegger

Struggles against the federal government and the Black Book underlined the changing nature of the gaming industry in the 1960s; the structural nature of Nevada gaming was beginning to work against former bootleggers with mob connections. Casino operators who borrowed underworld money faced a foe more redoubtable than the Department of Justice or Gaming Control Board: the reality of a dramatic increase in start-up and operating costs on the Strip. The difficulties that Caesars Palace encountered in securing investment capital underlined the new, tighter credit market of the 1960s. Thus, the elaborate pleasure palaces that underworld-backed operators built ended up pricing these very operators and their investors out of Las Vegas. This did not happen in one fell swoop, but as newer and more outrageous casinos began to rise on the Strip, the older houses needed renovation to stay competitive. Eventually, the costs of such renovations exceeded the means of underworld capital.

More important, many operators who retained connections to criminal syndicates simply aged and retired. Most of the operators who moved to Nevada in the 1950s were former bootleggers who belonged in a generation that had come of age with the advent of Prohibition in the early 1920s. These bootleggers were ambitious young men, primarily of Jewish, Italian, Irish, and Polish heritage. When Prohibition ended in 1933, this cohort was still relatively young and, as Mark Haller argues, "wealthy and ambitious upstarts."[40] After the lifting of Prohibition, many turned to gambling ventures as a quasi-legitimate profession. As older crime syndicate leaders died or retired in the 1940s, these men assumed leadership of America's criminal syndicates. In the 1950s, they were well into middle age and looking for stability and respectability. Many went to Las Vegas to find both.

By the 1960s, this ambitious coterie was in its 60s. The new criminal leaders poised to take control of the crime "families" of major cities did not share this cohort's experience in bootlegging and illegal gambling. Instead, criminal syndicates became heavily involved in illegal narcotics traffic. Though this form of crime was lucrative and supplied the new generation of criminal syndicates with money to invest, it did not prepare them in any way to operate gambling ventures. The cohort that had come of age as

G-Men Vs The Casino Resort

In 1961, Attorney General Robert Kennedy, responding to wide-spread media reports that criminal syndicates were siphoning money from Las Vegas, sought to have 65 federal agents be deputized as assistants to the Nevada attorney general. These agents were to simultaneously raid all major Strip casinos and, in Kennedy's words, close the "bank of America's organized crime." Nevada governor Grant Sawyer became understandably alarmed and promptly shuttled to Washington to avert the raid. Sawyer, pledging state cooperation against organized crime in Nevada, was able to forestall Kennedy's planned raid.[34]

Over the next five years, federal and state agents thoroughly investigated Nevada's casino industry for evidence of underworld infiltration. The FBI, IRS, Bureau of Narcotics, Immigration and Naturalization Service, Alcohol and Tobacco Tax Unit, and Department of Labor scrutinized every aspect of Nevada gaming and its licensees. This federal effort primarily investigated skimming. Ed Olsen, chair of the Gaming Control Board, recounted in his oral history that many federal agents had a fundamental ignorance about both Nevada and the underworld in general.[35] This may explain why the army of federal agents was less than efficient. The government won only one federal skimming case when, in 1973, Morris Lansburgh and others pled guilty to concealing Meyer Lansky's interest in the Flamingo from 1960 to 1967.[36]

The Justice Department's effort to "Get Las Vegas" represented an apparent paradox between Kennedy's two goals: to wage war against organized crime and to promote civil rights. A similar development, the inauguration of a special "Get-Hoffa Squad" within the Justice Department, would seem an incongruity in an administration dedicated to ensuring that all Americans received equal protection under the law. Indeed, Kennedy's critics for his prosecution of Hoffa and suspected racketeers are legion.[37] But if, instead, the war against organize crime and the struggle for civil rights are seen as two exemplars of an activist federal government crusading to correct situations that state and local authorities were remiss in addressing, Kennedy's Justice Department does not seem so schizophrenic.

In May 1963, the FBI turned over to the Justice Department a two-volume document that outlined massive skimming operations in many Las Vegas casino resorts. The bureau had obtained evidence of skimming via clandestine wiretaps. These wiretaps involved thorough electronic surveillance of homes and offices throughout Nevada. Not even other federal agents were to know of the wiretaps. The bureau was greatly chagrined, then, when the subjects of the surveillance received a verbatim copy of the FBI–produced report within three days of its delivery to Justice. In any event, wiretapping was illegal in Nevada and the hard-earned evidence was completely inadmissible in court.[38]

Under Olsen's leadership, the Gaming Control Board conducted its own investigation into skimming at major Strip casino resorts and concluded that the net losses to skimming were "less of a loss than Woolworth's sustains." To uncover skimming, investigators observed money being dropped into gaming tables boxes and compare their observations with the reported drop at shift's end. Though the four-year study revealed that some money was disappearing between the gaming tables and the counting room, allegations of millions of dollars being funneled to the underworld were proven false. In fact, Olsen claimed that losses were within the study's margin of error, as casinos frequently reported higher drops than the investigators' visual estimates.[39] Thanks to an assist from the state of Nevada, casino resorts prevailed against the most concerted challenge by the federal government to date.

bootleggers had, for the most part, sent its children to college and from there into the professions. Thus, the children of the former bootleggers who eventually settled in Las Vegas as casino operators for the most part did not follow them into the casino industry. Those who did enter the hospitality industry did so armed with business degrees.[41]

Allard Roen is a prime example of the passing of the generational torch. The son of Cleveland gambling operator Frank Rosen and a graduate of Duke University, Roen was actively groomed as the heir apparent of Moe Dalitz's Desert Inn syndicate during the 1950s. Roen had majored in business administration at Duke and was described in one booster account as a "young, urbane executive from the East." By 1954, he was a man of honor at the Desert Inn; in a vintage photo opportunity he accepted checks from Strip luminaries such as Gus Greenbaum, Clifford Jones, Jake Kozloff, Marion Hicks, Jack Entratter, Beldon Katleman, and Morris Kleinman to underwrite that year's Tournament of Champions.[42] When asked in 1955 why he would choose to work for the Desert Inn, a casino "built by the perfectly respectable Wilbur Clark but controlled by a one-time bootlegging and gambling combination," Roen waxed historical:

I feel that many of the biggest fortunes in our country were originated by men who ignored the laws of the time to take advantage of
the natural laws of supply and demand. These included fur trap-
pers, land poachers, cattle rustlers, early railroad barons and bootleggers, among others. But time and a new life within the law and
the raising of families placed their descendants among the blue
bloods of the Nation's society.[43]

This argument parallels Daniel Bell's (see footnote) by frankly recognizing
the violent and disreputable origins of many American fortunes. Roen was
being slightly disingenuous by masking his own role as the son of a former
bootlegger here, but clearly his education and polish enabled him to move
in circles that the erstwhile Mayfield Road Gang could not. He became the
chief day-to-day manager of both the Desert Inn and the Stardust in the
late 1950s.[44]

The meteoric rise of Allard Roen came to a halt, however, when he was
indicted along with four others, including convicted white-collar criminal
Alexander Guterma, in a stock-swindling scheme in April 1961. Roen, facing a possible $10,000 fine and five years in prison, pled guilty and cooper-
ated with prosecutors. He received two years probation and a $10,000
fine.[45] Still, his career as the golden boy of the Desert Inn was finished;
though he remained at the hotel, he was eased out of the top managerial
position into an advisory one. Allard Roen was eventually tarnished by
corruption, but he stands as an example of the "new generation" of casino
operators who stood ready to replace the former bootleggers, the men who
had built the casino resorts of the Strip.

A variety of factors combined to force the hands of former bootleggers
who had become casino operators. As this group aged, their children
proved unwilling or unable, for the most part, to carry on their ownership
interests. Some children of former illegal operators, like Allard Roen, were
at first glance indistinguishable from the college-educated children of first-
and second-generation immigrants who ultimately entered professional
life as doctors, lawyers, or businesspeople. Others lacked the creative verve
of their progenitors. Whatever the reason, the former bootlegger/boss
gambler would soon leave the scene.

The high-profile racial integration of Strip casino resorts in 1960 showed
how deeply tied those institutions were to the bedrock of suburban life
elsewhere. As suburban communities around the nation made at least
token efforts at integration, the Strip's resorts took the first steps toward
equality of accommodation for guests and opportunity for employees,
steps that communities and employers elsewhere took at the same time.

Casino resorts were more mainstream than is usually thought in other ways, as well. Though the hedonistic antics of the Rat Pack seemed to mock the staid lifeways of American bedroom communities, the group was wildly popular, and its records and films provided vicarious release from the mores of suburban America for many fans. That its members became the symbols of the sybaritic adventure palaces of the Strip is no surprise.

In the Copa era, the casino resort reached its apotheosis as the capital of the "wise-guy empire" of former bootleggers and "boss gamblers." These men, driven from Cleveland, New York, Miami, and a host of other cities in the early 1950s, built and staffed the casino resorts that became national vacation and convention destinations. These casino resorts, in turn, represented the "golden age" of the Las Vegas Strip, when Frank, Dino, and Sammy held court. As the erstwhile "boss gamblers" grew older, they looked to pass the torch to a new generation, one that had gone to business school and whose members were far removed from the floating craps games and speakeasy casinos of the Prohibition era.

The rising costs of casino operations, however, rapidly made the point of succession moot. The success of the lavish resorts of the 1950s such as the Tropicana and Stardust inspired even more expensive imitators like Caesars Palace in the next decade. By the time that casino operators needed $25 million to begin building a competitive casino resort, it was clear that casinos could no longer be bankrolled exclusively by traditional underworld sources. The successful casino builders of the 1950s and 1960s gradually priced themselves out of the market, thus preparing the way for corporate entrance into Nevada gaming and a new era for the casino resort.

CHAPTER 6

When the Suits Come Marching In
Meet the new boss, same as the old boss: the corporate era begins

The mob?
The last vestiges of organized crime faded from the Las Vegas scene in the late
1970s as giant public corporations took control of the famous resorts.
News account marking the 50th anniversary of the Flamingo, 1996

It's expanding, in every way, shape imaginable. . . . But they catered to you
more in those [precorporate] days; they're strictly business now. They were more
interested in your pleasure . . . to satisfy you in every way you wanted, whereas
nowadays, it's more cut-and-dried, business. It's better now, though. There's
more to see, more to do, and more entertainment.
Clifford Lorenz, industrial engineer and longtime
Las Vegas resident, on the new era, 1981

The curious frequently ask when the mob sold its last casino to "the corporations." This question greatly oversimplifies the true role of organized
crime in the development of the casino industry. "Mob" influence was not
so much about gravel-throated men smoking cigars while divvying up the
spoils of the Strip (a popular image, nonetheless) as it was disparate group
of investors with varying degrees of connection to the criminal underworld. This influence did not end with a pen's flourish and the signing of
the corporate gaming act. Instead, there was a more gradual process, where

the traditional syndicates of "boss gamblers" with underworld financing gave way or evolved into publicly traded corporations that were more palatable to mainstream investors. There was no sharp break to signify the start of a new era, but rather a comparatively smooth transition. The new owners kept in place operational procedures and marketing techniques (and sometimes less savory aspects of the industry) developed by their forebears, and the biggest changes in the casino resort that the new ownership groups brought were ones of scale rather than substance.

The recluse messiah?

One man is usually hailed as having rescued the casino resort from mob dominion—Howard Hughes. Those whose point of reference for Hughes is primarily that of the hirsute demented hermit of his final years cannot truly appreciate his impact on the American scene and, during the late 1960s, the Las Vegas Strip. Contemporary observers viewed his arrival in Las Vegas and subsequent entry into the gaming industry on a nearly Promethean scale. His actual contribution to the development of the casino resort, however, is less substantive than his high profile might suggest.

In November 1966 Hughes made a bizarre entrance into the casino scene, moving into a suite at the Desert Inn after a cross-country train journey. For four years, would remain in that suite's bedroom without leaving, receiving no visitors, attended only by a cadre of five male nurses/administrative assistants.[1] Robert Maheu, a former FBI agent and independent international consultant who had become Hughes's trusted right hand and public alter ego, had reserved the entire ninth floor at the top of the Desert Inn with the proviso that Hughes would remain no more than ten days. After arriving, the Hughes party rented most of the eighth floor as well. The management of the Desert Inn, understandably wishing to offer these choice suites to high rollers during the busy holiday season, first requested, then demanded, that Hughes leave. Maheu suggested that Hughes simply buy the hotel. After a fair amount of the haggling for which Hughes was notorious, he did just that. On March 22, 1967, the sale was closed. Hughes paid $13.2 million ($6.25 million cash, the remainder assumption of liabilities) for the Desert Inn, including its casino, hotel, and golf course. The Hughes era in Las Vegas had begun.[2]

The changing of the guard at the Desert Inn from Dalitz et al. to the Hughes organization has been celebrated as an epochal transition from shameful "mobbed up" practices to clear-headed business sense. Yet, in reality Maheu and the Hughes team held Dalitz's operation of the Desert Inn in the highest esteem. The transfer of the Desert Inn officially happened on March 27, but Hughes actually took control of the casino when the new financial quarter began on April 1. In a business with as much "liquid inventory" as a casino, tremendous sums of money can disappear, legitimately or not, in hours. Because Hughes and Maheu viewed Dalitz as a "hard-nosed businessman who let nothing escape his attention," they appointed him fiduciary agent for the interregnum, meaning that he was to square all accounts, inventory all assets and liabilities, and generally deliver an accurate account of what Hughes had bought. Maheu believed that Dalitz worked sedulously and honestly to do just this.[4] The selection of Dalitz as fiduciary agent speaks not only to Maheu's personal trust in the man but also to his faith in Dalitz's accounting skills. If Dalitz were honest but imprecise, it is unlikely that he would have received Maheu's trust. That Maheu believed Dalitz to be the best person for the job indicates that the erstwhile Mayfield Road gang member had developed management controls to rival, if not eclipse, those of the vaunted Hughes organization. Nor did Hughes plan any sweeping changes in the Desert Inn, or any of the five other casinos he would buy. Hughes's organization, when taking over the Sands, publicly acknowledged, "We are buying a very successful operation—which has been built by a successful management, executive, and employee team, which we welcome into the Hughes family. We plan no change in operation of the Sands."[5]

When considering Hughes's intentions regarding the gaming industry, it is important to remember that Hughes did not limit himself to the casino industry in Nevada. All told, he spent about $300 million on his casino empire (which included the Strip properties and Reno's Harolds Club), but also spent a considerable about on purchases that had nothing to do with gaming. His purchase of KLAS-TV to facilitate his yen for late-night movies was only one of a series of noncasino acquisitions. Hughes bought up vast, far-flung mining claims throughout the state, for which he paid over $20 million but which were largely worthless and the subject of almost immediate litigation. This was part of a greater scheme to acquire real estate. His holdings in and around Las Vegas alone were estimated at over 30,000 acres at the time of his death. By 1970, he employed over 8,000 Nevadans, making him the state's largest employer.[6] There was no attempt to specialize in casino ownership or management; the pattern seemed to be that Hughes bought everything near him. Since he made his abode in the Desert Inn, it was only natural that he purchase several casino resorts. But there was no grand vision for the gaming industry—merely a desire to acquire property.

Though Hughes didn't construct anything in Las Vegas, his administration of his four major casino resorts, the Desert Inn, Sands, Frontier, and Landmark, was championed as setting the pace for a new Las Vegas. Journalist Omar Garrison's boosterish account of Hughes in Las Vegas exulted in the professionalism of the "Hughesmen," who were "college-trained, technically oriented men who based their decisions on business-school criteria." Yet Hughes really changed little. One cannot imagine Charles Hirsch feeling out of place among this "new breed." Indeed, Hirsch moved to the Sands in 1970 and added a vigorous defense of Howard Hughes to his service club orations. The disjuncture between the "Hughesmen" and previous managers was less fundamentally severe than some had supposed. Even Garrison admitted that the gambling operators of the Strip were good at their jobs, though he claimed their expertise was based "partly upon instinctive judgments and partly upon cruel indifference to human weakness." Hughes-installed Edward Nigro, general manager of the Sands, continued to rely upon industry veterans like Carl Cohen, Sandy Waterman, and Charles Kandell. Admitting candidly his own ignorance of the business of gambling, he declared that "these guys who have been in gambling for twenty years have got a sixth sense. We haven't got enough time in our lives to learn what they know."[7]

Hughes was also purported to bring hardheaded business sense to the gaming industry. But his operations there were never profitable, and he consistently made poor decisions. In 1969, Hughes's Nevada operations lost $8.4 million. Some observers believed that Hughes was the victim of a massive mob skim; others claimed that his management team was incompetent. Robert Maheu suggests, however, that the real reason for the fiscal hemorrhaging was Hughes's own lack of acumen; he purchased properties on impulse, not foresight. His mining purchases, for instance, were wildly unprofitable and bordered on out-and-out fraud. Maheu cites the Landmark as a prime example. He had strenuously advised Hughes against the purchase; a study prepared by Moe Dalitz estimated that the casino would lose $5.5 million annually. In its first year of operation, the space age casino in fact lost $5.7 million. Hughes's $200 million Nevada investments were, as a whole, consistently unprofitable during Hughes's lifetime.[8] Within twenty-five years of his death, however, his land investments eventually yielded the Summerlin master-planned communities west of Las Vegas and a spate of other commercial and residential developments throughout the Las Vegas Valley. As was the case from the city's incorporation, the real fortunes to be made in Las Vegas were not in gaming, but rather in land speculation.

For all of the effusive press hailing Hughes as the savior of Nevada gaming in the late 1960s, he did not actually build any casino resorts. In his four years as the Strip's famous recluse, Hughes added nothing to the skyline in terms of new construction or renovation. Given the dramatic expansions that other properties undertook in these years and throughout the 1970s, Hughes's failure to build is noteworthy. Considering the tremendous reserves of capital that Hughes commanded, the lack of new casino projects can only mean that Hughes had no grand designs. Whether he bought from disordered compulsions or for tax purposes, he certainly did not intend to build a true casino empire or to change the structure of casino resorts.

Soon after his arrival, those who wanted to move Nevada's gaming industry forward championed Hughes as the catalyst for the "corporatization" of Nevada gaming, but the structural pressures that dictated a turn to corporate capital had been building since the late 1950s. Hughes in fact believed that he stood against the corporate monoliths, claiming that his was the only "competitive enterprise still functioning and holding out against the onrushing hordes of corporate giants."[9] Working Hughes into a teleological scheme leading from traditional syndicate ownership to publicly traded corporate control completely misreads his intentions and actions.

Though at the time Hughes seemed to herald the new era of the corporations, in retrospect he did little to change how casinos were owned and operated. The Hughes mystique was a public relations windfall for the Nevada's gaming industry and perhaps lessened the reluctance of corporate investors. Still, the mounting costs of casino operations and the dwindling utility of traditional underworld financing almost inevitably pointed toward a radical change in the gaming industry by the early 1970s. Hughes, the most visible "invisible man" of the twentieth century, was not an epochal figure in the development of the casino resort.

Stern and Kerkorian create the modern casino resort

Between 1967 and 1975, the casino resort was reconceptualized in two-and-a-half megaresorts that, thirty years later, remain the paradigm for casino developments. These resorts are the International, the MGM Grand, and the never-realized Xanadu. The first two were planned and owned by Kirk Kerkorian, belying his reputation as a "risk-averse businessman."[12] All three were designed by Martin Stern, Jr., an architect whose place in the history of the casino resort cannot be overstated. The traditional layout of casino resorts, a central casino/restaurant/theater surrounded by motel wings, had reached its apotheosis with the Stardust in 1958. Since then, builders had predictably gone up. The Riviera, built in 1955, was the Strip's first midrise at nine stories, and Caesars Palace had been built with a hotel tower, not motel wings. But even Caesars was relatively small-scale, with only 680 rooms. The gigantic casino hotels that Kerkorian demanded created new problems of design and function. Stern solved these problems, and most casino architects since him have been engaged basically in updating his designs.

The Hughes Casinos

The Desert Inn only whetted Howard Hughes's appetite for casino properties. Next, he bought the Sands, the fabled hangout of Sinatra and his Rat Pack, in late July 1967, for $14.7 million.

Hughes next turned to the latest incarnation of a Strip perennial, the Frontier, buying its hotel on September 22, 1967. In 1965, the New Frontier had been leveled and the Frontier, now shorn of descriptive adjectives, rose in 1967 to replace it. Interestingly, Beldon Katleman, who had previously renovated the property as the New Frontier only to immediately sell it, was one of the principals of the ownership group that sold to Hughes. The casino had not prospered since its reopening, and most blamed poor management. A 650-room hotel and casino, the Frontier sat on a sprawling 25-acre plot on the central Strip.[10] The Hughes organization also purchased two smaller Strip casinos, the Castaways and the Silver Slipper.

Hughes also purchased the Landmark, which had been languishing in preopening construction for the better part of the 1960s, and opened it. This casino, which was never truly successful, was imploded in 1995 to make way for a parking lot—perhaps a fitting commentary on Hughes's impact on the casino resort.

The International, whose construction began in 1967 and which opened in July 1969, initiated the Y-shaped triform hotel tower that is now ubiquitous on the Strip; it was an adaptation to the need to fit over 1,000 hotel rooms on a square plot in a way that would afford each room a decent view. Predictably billed as "the world's largest, most exciting resort hotel," the International sought to have something for everyone, as befitted such a large project. The International complex featured four entertainment venues, including the 2,000-seat Showroom International, the Casino Theatre Lounge, the Crown Room, a thirtieth-story dance club, and the Theatre Royal, Las Vegas's first "legitimate" theater, which ultimately bombed. The era of snug showrooms, in which the headliners could banter freely with guests seated feet away from the stage, was over, and the huge size of the International's showroom was an adaptation to the larger audiences for casino entertainment in the new era. The resort, like most others, offered more than just gambling and entertainment, and in the International, there was simply more of everything. In addition to a nearby golf course, the International itself boasted an outdoor recreation deck featuring swimming

Sinatra Leaves the Sands

Few things signified the new order in casino gaming as did Frank Sinatra's sudden departure from his once-treasured hangout, the Sands, after Howard Hughes purchased it. The reasons for Sinatra's dissatisfaction with the new regime remain open to speculation. Personal enmity for Hughes, desire for a more lucrative contract, and a host of other explanations have been offered. Since selling his points in the Sands in 1963, Sinatra had continued to perform there. Sinatra had not mellowed, though. If anything, his humiliating rebuff by Nevada regulators early in the decade had lifted all previous restraints on his behavior. Among other indignities, Sinatra staged numerous drunken tirades along the Strip as his public persona shifted from the swinging liberal hedonist of the Jack Pack days to the surly, rancorous character parodied by Phil Hartman on *Saturday Night Live* decades later.

Frustrations came to a head in September 1967 when Sinatra was denied an extension of credit in the casino after losing over $50,000. In retaliation, he pulled all the wires out of the phone switchboard at the Sands and drove a golf cart through a plate glass window. He also endangered the human capital of the Sands, threatening to break a blackjack dealer's legs and embarking on profane tirades against Hughes and the management. Sinatra declared he would not finish his engagement. Casino manager Carl Cohen attempted to reason with the singer, but Sinatra, enraged, attempted to assault him with a chair. Cohen ducked, counterpunched, and chipped two of Sinatra's teeth, knocking the now-unconscious star to the floor. Sinatra did, in fact, not finish his engagement and signed with Caesars Palace. That no one came to Sinatra's aid says enough about both Cohen's reputation and Sinatra's. Later, Sinatra admitted that the embarrassing episode, which was never again referred to in his presence, taught him that he should "never fight a Jew in the desert."[11] In keeping with the reality of the continuities in the casino world, however, Sinatra moved a few blocks south to Caesars Palace's Circus Maximus Showroom and continued to draw audiences to Las Vegas at his pleasure until well into the 1990s. Today, the day of Sinatra's birth is a municipally sanctioned holiday in Las Vegas and those in the entertainment and gaming industries still speak of "Mr. Sinatra" in reverent tones.

Architect Martin Stern, Jr.'s designs have become the standard for casino architecture. This is the original presentation drawing for his first "modern" casino for Kirk Kerkorian, the International (now the Las Vegas Hilton). Stern's design seamlessly integrated the traditional functions of the casino resort into a titanic hotel and resort. Courtesy UNLV Special Collections.

pools, four tennis courts, badminton ranges, ping-pong tables, and a health spa. Seven restaurants served patrons, including the gourmet Imperial Room, Benihana of Tokyo, an Italian restaurant, a Bavarian eatery, a steak house, and a coffee shop.[13] The International was the largest casino resort built yet, but it was only a harbinger of the new era.

Comparing the International to its nearby rival, the Landmark, is particularly instructive. Builder Frank Carroll of Kansas City had begun planning the building, conceived as a complex of apartments, shops, and a hotel tower, as early as 1959.[14] Construction on a fourteen-story hotel tower inspired by Seattle's Space Needle began in 1961, but came to a halt when Carroll chose to add floors in order to make it Las Vegas's tallest structure, a distinction that the fast-rising Mint (coincidentally, another Stern design) had stolen. As the Landmark grew from fourteen to thirty-one stories, original architect Gerald Moffit quit in protest. Carroll encountered the capital problems typical of the era, and he was ultimately denied a gaming license because of alleged links to reputed organized crime figures. Some have charged, that the entire Landmark operation was a scam; the building was planned to look promising to investors, not to ac-

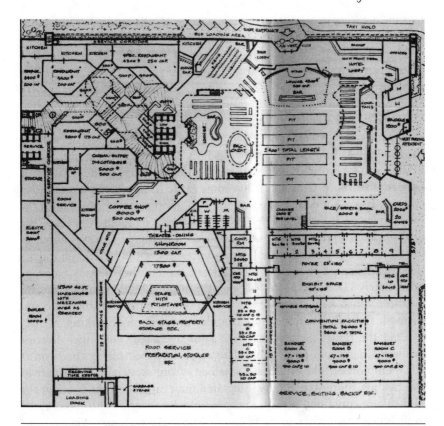

Stern's designs efficiently used interior space to maximize casino square footage while allowing for the many ancillary attractions of the casino resort. This the original rendering of the casino level of the unbuilt Xanadu. Courtesy UNLV Special Collections.

tually open. Howard Hughes bought the hotel against the advice of Moe Dalitz and opened it on July 2, 1969, the same day as the International.

The Landmark's unwieldy design (part of its casino was in the enlarged dome at the top of the tower, part on the ground floor; the pie-shaped guest rooms were awkward) doomed it from the start. Its showroom, for example, was about a quarter the size of the International's, too big to be friendly but too small to accommodate huge crowds. The property itself seemed to exude an odor that was not quite right, as casino host Mort Saiger recalled that many Desert Inn and Frontier guests who tried the Landmark told him politely that the new casino was not their "cup of tea."[15] In the end, it was not annexed by casino operators or even cannibalized for potential convention space by the adjacent Las Vegas Convention

Center; it closed in 1991 and was razed in 1995. The failures of the Landmark illuminate the ingenuity and influence of Stern's resorts.

The MGM Grand, Kerkorian's next project, opened in December 1973. At almost twice the size of the International, it ventured even further into new design frontiers. It also represented a return to the casino resort's Southern California roots; Kerkorian had bought the fabled Metro-Goldwyn-Mayer movie studio in 1970 and the new casino was envisioned as a fusion of Hollywood and Las Vegas (the casino's name was taken from the 1932 MGM film *Grand Hotel*), certainly not a new concept. But the 2.5 million square foot complex was, at the time, staggeringly huge. When it opened, the MGM Grand's 2,100 rooms made it the world's largest hotel (though it was soon surpassed by the Hilton's phase two expansion). Its casino boasted 10 craps tables, 70 blackjack tables, 6 roulette wheels, 3 "Big Six" wheels, 16 poker tables, and 1,000 slot machines. This was about as large a table games component as casino resorts would have; even today's megaresorts sport about 100 table games, though they usually have approximately 3,000 slot machines. Since the original MGM Grand, there has not been much new attempted in casino design outside of thematic and cosmetic flourishes and the more complete integration of parking.

Even the resort's executives were a bit overawed. Personnel director William Champion, in revealing language, described hiring the casino's 4,500 employees "like building a small city from scratch."[16] Stern-derivative casinos, more structurally integrated than earlier resorts, brought the idea of self-contained pleasure palaces into a new era. With new capital available at last thanks to mainstream financiers such as Kerkorian, the casino resort began to assume gargantuan dimensions, and insularity remained its trademark.

The MGM Grand was, like the International, a glimpse into the future of the casino resort: a large casino surrounded by thousands of hotel rooms geared toward the convention trade and international patronage. These casinos were not only bigger but also more self-contained than the original nightclub-and-bungalow resorts of the 1950s. One literally did not see sunlight after parking and entering the building—it was possible to spend a weekend eating, shopping, lounging in a spa, and being entertained without leaving the same building, and without leaving the vicinity of the casino. The unrealized Xanadu would have continued this trend and brought an Asiatic pleasure-dome theme to the Strip fifteen years before the Mirage. It also would have solved the problem of parking, as the resort's designs included covered garages as an integral part of the structure, something that other casinos began to do in the 1980s. This fully integrated structure would set the paradigm for the resorts to come in Atlantic City in the 1980s and on the Strip in the 1990s.

The Stern/Kerkorian models are still a part of the casino world, more than thirty years after their creation. Stern's two Las Vegas megaresorts, today known as the Las Vegas Hilton and Bally's, have both expanded but still retain much of their original appearance, something that is not true of other resorts built in the era, such as Caesars Palace or the Holiday Casino. The casino resorts designed by Kerkorian and Stern became the favored models for both the next generation of Strip resorts and the resorts that, after 1978, could be found throughout the United States. When you enter a casino with a sweeping porte cochere, attached parking garage, barn-like casino/entertainment/retail complex, and high-rise hotel towers, you are in a design first realized by Stern and Kerkorian.

Laying the foundations and reaping the benefits

These new behemoths could be built only after a capital crisis had been re-solved. By costing so much to build, they priced those without access to ex-pansive funding out of the ownership picture. The tight money supply of the 1960s, which limited expansions, also kept the Landmark unfinished for eight years, and forced Caesars Palace and Aladdin to seek emergency injections of capital shortly before their openings. As the casino operators of the Strip sought to refresh their physical plants to remain competitive for tourist dollars they had precious few avenues for financing. By permit-ting publicly held corporations to legitimately own and operate casinos, the legislature hoped to make the casino industry more amenable to main-stream investment.

A more public crisis of reputability, though, obscured the capital crisis. The issue of reputability and mob influence has fired the public imagination more than the frankly unexciting saga of bond markets and mortgage notes that presaged the real changes in the casino industry. Though casino man-agers of Moe Dalitz's ability had built successful resorts and executives of Charles Hirsch's integrity had run them efficiently, charges of mob affiliation and infiltration continued to dog most casino resorts. The federal govern-ment maintained that skimmed casino revenues added millions annually to underworld coffers, though Nevada regulators' own investigations refuted these accusations. Still, Nevadans continued to see the threat of federal inter-ference as a dreadful possibility. Lest this nightmare vision become a reality and the feared federal action hobble or crush completely Nevada's major in-dustry, Nevada politicians wanted "respectability" for casino gaming. They assumed that corporate investment in Nevada's gaming citadels could in fact bring a measure of legitimacy to the gaming industry, hence protection against federal action. Since the 1940s, Nevadans had hoped that successive waves of development would bring newfound legitimacy to legalized gaming

Elvis Becomes a Casino Icon

Kirk Kerkorian lured one of the giants of twentieth-century Americana to the Strip in a move that redefined Strip entertainment and provided a fitting symbol of the new homogeneity of the 1970s. Elvis Presley, who had shunned public concert appearances for the better part of a decade, made his return to live entertaining at the International in 1969, succeeding Barbara Streisand in the hotel's mammoth showroom. The King's rebirth on the Strip was a personal career milestone as well as a statement of what and who the Strip had become. Elvis was the epitome of the new homogeneity of the casino resort. At the helms of casinos, the "Runyonesque" former bootleggers were being supplanted by suit-and-tie, ethnically bland corporate types. Just as Elvis's stint in the army had reassured older listeners and fans that he was not so radical, his appearances in Las Vegas assuaged fears that the city was a sinkhole of mob money. By this time Elvis was no longer a gyrating teen idol; his mature appeal spoke to the broad center of American popular culture. Within less than a decade, the cool consensus of the Rat Pack had been outshined by the big money superstardom of Elvis. The image of Elvis, wearing a magnificently jeweled jumpsuit, triumphantly striding onto the stage of the International's showroom to the epic strains of "Also Sprach Zarathustra" captures the zeitgeist of corporate gaming.[17]

The new Elvis found the new Las Vegas to be a perfect showcase. Before Elvis even played the International, the casino's marketing department mass-mailed "signed" postcards bearing a rather formal photograph of Elvis in a three-piece suit and a neatly penned message from the King:

> Hi—
> Just took a tour of the new International Hotel. It's the greatest. I'll be there late this summer.
>   Elvis[18]

In the 1970s, Elvis's maturity as a performer and his mammoth fan base lent itself well to the International's 2,000-seat showroom. He logged a Las Vegas record 837 consecutive sold-out performances. He regularly performed in Las Vegas until his death in 1977, redefining both himself and Las Vegas. In September 1978, the Las Vegas Hilton unveiled a 400-pound life-size bronze statue of Elvis that still graces its upper lobby area as an eternal monument to the casino's largest showroom headliner.[19] His popularity in Las Vegas outlasted his lifetime; Elvis imitators continued to sport sideburns and white studded jumpsuits into the next century. Within a generation of his inaugural appearance at the International, popular culture conflated Elvis and Las Vegas, and the resort city rivaled Memphis as a center of Presley adoration. The popularity of the Elvis imitator in Las Vegas says everything about the resort's new identity. He, not Howard Hughes, was the true symbol of the new Las Vegas, just as Frank Sinatra, not Ben Siegel, was the real embodiment of the "old" Las Vegas.

and the casino resort. The embrace of publicly traded corporations in the late 1960s was yet another manifestation of this evergreen trend.

Even as Hughes made his splash in casino real estate in 1967, the Nevada legislature moved to amend gaming legislation with the perennial goal of eliminating "undesirable elements" from the state's gaming industry. In that year the legislature gave the Gaming Commission the power to levy fines of up to $100,000 per casino and $50,000 per individual for violating gaming regulations. Previously, the Gaming Commission could merely reprimand offenders or suspend or revoke outright their licenses. In addition to granting regulators this new punitive power, the legislature formally established the "List of Excluded Persons," (i.e., the Black Book) thereby making this effort at containment of "undesirables" part of the state's regulatory framework; that the Supreme Court had confirmed the power of the Black Book with its refusal to review the Marshall case in that year only added to the power of this tool.[20]

The legislature also amended gaming statutes to facilitate corporate ownership and operation of casinos. Though Nevada statutes had never specifically banned corporate ownership of casinos, requiring each owner, no matter how small his or her share, to be licensed by the Gaming Commission obviously precluded publicly traded corporations with thousands of shares of stock in constant flux from receiving licenses, which in turn shut them out of casino ownership. Of course, some major corporations, like Del Webb, had found ways around these restrictions, but the shell game of dummy operating companies and leaseback agreements must have been a bit off-putting, particularly to those who already believed casino gaming to be a less-than-legitimate business.

Other early experiments with corporate ownership involved the distribution of what were, essentially, stock options to important employees. In

1960, the Sahara was organized as a publicly held corporation, the first casino resort to do so. Key executives were given stock in the company as part of their compensation packages, and the ownership pool remained finite.[21] But such arrangements still precluded the possibility of transferring shares without regulatory approval, often a cumbersome task. Whether intended or not, major corporations had the impression that they were not welcome as casino resort owners.

The Corporate Gaming Acts of 1967 and 1969 changed this. The legislature at last amended the gaming code to permit publicly traded corporations to fully enter into the gaming industry. These amendments waived the requirement that all stockholders receive gaming licenses but still required the licensing of controlling stockholders, officers, and directors of a corporation seeking to operate a casino. The state reserved the right to remove any stockholder from a corporation if his presence in the gaming industry was deemed "contrary to the best interests of Nevada."[22] Seemingly a violation of due process, this article of the gaming code assuaged fears that gangster elements might use dummy corporations as Trojan horses to furtively invade Nevada gaming. It was the latest example of Nevada's efforts to contain "undesirable elements." With containment through exclusion extended to casino operators, patrons, and stockholders, regulators hoped that their vigilance would safeguard the reputation of the state's chief industry.

The renewed vigor and enthusiasm directed toward gaming regulation was reflected in an increased scope of economic research and analysis directed at the gaming industry. A 1966 general revenue fund study by accounting firm Lybrand, Ross Brothers, and Montgomery, commissioned by the state legislature, devoted nearly half of its bulk to gaming. The state was attempting to optimize the tax burden on the gaming industry; the study was essentially designed to discover how much more taxation the industry could bear without negative fiscal repercussions. The Lybrand report recommended more thoroughly detailed analysis of gaming revenues and finances, particularly uniform accounting charts and standardized financial reporting forms. As a result, the legislature created the Economic Research Section of the Gaming Control Board, which was charged with collecting and analyzing statistical data. This data's purpose was "either to measure the efficiency or economics of individual operations, or to appraise economic conditions that have a bearing on the industry."[23] Beginning in 1972, the Economic Research section issued what has become an annual accounting of the gaming industry, the *Nevada Gaming Abstract*. Such state-sponsored accounting has become the norm for non–Native American casino resorts as a way for state authorities to track revenues and, therefore, tax monies.

The state of Nevada was not a disinterested regulator of the gaming industry. By the 1960s, it was apparent to even the most obtuse observer that

Nevada's economy rose and fell with the tourism predicated upon the casino resort. State and county governments in Nevada became increasingly reliant upon the indirect growth created by casino resorts as well as the taxes levied directly upon gaming. Direct levies on Nevada gaming climbed steadily during the first decade of the corporate era. By 1970, the tax schedule of casino resorts had been more or less cemented and Strip casino operators found themselves contributing regularly to the U.S. Treasury, Nevada General Fund, and Clark County General Fund.

The federal government levied a $250 fee per slot machine (the state later assumed this tax), a $50 wagering stamp on principals and agents involved in race and sports betting, and a 10 percent excise tax on bookmaking. Nevada extracted flat fees per game and machine as well as percentage taxes on gross revenue in the form of quarterly license fees. Casinos also paid, directly or indirectly, for manufacturers and distributors' licenses, race wire fees, and investigative fees, as well as any penalties incurred for gaming infractions. Clark County demanded quarterly county license fees and casino resorts located within Las Vegas city limits were assessed additional city license fees. Total gaming levies in Nevada climbed from over $20 million in 1960 to approximately $48.8 million in 1969. The advent of corporate capital and perhaps a moderate reduction in skimming vastly enhanced casino gross revenue and levies on it; by 1977, total levies on Nevada gaming exceeded $122 million. Considering the national economic stagnation of the 1970s, this growth was remarkable.[24]

It was this growth that other jurisdictions envisioned when they later turned to casino gaming for revenue replacement. When casino gaming advocates spoke of casino resorts as engines of local redevelopment and guarantors of governmental fiscal solvency without tax increases, these were the statistics they cited. They didn't usually mention that the casino resorts of the Strip enjoyed the benefits of infrastructure improvements that hadn't come cheaply, or that the growth resorts sparked might overburden local social services. The resorts of the Strip have also historically labored under a much lighter tax burden than casinos proposed in other areas of the nation. Finally, it is important to consider these numbers in context; they represent the performance of casino resorts in a primary tourism destination, at the hub of a regional economy more or less based on casino gaming.

New Age Outlaws: Corporations buy in

With the stage thus set, large corporations would begin to own and operate casino resorts. Within a generation, legends of the unseating of pinstriped mobfathers by power-tied corporate sharks would shroud the actual slow process of industrial maturation that the casino industry underwent during the 1970s, a process that would eventually change the way casinos looked but not substantially alter their basic premise—to entertain and divert a captive gaming audience.

One of the biggest myths in the history of the casino resort is that, with the enactment of the corporate gaming laws, hotel corporations from outside Nevada swooped in and bought all the resorts of the Strip. In actuality, the first publicly traded corporations in Nevada gaming were not large hotel operators. In 1969, the Showboat casino went public, retaining its chief owners and managers but offering stock to the public. Del Webb was able to drop the legal fiction of the Consolidated leaseback and own its casinos outright. William Harrah in Reno pursued the same strategy as the Showboat, retaining control over his operations while offering shares to the general public. Public ownership did not necessarily mean any major changes in the management or personnel of casinos.

When outside corporations did move in, they were not always hotel-based. Lum's, a Florida-based corporation, purchased Caesars Palace in·late 1969. The company owned and operated 440 restaurants and 110 retail discount stores. Signifying its new focus, Lum's officially changed its name to Caesars World Inc. in 1971 and sold off its restaurant franchise chain. The impact that Lum's/Caesars World had on the resort was immediate and obvious; the resort was to expand five times by 1980, from Jay Sarno's original crescent-shaped tower to an unbalanced (but profitable) jumble of expansion towers.[25] Clearly the capital infusion of the corporation that became Caesars World solved the tight finances that had characterized the lavish resort since before its opening. Despite its far-flung hot dog and beer eateries, Lum's management looked to Caesars Palace to become its chief enterprise; even before purchase, Lum's executive vice president publicly estimated the casino to represent about 45 percent of the corporation's anticipated profits.[26] The 1971 decision to concentrate on gaming reflected the central place that Caesars Palace had assumed as the corporation's cash cow.

The first major hotel chain to move into the gaming industry, though, could not have picked more symbolic properties to buy. In 1971, Hilton Hotels bought Kerkorian's Las Vegas properties, adding the Hilton suffix to the storied Flamingo and renaming Elvis Presley's Las Vegas home, the International, the Las Vegas Hilton and expanding it to a then-unreal 3,000 rooms. Hilton executives married the Flamingo's reputation for gambling and entertainment with the Hilton tradition of upscale accommodations and service, creating what would eventually become a near-franchise of Flamingo Hiltons in other Nevada gaming centers such as Reno and, later, Laughlin. The notion of a "Flamingo Hilton" underscores the managerial and operational splicing between hotel corporations and "casino people" that went on in the 1970s. The resort was now no longer the Flamingo, but it wasn't quite a Hilton, either. Instead, it was a little of both.

Another hotel corporation's later entrance into gaming is equally instructive. Ramada Inns, Incorporated, moved into Nevada gaming in 1979 with the purchase of the Tropicana Hotel and Country Club in Las Vegas for approximately $70 million. Ramada also began construction of a "spectacularly modern" casino, also called the Tropicana, in Atlantic City, New Jersey. In their 1979 annual report, the directors of Ramada forthrightly declared that this "new era in its corporate growth" would "dramatically expand Ramada's potential earnings base in the 1980s." But they cited deeper reasons, as well:

> Ramada's decision to join the fast-growing casino gaming industry was based on more than earnings potential. We selected gaming because it is a logical extension of our long-time experience in the hospitality industry. We picked it, too, because casino gaming appears to be recession-resistant if not recession-proof. We also selected gaming because of the superior pre-tax profit margins that are possible in Las Vegas and Atlantic City.[27]

The "recession-proof" claim was no small part of the casino industry's attractiveness in the late 1970s. The rationale that Ramada offered its stockholders, that the gaming industry made good economic sense, stood the conventional wisdom of the previous generation on its head; in the 1950s, mainstream businesses for the most part considered the casino industry too risky for investment, despite the profits to be earned. By 1979, the casino resort had gained a measure of fiscal legitimacy unthinkable fifteen years earlier.[28]

The liberalization of the gaming code to elicit corporate investment was successful in solving the capital problem for the gaming industry. By 1976, twelve publicly traded corporations owned nineteen casino resorts grossing over $10 million each annually. These corporate casinos accounted for just under $1.1 billion in revenue in 1976, a sizeable portion of the $1.6 billion in revenue that the major casinos of the Strip generated that year.[29] The arrival of corporate capital and prestige brought an appearance of stability and respectability that made possible the controlled growth of the casino industry in the 1970s. The "new age outlaws," corporate casino owners, paced the industry's expansion and inspired a new public confidence in the casino resort. The publicly accepted truism that the corporations had driven out mob interests and made gaming respectable, while a powerful idea that itself served to legitimize the industry, camouflaged the true crisis that corporations had solved, that of capital.

In ways that couldn't be entirely foreseen, corporate ownership changed the public discourse on casino resorts and, more than anything, paved the way for their appearance outside of Nevada. The antigambling paradigm espoused by Senators Kefauver and Tobey was completely irrelevant to the national discourse on gambling with the advent of ownership by publicly traded corporations. A cohort of former bootleggers no longer controlled the action, and no one could argue that the wealth of America was being siphoned to support criminal conspiracy. Instead, any American who had a stock portfolio was, potentially, a casino owner. As a result, Americans from outside Nevada, who had always found casino resorts acceptable vacation spots, began to think of casinos as solid investments and, eventually, decent neighbors. Within a decade, the casino resort would no longer be confined to Nevada, and within a generation, it would be ubiquitous.

"If Bugsy could see us now?"

The transformation of the Flamingo Hilton in the 1970s and 1980s encapsulated the corporate transition. Its vintage low-rise motel wings were replaced with gigantic, blankly modern hotel towers (the design of Homer Rissman, Martin Stern's chief rival for Strip contracts), its casino enlarged, and more restaurants and convention space added, among a host of other changes, essentially, a new structure replaced the original Flamingo. But the essential elements of the "new" Flamingo Hilton could have been found in the "old" Flamingo or, for that matter, Thomas Hull's El Rancho Vegas. Just as the Stern-derivative casino resorts siphoned the functions of older resorts into larger, more integrated designs, the transition to new corporate owners, while it often coincided with innovations in operations, did not appreciably change the essential function of casino resorts.

Who worked in these new megacasinos? Frequently, they were the same men and women who had staffed Strip casinos for the past two decades. One of those who prospered under the new regime was a longtime Las Vegan, Jimmy Newman. Newman had come to town in 1947 from Amarillo, Texas, ostensibly to vacation and play some poker. After ten days, he had lost his bankroll and, in dire need of money, began working as a blackjack dealer. He subsequently switched to craps, a more difficult but more lucrative dealing job. After working at several downtown clubs, he graduated to the Strip and the Sahara, where, beginning in 1953, he climbed the casino career ladder:

> I was employed [initially] as a crap dealer at the Sahara. . . . I worked there as a dealer, was promoted to a boxman, from a boxman to a floorman, from a floorman to a pit boss, pit boss to shift manager, and in the latter part of the 1950s I was able to purchase a small percentage of the hotel.[30]

Like much of the Sahara's management team, Newman followed Sahara president Alex Shoofey when he left Del Webb to work for Kirk Kerkorian in 1967. Kerkorian offered Newman the chance to purchase 2 percent of the property and the position of casino manager. After Kerkorian formed a public corporation, International Leisure, and transferred ownership of the Flamingo to it, Newman and several of his associates from the Sahara bought into the Flamingo and worked there as key personnel.[31]

After Kerkorian opened the International, Newman and most of Shoofey's Flamingo staff transferred there. When Hilton fully acquired the property from Kerkorian in 1972, Newman remained. By 1978, he had become the Las Vegas Hilton's executive vice president and casino manager. He reported that his organization "consisted of, you might say, the young and the old as far as the gaming business is concerned."[32] Those who had advanced through the ranks in the pits worked alongside the new corporate leadership, often imported from outside, and some, such as Newman, wielded considerable power. New ownership did not mean the overnight dissolution of the old order.

In fact, there was a great degree of carryover between "traditional" casino management forged in the 1950s and the new corporate ways. Sources on casino management, from active casino executives like Charles Hirsch to industry analysts like Bill Friedman, viewed the changes of the early 1970s as typical of maturation rather than sudden innovation. Many alterations in casino operations were adaptations to new technologies. The use of closed circuit television cameras for surveillance supplemented and eventually supplanted direct catwalk observation of the gaming pits and allowed casino managers a ubiquitous all-seeing eye on the casino floor. Similarly, slot machines evolved into sophisticated computer-driven automata, but this change had less to do with corporate ownership than general technological advances.

When mainstream corporations bought existing casinos, they also purchased the human capital of their managers and employees. Clifford Perlman, chairman of Lum's Board of Directors, stressed at the time of Lum's purchase of Caesars Palace that no changes were planned in casino management, including gaming and entertainment policies.[33] Indeed, then-president William S. "Billy" Weinberger remained confidently at the helm of Caesars Palace; his career in the gaming industry, which also brought him to Atlantic City, was long, distinguished, and marked by deep involvement with the community. Floor-level managers like Mike Velardo and Tony Grasso, when asked about changes in their jobs since corporate investment, often stressed the similarities. When queried about the corporate changes, Grasso could not think of any that substantially changed the casino floor. "The gambling part never changed," he said. "The method of operation changed."[34] The maturation of management techniques that had been pioneered by Charles Hirsch and others since the 1950s intensified, but in most cases casinos continued to operate under the same basic premises.

Likewise, casino operators continued to use sex to sell the casino resort experience. Seminude revues continued to be the extravagant centerpieces of Strip showrooms, the Las Vegas News Bureau persisted in churning out "cheesecake" photos of smiling nubile young women in Las Vegas, and promotional advertisements and brochures, if anything, became racier in the corporate years. A 1977 Aladdin promotional brochure, for example, featured an attractive, bikini-clad woman emerging from a swimming pool and lounging on a bed. The brochure's cover was dominated by a large representation of an exotic, raven-haired, bosomy woman (barely) wearing gauzy, jeweled, and revealing lingerie. This Aladdin fantasy woman was shown lounging next to a treasure chest, waving from a magic carpet, and beguilingly holding a room key while sitting on a pile of luggage. Few images better capture the enduring use of sex to sell a casino resort vacation.[35]

At the same time, casino resorts continued to provide a unique brand of marriage tourism. Visitors to Las Vegas in the 1970s could be married at small roadside chapels, like the famous Little Church of the West, which was moved in the late 1970s to the far south of the Strip near the present-day Mandalay Bay. But many chose to hold their nuptials in casinos. Sam Boyd, one of Las Vegas's most successful operators, described the manifold ways to be wed in Las Vegas:

> Well, we get lots of people come up here to get married and nearly every week we have people staying here [at the downtown California Hotel and Casino] and some of them are married in our suites and we call in a local minister for them and there's a lot of people who like to go to the Little Church of the West for their wedding ceremonies and still others come and inquire about it and there is a marriage counselor next to the city clerk's office, a lot of them just go over and get their license and get married without benefit a clergyman.[36]

Room service weddings? Outside the casino resort, crafty operators began, by the next decade, to operate drive-in wedding chapels. Within Nevada resorts, the wedding chapel became a ubiquitous feature of casino design and a standard element of casino vacations. Outside of Nevada, casino resorts are often choice spots for wedding receptions because of their convention facilities, but they lack the strong ties to the wedding trade that Nevada resorts have.

While continuing marriage tourism and other traditional methods of drumming up business, corporate ownership did not substantially modify casino promotion. Casinos continued to be pitched as solid vacation bargains for the middle class or, as a 1977 Flamingo Hilton ad put it, "paradise at an affordable price." A 1976 Flamingo Hilton full-page advertisement neatly captures the zeitgeist of a casino resort in transition. The top of the page advises, "if it's happening in Las Vegas ... it's happening at the FLAMINGO HILTON." The featured attractions included "Hooray '76 (A BI★CENSATIONAL REVUE!)," which was described in glowing terms that evoked the patriotic heartland as well as European sophistication:

> As dazzling as the Fourth of July! Cast of 50! Including America's most gorgeous girls. A multitude of spectacular sequences, incredible staging, magnificent costumes from Paris and other European centers[37]

This gala which included two cocktails cost the patron only $5.95. The same page extolled the "famous Crown Buffets" ($2.95 for dinner including roast beef), and prime rib and T-bone steak meals at the Speakeasy skyroom and restaurant. The Speakeasy is itself a telling commentary on corporate attitudes toward the murky past of casino gaming; of course, it evokes Prohibition-era bootleggers and elegant, though illegal, nights out. By the next year, the Flamingo's advertisements explicitly referenced the casino's past with a wink. At the bottom of a page-long advertisement promising Pot of Gold jackpots, the perennial buffets, and nightly disco dancing, a caption beneath a picture of the casino's new façade, reads, "If Bugsy could see us now."[38] Certainly, the Flamingo's real founder, Billy Wilkerson, might have been taken aback by the imposing new façade, disco dancing to live music, and the monolithic hotel towers. The ad's tag line can read as smirking irony (the morbid might even make a connection to the gruesome details of Siegel's grisly demise). But it was most probably a genuine attempt by the Flamingo to reconnect with its fabled past; now that the bugbear of "Mafia infiltration" had been laid to rest by corporate ownership, casino operators felt it was safe, and even amusing, to capitalize on the sordid past.[39]

The embrace of a cartoonish "gangster" past by casino operators, beginning in the 1970s, is more a creature of public relations than a legitimate effort to understand the past of casino resorts. Certainly it was not the real Ben Siegel, murderer, rapist, and extortion artist, that the Flamingo Hilton paid homage to, but an idealized rakish criminal entrepreneur. Tellingly, evocations of the "mob past" of the gaming industry recalled a strangely fused animal—the benevolent, romantic Mafia don played by Marlon

Brando and the hot-blooded, tommy-gun toting bootlegger. The real presence of organized crime in casino resorts, though, was marked more by middle-aged white collar criminals, tax evaders, and far-off racketeers looking for good investments than by the swashbuckling heroics that are usually imagined. But in doing so, the "new" owners of the 1970s could distance themselves from a past that certainly had its bleaker points, including corruption and racial segregation.

Though they distanced themselves from their forebears, the new corporate regimes brought some new marketing expansions that were little more than elaborations of earlier trends. In the 1970s, perhaps in response to domestic economic malaise, casinos began to reach farther afield in search of patrons. Beginning in 1973 with a Hong Kong junket, the Las Vegas Hilton began importing premium international players en masse. Hong Kong, Japan, and Thailand represented the major Asian markets of that era; Beirut topped the list of Middle Eastern targets. These players were originally provided with interpreters, but, with time, casino resorts began hiring staff members to work specifically to attract and keep premium foreign players.[40] Eventually international marketing developed into an essential component of Las Vegas and Atlantic City casino resorts.

Despite the dollars-and-cents reputation of corporate casinos cited by Clifford Lorenz in the quotation at the beginning of this chapter, according to one longtime casino manager, casinos of the 1970s were actually looser with credit than their earlier counterparts. Mike Velardo, an assistant casino manager at Caesars Palace in 1976, believed that casinos granted far more credit in the 1970s. Whereas in the 1950s a $20,000 credit line was astronomical, by the 1970s it was commonplace. Even allowing for inflation, Velardo believed that credit gambling was a bigger part of 1970s operations than earlier ones. He posited that the presence of "bigger businesspeople" visiting the Strip led to the extension of greater amounts of credit.

An increase in blackjack tables and slot machines, which he also noted, can be attributed to the intensification of a long-standing Las Vegas trend, catering to casual gamblers. According to Velardo, the expansions of the 1970s largely foreswore new craps tables but instead added blackjack tables, a less intense and less intimidating table game. Certainly the expansion of the convention trade, which continued in the 1970s, brought "bigger businesspeople" into town who may not have been entirely familiar with the nuances of craps.[41] Another reason for the growing popularity of blackjack was the appearance of books like Edward Thorp's *Beat the Dealer*. Thorp, a University of California, Irvine, math professor, published a statistically proven method of card counting that could give an astute player an edge.[42] "Skill players" soon became the bane of pit bosses, and the number of blackjack players skyrocketed, though most continued to lose at blackjack—still the most reliable way to leave a casino with a small fortune was to arrive with a large one.

Two advertisements for the Desert Inn, separated by about twenty years, show the evolution and continuity in casino resort promotion. Printed on the back of a "souvenir menu," the 1950s ad depicted a visual cornucopia of leisure activities. Its text read:

> A world of fun and pleasure is yours at Wilbur Clark's Desert Inn! America's finest desert golf course • Beautiful Olympic-size pool • Pool-side service • Boating and Fishing on Lake Mead • Horseback riding • Sky Room Lounge • Chuck Wagon • Three great dining rooms • Extravagant floor shows nightly • Dancing • Health Club • Complete shops and personal services

The advertisement from the 1970s, a full magazine page, is more focused and sophisticated, yet follows the same fundamental arc. A single incongruous image of a couple dining by candlelight at an elegant table in the desert framed the text:

> When you dine at the Desert Inn you'll hardly believe you're in the desert. The Desert Inn features six great restaurants including the magnificent Monte Carlo Room . . . truly an epicurean adventure! In addition to the finest in dining, the Desert Inn features the world's greatest entertainment in the lavish Crystal Room, golf on two 18-hole championship layouts, tennis, health club and other outstanding facilities. Come and join the "Inn" crowd . . . just to get away from it all.

Though the later advertisement is unquestionably slicker, both advertisements stress the Desert Inn's dining, entertainment, and golf. Both completely avoided any mention of gambling. Though casino promotions had become more refined, they remained substantially the same. This is because they both spoke to the same fundamental audience: the middle-class suburbanites who had been the target of Strip promotions from the El Rancho Vegas days.

Reactions to the new era

The most marked change in the casino industry was not one of substance but of scale. "The whole town's growing," Aladdin manager Tony Grasso said in 1980, and he meant more than the population of Las Vegas.[43] As evidenced by the gargantuan new International and MGM Grand and a spate of hotel additions and expansions, casino resorts became much larger in the 1970s. The Flamingo, Hilton, Aladdin, Caesars Palace, Hacienda, and

Dunes were among the largest expansion and renovation projects of the decade. The impetus to build larger casinos and more hotel rooms was inspired to a great degree by an expansion of the convention trade, and the access of casino operators to more regular streams of capital made these expansions possible. The ending of Nevada's monopoly on casinos by New Jersey's legalization in 1976 also changed the mood. It created a feeling that the Strip was no longer a lone outpost of casino glamour, but rather the center of an industry growing throughout the nation.

The major corporations that invested in the 1970s did not want to operate several competing small-scale operations, but instead concentrated their investment into one to three large casino resorts. In order to maximize profits from the lucrative convention trade, individual Strip casino resorts expanded to an extent that has not been found elsewhere. The necessity of attracting the bulk volume of convention guests caused Las Vegas casino resorts to have larger hotel components than those later built in other jurisdictions. For example, by the late 1990s Las Vegas's largest casino resort, the MGM Grand, boasted over 5,000 rooms, whereas the largest in Atlantic City, the Tropicana, had only slightly over 1,600. The abundance of hotel rooms in the Las Vegas casino resort was an adaptation to the specific reliance upon conventions in that market.

This larger scale of casino operations led inevitably to what many considered the depersonalization of the casino experience. Both employees and patrons nostalgically recalled the "good old days" in which everyone knew everyone and the personal touch extended to all aspects of a casino resort vacation. John Haines, who had worked in Nevada gaming since its 1931 legalization, ambiguously recalled the precorporate days while unambiguously decrying the state of Nevada gaming in the early 1970s:

> I had one of my bosses, I won't say his name, make me hire some of these hoodlums on one of my shifts. I asked him what was going on and he told me, "Johnny, when they say put him to work, there's nothing you can do but give him a job." It's a good thing I never got mixed up with them—I probably could have been a big man, but more than likely, I would have ended up out in the desert under some sagebrush. This is the problem with the gambling in Las Vegas. These people don't know how to treat people, except kill them if they get out of line, and the corporations don't know anything about the gambling business. Used to, when you had one owner, he'd take his share off the top, give the bosses some, give the players some—he'd come sit down and talk to the dealers . . . the whole atmosphere has changed and I'm just glad I'm retired.[44]

Haines's comments should be taken with the caveat that, in general, he comes off as quite embittered throughout his oral history interview. Still,

Haines's characterization of old-time operators as ruthless but munificent reflected the feelings of many Strip workers and patrons.

But not everyone found the new corporate managers to be heartless ingrates. Jimmy Gay, a communications and human resources specialist who had been with the Sands for fifteen years in the early 1970s, was treated to a gratis wedding for his daughter by Sands management. Gay stated that "as a showing for their appreciation for my service with them," the Sands management, then headed by the Hughes organization, gave Gay's daughter a $30,000 wedding, with 800 to 900 guests at the dinner reception. An obviously grateful Gay beamed at the size and splendor of the nuptials, which he characterized as "the most beautiful wedding." The new regime was not always as cold-hearted as was often believed.[45]

Though some yearned for the "good old days," the corporate era coincided with expanded opportunities for minorities and women in casino resorts. Gay, for example, was a black man whom the Sands publicly feted for his years of loyal service. His employment had started in the precorporate era, but his recognition came in the new era. Not only did exceptional employees like Gay reap benefits from new opportunities in the 1970s. As the result of a federal mandated consent decree, Strip casino resorts agreed to hire at least 12.5 percent African-American employees. Casino resorts also implemented training programs and began to hire minorities into positions of greater authority. Also in the 1970s, the on-again/off-again ban on women dealers permanently crumbled, as women dealers were hired and promoted at all Strip casinos. When interviewed in 1978, casino manger Jimmy Newman struggled to fit the new realities into an outdated vocabulary:

> In fact, recently we had a couple women security guards in the casino, we've had two women who are bell-women, bellmen, bell-men or bell-women. . . . I have a woman who is a slot floorman, slot floor- (laughter).[46]

Newman's interviewer, a woman, laughingly responded, "A slot floor-person, right? That's hard to say." Opportunities for women, as for minorities, began to expand in the 1970s, but it would take years for these changes to become readily apparent. When authorized in new jurisdictions, like Atlantic City, casino operators were frequently charged with maintaining hiring and promotions quotas based on race and gender, as legislators sought to use the casino resort to promote opportunity, an idea that Estes Kefauver and other antigambling stalwarts of the early 1950s would have found incomprehensible.

The new corporate era of the casino resort brought no fundamental change in their construction as integrated—and usually insular—institutions. Though development along the Strip reached skyward in the 1970s, the discrete pleasure islands of individual casino resorts did not mesh into a genuinely urban fabric. In addition, the casino resort's insularity extended increasingly to downtown gaming. A 1975 status report on downtown Las Vegas authored by that city's Department of Community Development took a sanguine view of "Casino Center," noting that while other cities, whose downtowns were largely industrial, had declined in recent years, Las Vegas's downtown, based on tourism, had experienced phenomenal development. Between 1960 and 1975, the report estimated that $104 million had been spent on new constructions and renovations.[47] Most of this money was shunted into development related to casino resorts and not "traditional" retail sectors. The report admitted that downtown retail business had been lost to suburban shopping centers but stressed that the idiosyncratic development of Las Vegas as a tourist center was a viable option for development.

The report favorably compared the accessible, pedestrian-friendly downtown with the Strip. Yet Fremont Street had already been transformed into a hub for casino resort development. Any pretensions toward a "real" downtown of shops and restaurants seemed to be lost. The report urged "a recognition of the fact that the loss of the retail function as the dominant function of downtown is not necessarily catastrophic—*a recognition of the changes that are taking place, and a willingness to work with these changes.*"[48] In other words, any kind of development, even that of casino resorts that stunted the growth of the surrounding urban area, was to be welcomed. The report concluded with a final vision of greatness: "*Universal recognition of the fact that downtown Las Vegas is progressively approaching its destiny as the vital heart of the city.*"[49] But new developments such as the Sundance, Union Plaza, and California hewed closely to the Strip's casino resort paradigm. Existing casinos like the Golden Nugget, which had been strictly gambling halls, incorporated hotel towers into their designs in the 1970s. Within twenty years, that "vital heart" was turned into a roofed mall as part of the Fremont Street Experience development in a quest to remain competitive with the Strip. No matter where its was extended or who owned it, the casino resort remained indivisibly insular.

Because of its success as an economic generator and entertainment locale, the casino resort began to receive favorable attention from national policymakers in the 1970s. Twenty years after Estes Kefauver concluded that Nevada's history spoke "eloquently in the negative," another federal body, with less jaundiced intentions, concluded that Nevada gaming was not such a bad thing after all. The Commission on the Review of the National Policy toward Gambling met, held hearings, and conducted research from 1974 to 1976. It was charged with studying existing gambling and federal, state, and local policies toward it. The diverse gambling genres examined by the CRNPG included lotteries, horse racing, off-track betting, sports betting, dog fighting, and casino gaming. In addition to its survey of current gambling practice, the CRNPG was also to review the effectiveness of law enforcement, judicial administration, and corrections and consider alternatives to them. The shrill moralizing of the Kefauver Committee gave way to a genuine desire to better understand gambling as a social, legal, and economic phenomenon. One can sense that any strictly moral authority that the government may have once possessed had been irrevocably swept away by the Vietnam War and Watergate. The CRNPG reported its findings to a markedly different America than had Kefauver.[50]

The CRNPG thoroughly studied Nevada gaming. Whereas the Kefauver Committee had conducted a few hours of hearings in Las Vegas primarily for publicity purposes, the CRNPG diligently researched Nevada gaming and held four days of hearings. The commission's avowed aim was to sweep away the "rumor, innuendo, and exaggeration" that had shrouded Nevada gaming with a truly objective study. Thirty-eight witnesses, including industry spokespeople, law enforcement, agents, regulatory officials, and community leaders were called before the CRNPG in its Nevada hearings. The CRNPG was nothing if not comprehensive in its treatment of Nevada.[51]

On the whole, the commission's conclusions were favorable to Nevada gaming and the casino resort. Significantly, the CRNPG decided that "although organized crime once was a significant factor in some Nevada casinos," its influence had declined over the previous ten years and its current presence was "negligible." Within this period, "stringent accounting regulations and sound internal control mechanisms" had developed to minimize the possibilities for skimming. Gambling was not to be held solely, or even primarily, responsible for the higher-than-average crime rates in Reno and Las Vegas. A casino survey conducted by the CRNPG revealed that a majority of Americans favored casino gaming. In sum, the CRNPG declared that the system of gaming regulation and control that had developed in Nevada was "sufficiently stringent and enforcement [of gaming regulations] is effective."[52] Casino resorts had been successful in transforming gambling from a pariah business to an exemplar of successful state-industry cooperation, at least in the committee's view. With this endorsement, the casino resort was primed to enter a new phase, that of government-sanctioned economic savior.

The developments of the corporate era did not constitute a reversal of earlier developments so much as a culmination. Since the 1940s, casino floor operations have been laboratories for the development of new managerial techniques and cash controls. As the gaming industry grew in the 1950s and 1960s, Nevada's regulatory regime expanded precipitously. The redefinition of a consumer market has been a constant of the gaming industry. Casinos promoted marriage tourism and they persisted in using sex to sell their product. Even as air travel to Las Vegas expanded, the city's relative isolation insulated corporations from charges that they would ruin urban America by underwriting gambling. All of these existing features enticed major corporations into the casino industry in Southern Nevada. Ultimately, the success of the Las Vegas Strip would lead to the transformation of gambling from urban menace to urban savior.

CHAPTER 7

The Casino Archipelago
Success brings imitators, and the casino resort brings gambling back to America

The work of this Commission . . . was undertaken against a background of developing interest, both in this State and nationwide, in the potential benefits of legalized gambling. The reasons for this interest . . . are essentially threefold:

1. *In an era of fiscal stringency, legalized gambling holds forth a promise of providing substantial revenues through as nearly a "painless" method as can be conceived.*

2. *In an era increasingly vexed by problems of crime and corruption, legalization of gambling is put forward as a means of (a) undercutting organized crime by depriving it of the revenues which it now derives from illegal gambling, most of which it controls; (b) freeing law-enforcement manpower and resources for use against both the "organized crime" and the violent "street crime" which alarm the citizenry and undermine social order, and (c) eliminating opportunities and temptations for the corruption of various public officials whose protection or connivance is necessary to the survival of most illegal gambling operations.*

3. *In an era when assertion of personal liberty against state control has been ever more vociferously expressed, the legalization of gambling would remove restrictions on personal action which many people resent as puritanical, hypocritical, repressive and archaic.*

State of New Jersey Gambling Study Commission, 1973

NGISC [National Gambling Impact Study Commission] reported that in 1996, the legalized gambling industry employed more than a half a million people who earned more than $15 billion in salaries. . . .

> NGISC noted than most local and tribal government officials from communities with casino gambling testified that casinos had a positive economic impact on their communities. NGISC also cited the testimony of employees who said that, with the introduction of casino gambling, they were able to find better jobs with health and retirement benefits. (p.16)

> Neither NGISC nor our Atlantic City case study was able to clearly identify the social effects [of gambling] for a variety of reasons. . . . While NGISC and our case study in Atlantic City found some testimonial evidence that gambling, particularly pathological gambling, has resulted in increased family problems (such as domestic violence, child abuse, and divorce), crime, and suicide, NGISC reached no conclusions on whether gambling increased family problems, crime, or suicide for the general population. Similarly, we found no conclusive evidence on whether or not gambling caused increased social problems in Atlantic City. (p. 3)
> United States General Accounting Office, April 2000.

Until Memorial Day 1978, the casino resort was a Nevada curiosity. Though many Americans enjoyed their vacations in casino resorts on the Strip, they could see no reason to move the action closer to their homes. With the memories of urban gambling's corruption still fresh, they felt a lingering social anxiety and moral revulsion at the thought of a casino in their own neighborhood. But beginning with Atlantic City, New Jersey, several jurisdictions sought to channel for social good the public's appetite for gambling within the casino resort. Shifting public sentiments toward gambling and the fiscal realities of deindustrialization prompted sober-minded, conscientious public officials to embrace casino gaming as a positive public good. By the end of the twentieth century, Las Vegas Strip–style casino resorts could be found on the shore of the Atlantic Ocean, on the Gulf Coast, in the Rocky Mountains, along the Mississippi River, throughout California, and many points in between. This would bring the casino resort to new locales, and shatter the original premise of the casino resort—that it couldspatially and culturally contain gambling.

Atlantic City rolls the dice

Given the success of the Strip and the boom in Southern Nevada that casino resorts engendered, it was perhaps inevitable that other jurisdictions would begin to explore the feasibility of following Nevada's lead and legalize, regulate, and promote casino gaming In 1976, New Jersey voters chose via referendum to legalize casino gaming in Atlantic City. From this East Coast beachhead, the casino resort would, within twenty years, establish itself in every region of the country. A combination of social, political, economic, and historical factors pushed Atlantic City onto the stage of history as the first jurisdiction outside of Nevada to embrace legal casino gaming.

Atlantic City had a history as a seaside resort dating back to the nineteenth century. Its origins paralleled those of Las Vegas. It was a railroad town, founded in the 1850s in a fit of land speculation by railroad interests. However, unlike its desert cousin, boosters promoted it from the start as a vacation getaway, drawing on the affluent and laboring classes alike. From its earliest days it constituted an innovative cauldron of seaside tourism marketing; early Atlantic City innovations include the nation's first boardwalk, which made it possible for strollers to enjoy the sea air and shop, and saltwater taffy, reportedly born when a flood tide baptized a boardwalk merchant's candy stock. City merchants, eager to extend the tourist season into the week after its traditional end at Labor Day, created the Miss America Pageant, an institution that still calls the city its home. From the 1860s to the 1890s, the city's hotels, restaurants, and piers became world famous as vacation destinations.[1] After its initial heyday in the Gilded Age, the resort successfully made the transition into the twentieth century, with new hotels and new attractions. The city also became a noted convention town. During the flush years of the mid-1920s, it averaged 400 different conventions and a total of 12 million visitors per year.[2] The city's nightlife was resplendent, with nightclubs located throughout the city, many of which also had gambling in back rooms. Through the 1950s, Atlantic City was a national center for vacationers, conventioneers, and those seeking a good time.

By the 1960s, competing resorts (including Las Vegas), a crumbling infrastructure, and deteriorating hotel facilities made the town a shadow of its former self. Atlantic City, once billed as the "World's Playground," had fallen on hard times. Its low ebb came with the 1964 Democratic Party Convention, which revealed it to the nation as a city with decaying hotels, an inadequate infrastructure, and few attractions. Ironically, the proliferation of cheap air travel, which had brought sustenance to Nevada casinos, was one of the chief reasons for the decline of Atlantic City as a tourist destination. As more and more people could afford to hop on a plane to Nevada, Florida, or the Caribbean, fewer found a vacation in Atlantic City's aging hotels attractive. A local coalition of business interests and citizens clamored for the introduction of legal casino gaming, reasoning that casinos would jump-start Atlantic City's economy by providing employment and increasing its appeal to potential tourists. Additionally, gambling proponents stressed that state revenue garnered from casino taxes could be used to benefit citizens of the entire state.

Although a referendum that would have legalized state-run casinos throughout the state failed in 1974, the measure, in truncated form, was put to the voters again in 1976. This referendum specified that casinos would be privately owned, state regulated, and restricted to Atlantic City. Tax revenue raised by casino gaming would be dedicated to programs that assisted the elderly and disabled. As the result of vigorous lobbying and voter education efforts by a number of groups, the referendum passed. The Casino Control Act, the enabling legislation that set up the state's superintending of Atlantic City's legalized gaming, declared that casino gaming was a "unique tool for urban redevelopment" that would "facilitate the redevelopment of existed blighted areas, and the refurbishing and expansion" of the region's tourist facilities.[3]

The Casino Control Act further specified that all gambling in Atlantic City was to take place within the confines of casino resorts. The act declared that the "rehabilitation and redevelopment" of Atlantic City's resort business would offer a "unique opportunity . . . to make maximum use of the natural resources available in Atlantic City" to effect "the restoration of Atlantic City as the Playground of the World and the major hospitality center of the Eastern United States." Regarding the structure of the casino industry, the act stated:

> Restricting the issuance of casino licenses to major hotel and convention facilities [casino resorts] is designed to assure that the existing nature and tone of the hospitality industry in New Jersey and Atlantic City is preserved, and that the casino rooms licensed pursuant to the provisions of this act are always offered and maintained as an integral element of such hospitality facilities, rather than as the industry unto themselves that they have become in other jurisdictions.[4]

Thus, Atlantic City represented more than the laissez-faire legalization of gambling. The state, with full public approval, actually mandated that casinos hew to the casino resort paradigm to promote development and created a very proactive regulatory regime that involved state officials in the day-to-day operation of ostensibly private businesses.[5]

The first casino resort, Resorts International, opened Memorial Day 1978 in a renovated hotel, Chalfonte-Haddon Hall.[6] That year, the traditional start of the summer tourist season signaled absolute bedlam, as gamblers flocked to the casino, forming lines just to get in, that stretched along the boardwalk and lining up three deep at the craps tables. The profits were even larger than had been imagined; casino cage personnel struggled to count the deluge of cash. Resorts's wild success encouraged an explosion of casino development, as new operators, eager to start raking in the profits themselves, frenetically put together proposals and began building casinos of their own. The process was far from orderly. Some projects, like the Atlantic City Dunes or Penthouse, ran out of money in the earliest stages of construction and stood unfinished along the boardwalk for years. Others, like Playboy and Hilton, completed their buildings but were denied licenses by a Casino Control Commission with stricter standards than Nevada's Gaming Commission. Hilton, not allowed to open its marina district casino, sold the property to Donald Trump, who opened it as Trump's Castle. Playboy actually got to run its casino before selling it to the Elsinore Corporation, which renamed it the Atlantis. Perhaps it was an ill-starred choice, because the Atlantis, after its hot beginnings as the Playboy, sank into an ocean of gloom from which it never emerged. After acquisition by Donald Trump and operation as a noncasino hotel—the Regency—and a casino—the World's Fair—the building was razed in 2000, the first Atlantic City casino resort to disappear.

The casinos themselves were typical Stern derivatives (several, in fact, were designed by him, including the Playboy, Showboat, and Harrah's Marina) with gaming, lodging, and entertainment along with an attached parking garage and showy porte cochere. As the market has expanded, though, most Atlantic City properties have added additional hotel towers and gaming space, thus re-creating the hodge-podge architecture of the Strip. Trump Plaza, as representative of the typical Atlantic City casino as any, followed this pattern. It opened with a 555-room, 31-story tower but has since added another hotel tower (part of the failed Penthouse casino project) with 349 rooms and suites. The casino itself was about the size of Strip ones, with a similar number of table games and more slot machines.[7] Other attractions included a small convention center, a 750-seat theater, four cocktail lounges, ten restaurants, a health spa, and retail shopping. It looks like a typical older Strip or downtown Las Vegas casino with one exception: it has a bus center with fourteen gates, and it draws about 35 percent of its visitors from bus patrons.[8] With this adaptation to the greater proportion of bus-in patrons available in the mid-Atlantic region, the casino resort was easily transplanted onto Absecon Island.

Drawing on an expanded "locals" market that includes a large chunk of the mid-Atlantic region, Atlantic City casinos have established a strong market niche and secured the city's reputation as the casino capital of the East and the number two gaming market in the nation, behind of course the Las Vegas Strip. By the early 1990s, the city hosted thirteen casino resorts along the boardwalk and in its Marina section. Until the 1999 openings of Paris, the Venetian, and Mandalay Bay on the Strip, Atlantic City consistently out-earned the Strip in gaming revenue. However, the gaming industry in Atlantic City has failed to make the jump, as have newer Strip properties, to significant nongaming components. While nongaming revenue comprises over half of the Strip's total revenue, it accounts for less than one-fifth of Atlantic City's earnings.[9]

The casino industry spurred a dramatic revival of Atlantic City's tourist trade; around 35 million visitors a year now go to the city. These numbers, though, must be noted with the caveat that many of these "tourists" never leave the confines of casino resorts. A walk on the boardwalk is no longer the sine qua non of a trip "down the shore;" playing the slots is. Still, casinos have undeniably helped Atlantic City. They have directly created over 50,000 jobs in Atlantic City and attracted billions of dollars in investment. Their municipal taxes have been put to good use: there have been a host of civic improvements, including the construction of new housing, the addition of a new convention center, the renovation of the hallowed boardwalk convention hall, and the attraction of minor league sports franchises. Much of the city's dilapidated housing has been demolished or upgraded, and infrastructure improvements, including the revival of rail service, have made the city (and its casinos) more accessible. The tax revenues produced by casinos were directed toward a number of socially useful programs, including the Casino Redevelopment Authority and programs for seniors. In several regards, Atlantic City's turn to the casino resort was more successful than could have been imagined.[10]

But critics of the casino resort in Atlantic City charge that gaming there has enriched casino operators, real estate speculators, and other interested parties at the expense of the citizenry of Atlantic City. Astute critics have realized that the very instrument of Atlantic City's boom, the casino resort, is also responsible for its relative lack of redevelopment:

> The laws that established casinos made them islands unto themselves; they were constructed to be self-contained cities. The purpose of the casino was to gamble. To keep the public gambling, everything had to be provided within the casino: drink, dining, exercise, sleep, entertainment, and shopping.[11]

This is exactly what Tommy Hull had first designed the El Rancho Vegas to do: keep people in the casino. It is no surprise that these casinos, when run properly, are wildly profitable. But the essentially nonurban institution that had sparked the growth of Las Vegas, the casino resort, could not be expected to produce an urban revival. In simple terms, casino patrons could not, or would not, venture outside the casinos in great numbers, thus stultifying any attempts to rebuild a noncasino commercial base.

One of the tenets of the original pro-casino campaign was that the construction of casino resorts would restore an urban structure where restaurants, retail stores, and other amenities might flourish amidst a garden of casino resorts. The middle class would return to the revitalized neighborhoods of Atlantic City and witness a millennium of civic tranquility. This didn't happen. If anything, casino resorts have further rent the urban fabric of Atlantic City. Pacific Avenue, which once boasted a resilient, if not thriving, line of restaurants and businesses, is now dominated by casino resorts that have in most cases swallowed up all the land around them. The spectacle of casinos consuming the very businesses that they were supposed to revive is evidence of the suburbanization of Atlantic City—to "save" the city and make it a better host to casino resorts, it will eventually be rebuilt as a series of resorts with a few support businesses nearby, as near a facsimile of the Las Vegas Strip as can be imagined. Only in Atlantic City, builders will not be working from barren desert, but from the remains of a once-booming seaside community.

But critics who observe the remnants of urban blight in Atlantic City and conclude that the "Atlantic City Experiment" had failed should consider the city within the context of the larger region. Like Las Vegas and indeed most of the nation, much of the growth in Atlantic City has been in its "suburbs" (it is a bit awkward to speak of a municipality of 36,000 as having suburbs). When considered on the regional, rather than local, level, casino resorts in Atlantic City have excelled at creating jobs, enhancing state revenue, and promoting development—precisely the things that casino advocates promised in the 1976 campaign. That the areas zoned for casinos have become dominated by casinos should not be surprising—after all, that is the most logical use of the land and, for the state, the most profitable.

Paradoxically, then, Atlantic City casino resorts are simultaneously trumpeted as having ushered in two decades of soaring revenues, booming development, and rising employment and criticized for causing urban businesses to decline. The ripples of development caused by the casino resorts have neither fully redeveloped the "city" nor erased its social and economic problems, though they have promoted suburban growth in its environs. But looking at the thirty-plus year history of resorts on the Strip should have yielded a few lessons for New Jersey planners. Though resorts on the Strip, and even on Fremont Street, certainly created revenues and development in the region, they did nothing to prevent urban blight from claiming the city's existing downtown, the area that was most similar to Atlantic City itself.

Those overseeing New Jersey's casino industry have only recently begun to acknowledge what should have been clear from the history of the casino resort on the Las Vegas Strip: as single nodes in a larger metropolitan system, casino resorts can work spectacularly well, but they are not effective anchors for urban development. James Hurley, former chairman of the

Casino Control Commission, acknowledged during a ceremony to celebrate that body's twenty-fifth anniversary that Strip-style casino resorts actually impeded urban redevelopment in Atlantic City. "The legislation was a mistake," Hurley said, in that the Casino Control Act required casinos to become "contained little cities" with required amounts of hotel, retail, dining, and convention space.[12] Though casino resorts have created both revenues and jobs in Atlantic City, it is clear that their very design prevents them from truly revitalizing the city as a traditional urban vacation resort.

On the reservation: Casinos for economic development in Indian country

Seizing on the example of Atlantic City—that casino-style gambling could be profitably run outside of Nevada—Indian tribes, slowly and almost by default, began moving into the casino business. By using reservation land for casino resorts, Indian tribes can make the marginality of their lands an asset. The notion of Native Americans profiting from Anglo-American profligacy gives the past 300 years of Euro-Indian relations an ironic kick. Indian gaming began to evolve in the late 1970s. Initially, Native American tribes conducted charity gambling events in accordance with state rules for such activities. In 1978, though, Seminole bingo operators in South Florida waived the state limits on their bingo, thus undercutting the trade of other charity bingo halls. This clearly violated the laws of Florida, but in *Seminole Tribe of Florida v. Butterworth*, a federal court of appeals ruled that games permitted elsewhere by states could be allowed without limits on reservations. Thus, unless states banned gambling entirely, they had no power to close gaming halls on Indian reservations.[13]

Over the next decade, Native American tribes across the nation turned to casino gaming as an engine of economic self-sufficiency. In 1987 with the Cabazon case, the U.S. Supreme Court turned aside another legal challenge to Indian gaming. The Court ruled that not only could states not regulate or close Indian gaming casinos but also that Indian gaming was actually consistent with federal efforts at economic development. In fact, the Bureau of Indian Affairs had given some tribes grants for casino construction. As a result, Indian gaming expanded dramatically.[14]

Congress moved to regulate Indian gaming in 1988 with passage of the Indian Gaming Regulatory Act (IGRA). This legislation established a three-member National Indian Gaming Commission and declared that casino gaming was to be regulated under rules established by compacts between state governments and individual tribes. The act delineated three classes of gaming. Class I gaming included low-stakes games played among tribal members and was to be regulated only by tribes. Class II gaming included bingo and similar games as well as nonbank card games such as poker, where players bet against each other rather than the house. Class II gaming is initially regulated by the commission, but successful operations can eventually apply for self-regulation.[15]

Class III gaming subsumed casino gaming, the most profitable form of gambling. For tribes to conduct Class III gaming, according to the IGRA, they must enter a compact with their states. Such a compact would specify the exact nature of the games to be allowed on the reservation and provide for the regulation of the gaming. Tribes were free to contract non-Indian companies to manage reservation facilities, though limits were placed on the share of revenue that this outside company could receive. States were given no power to tax Indian gaming and thus no effective power to regulate it. Thus, many Indian tribes were free to use their marginal lands and remote locations for economic development in a way that few could have foreseen before the 1980s.

The economic development engendered by Indian gaming has been incredible. Probably the most outstanding example of the success of the casino resort on Indian land can be found in Connecticut. What is now the world's largest casino, the Mashantucket Pequot tribe's Foxwoods Casino Resort, opened in 1992 and quickly became a gaming superpower, employing over 8,200 people and earning annual revenues of over $1 billion by 2000. The complex boasts a gargantuan casino (320,000 square feet, with over 5,800 slot machines) that is about three times as large as the average Strip casino, as well as lodging, restaurant, and convention facilities. Gaming revenues have permitted the tribe to build a community center and child-development facility. Each of the 280 members of the Pequot tribe receives approximately $400,000 annually from gaming revenue.[16]

Located on reservations with little existing commercial or industrial development, Indian gaming has been touted as highly successful. Benefits include the obvious tribal profits as well as increased non-Indian regional employment. Some tribes, as part of their compacts, pay states for the privilege of holding a gaming monopoly.[17] Indian casinos can be found throughout the United States, from Connecticut and New York to Florida, from Michigan and Wisconsin to New Mexico and California. Many of these casino resorts, like Mystic Lake in Minnesota and Ho-Chunk in Wisconsin, also feature convention centers, which offer groups lower rates and quieter settings than traditional convention markets, like Las Vegas.[18] They have thus completely absorbed the most recent phase of casino-resort development and have successfully applied it in relatively desolate areas without the accumulated attractions of Las Vegas.

The Indian casinos of Wisconsin, Michigan, Minnesota, and other states have successfully generated revenues and improvements despite their relative remoteness. The opening of the state of California to Indian gaming promises even greater profits for operators. Indian tribes in California originally ran casinos with games that were legal in California card casinos. These games differ from standard casino games in that they are player-banked (players bet against each other, not the house). Because the state operated electronic lottery machines, Indian tribes began to install gaming devices in their casinos. State authorities disputed the Indian tribes' right to offer these kinds of games, and efforts at working out a compact between the state and Indian tribes failed. Indian tribes therefore put Proposition 5, which would legalize "Vegas-style" Indian gaming, before the voters in 1998. The measure passed by a clear margin but was challenged in the courts and later ruled unconstitutional because the state constitution expressly forbade slot machines. Indian tribes pressed the issue and drafted a new referendum, Proposition 1A, which California voters passed in March 2000. This proposition amended the state constitution to permit tribes to run "Vegas-style" casino gaming on reservation land.

This opened a huge market to casino gaming. The state of California has long sent more visitors to Nevada than any other. As late as 2001, 25 percent of all visitors to Las Vegas were from Southern California.[19] Capturing even a piece of this market promised to be very lucrative. Tribes rushed to build casinos after March 2000, and commercial gaming interests, instead of opposing them, often joined with them. Gaming operators like Harrah's Entertainment, Park Place Entertainment, and Trump Hotels and Casino Resorts have inked contracts to manage Indian-owned resorts on reservation land. The casinos that they run promise to be integrated casinos resorts that are smaller than those on the Strip, but essentially similar to them.

In a sense, casino resorts on Indian land represent the ultimate application of the casino resort idea. Most Indian reservations, after all, are on extremely marginal lands with few natural resources and even fewer avenues for economic growth. They have traditionally had high unemployment rates, with little or no prospects for many residents. Reservation land is usually somewhat isolated, or at the very least removed from large cities. Not subject to state police authorities, it is also legally distinct. While Atlantic City and other casino towns like Biloxi, Mississippi were both underdeveloped before casino gaming, they shared a bond of governance with the rest of the state. Indian lands do not. Economically, socially, and politically, they are some of the most marginal of lands in the United States, and therefore have been ideal hosts for casino resorts, originally developed to thrive in a marginal desert-scape.

Indian gaming has been largely successful in promoting economic development on reservation lands, and it has become a popular choice for many tribal councils. By the early 1990s, several Native American tribes and states had gambled on gaming as a boon to both parties. Over 170 tribes had legalized gambling, with over 145 tribes spread over twenty-four states conducting Class III (casino) gaming. In 1997, it was estimated that $40 billion was wagered in Native American casinos, with net revenues of between $5 and $6 billion dollars.[20] By 2001, estimated Indian gaming revenues were $12 billion, and the industry employed about 300,000 people. For many policymakers, Native American gaming is a "painless" solution to the problems of endemic underdevelopment. Although there is always the possibility that the underregulated Native American casinos could be infiltrated by organized crime or other undesirable elements, or that competition from non-Native American casinos will cause profits to decline, it appears that the turn to Indian gaming has been an unmitigated success for most tribes.

The profits from casino operations have brought with them other things to Indian reservations: political influence, improved living conditions, and hope. After decades of failed federal policies aimed at improving the lives of Native Americans, spanning from the Dawes Act (1877) to more recent attempts at encouraging development, many reservations are finally seeing economic growth. A 2002 study on the impacts of Indian casinos in the state of Washington stated unambiguously: "Tribal gaming is good for Tribal members, for Tribes, for the surrounding communities, and for the state of Washington." The study noted that since the introduction of Indian gaming in that state, employment rates and median incomes had risen while poverty rates had fallen. The study's authors also concluded that tribal gaming had allowed tribal governments to stabilize and expand and had allowed the most successful tribes to achieve significant economic diversification, moving them close toward self-sufficiency and self-determination.[21]

The burgeoning economic and political clout of empowered Indian tribes can be seen in the National Indian Gaming Association (NIGA), a trade association that represents over 180 tribal nations. NIGA does many things that one would expect a lobbying group to so, such as favorably presenting its members' agenda to the public, press, and politicians. However, it also strives to "advance the lives of Indian people—economically, socially, and politically." To do this, NIGA offers many educational resources for tribal members, policymakers, and the general public (particularly through its website, www.indiangaming.org). NIGA also facilitates charitable contributions between tribes: in July 2002, the organization raised over $1 million from members for the White Mountain Apache tribe, whose lands had been recently devastated by wildfires.[22] Harnessing the casino boom has enabled many American Indians to improve their lives in very real ways.

The Native American gaming industry is not without its detractors. A one-sided 2002 cover story in *Time* magazine summarized the major points of casino opponents by stressing the uneven distribution of casino revenue and the "fraud, corruption and intimidation" that has reportedly accompanied the development of the industry.[23] While some of the arguments against Indian gaming are specific to the issue, such as the debate over who is a "real" Indian, much of the rhetoric employed against Indian casinos is eerily similar to the antigambling cant of the 1950s. Issues of corruption and lack of oversight, for example, kept most states from legalizing casinos until Nevada and New Jersey proved that regulation could work. Today's Indian casinos, like yesterday's commercial casinos, have difficulty in securing loans from American banks (chiefly because reservation property cannot, by law, be used as collateral). Therefore, they turn, as did the early casino operators, to nontraditional sources of capital, including financing from Malaysian billionaire Lim Goh Tong (Foxwoods) and South African casino entrepreneur Sol Kerzner (Mohegan Sun). Consequently the industry is very sensitive to charges that profits from Indian casinos flow to "hidden money men."

The most workable way to quiet the detractors of Indian casinos would be to open the industry to the same level of public scrutiny as the commercial casino industry. The casino industry has become legitimate, in part, because it has made itself transparent—accounting procedures are routine and subject to state control. The language of Indian casino opponents is rife with references to opacity—loan deals not open to the public are "shadowy," for example. Strengthening the National Indian Gaming Commission may be one way to achieve this, but it is hard to imagine any national system that would be able to police Indian casinos from coast to coast with the same focus as the New Jersey regulation, which watchdogs twelve casinos in a single city. Any efforts to regulate Indian gaming, finally, must square not only with popular (non-Indian) opinion but also must be constitutionally compatible with accepted principles of Indian sovereignty.

Some see irony in the fact that Native Americans are using a relatively marginal industry, gambling, to enter the political and economic mainstream. But the previous three centuries of Euro-Indian relations, which systematically deprived Indians of all but the most marginal lands, really left few other options. That tribes use of casinos to return to economic self-sufficiency and reclaim their identities is a testament to their peoples' endurance—and the broad appeal of casino resorts.

Rolling on the river: The casino resort comes to the heartland

As the implications of the IGRA became clear and Indian casinos began operating, jurisdictions around the United States began to look enviously at the burgeoning success of Indian casinos. Authorities in New Jersey had proven by the early 1980s that a state with a large and diverse economy could handle the regulation of a casino industry and that casino resorts could effectively be used as tax farmers and job factories. The failure of suicide and bankruptcy rates to skyrocket also suggested that casino gaming's proximity to major metropolitan areas was not a recipe for disaster.[24] As states looked for ways to channel the casino resort's economic vibrancy into an acceptable form, many of them hit upon the idea of reviving riverboat gambling.

The celebrated Mississippi River has produced several lasting contributions to the national fabric. One of these was riverboat gambling. Riverboats plied the Mississippi and other waterways in the nineteenth century, ferrying passengers and cargo. On them, "gentlemen travelers" and assorted other wayfarers frequently gambled. The same was true for other forms of public transportation such as railroads, but for aesthetic reasons riverboats remained fixed in the public mind as exemplars of America's glorious gambling heritage. Of course, this past was mythic and exaggerated, but that has never stood in the way of the commercialization of "history." In many jurisdictions, the introduction of gaming on riverboats represented a compromise. Gambling on the boats would presumably be more manageable and would not sully the land with the social problems associated with both gambling and tourism—an interesting twist on the original Strip paradigm of containment.

For those areas that were desperate for economic stimulus but not quite ready to become full-fledged casino towns, riverboats seemed propitious. With ties to regional history, they were not quite as radical as the sudden creation of a Las Vegas Strip or Atlantic City Boardwalk in the middle of farm country. Keeping gambling on boats, some argued, would make it easier to control. With laws prohibiting dockside gambling, would-be gamblers had to arrive in time to board for a specific cruise, something that should have discouraged casual gambling. Entry fees also discouraged some from merely stopping by on the way home from work. Riverboat gambling, its proponents hoped, would provide those who wanted to gamble with a controlled environment in which to do so and would hopefully attract tourists who would, in turn, patronize local restaurants and cultural events and otherwise spend money in depressed areas.

Hit hard by the farm crisis of the 1980s, Iowa became the first state to legalize riverboat gaming, and others quickly followed suit. By the late 1990s, six states had variants of riverboat gambling: Iowa, Illinois, Indiana, Missouri, Louisiana, and Mississippi.[25] However, many "riverboats" are boats in name only, as many states have abandoned the early regulations that required boats to actually cruise the river for more lenient rules that permit gaming on permanently docked barges. Sometimes, these barges are part of a larger hotel-entertainment complex—a casino resort with a "floating" casino, but a casino resort nevertheless. They are often run by publicly traded gaming operators, some of them relatively small, like Isle of Capri, and some of them quite large, like Harrah's Entertainment. In many states, wager and loss limits have been dropped, and the limited gambling originally envisioned has fallen victim to the need for greater revenues. Inevitably, these casinos will share marketing strategies and operational procedures with their land-based cousins. So even this form of gambling, which would seem as removed from a dusty desert strip as possible, has converged with the casino resort that originated outside of Las Vegas.

Other jurisdictions in the central United States lacking access to the water needed for a riverboat gaming industry decided to experiment with legal casino gaming. In 1989, South Dakota permitted limited casino development in Deadwood as a means of promoting tourism in that town.[26] The Colorado legislature voted in 1990 to allow limited stakes gambling (maximum bets of $5 on slots, blackjack, and poker) in three cities: Cripple Creek, south of Denver; Black Hawk, seventy miles west of the Mile High City; and Central City, located beyond Black Hawk. Within a year of gaming legalization Colorado had seventy-five casinos, but by 2001 the number of operating casinos had contracted to forty-three.[27]

Colorado is important to the study of the casino resort because in two cities, Cripple Creek and Central City, casinos do not conform to the casino paradigm. Visitors to Cripple Creek quickly find themselves on Bennett Avenue, once the thriving business district of the mining town, and they discover that most of the storefronts now contain slot parlors. A few of the casinos offer blackjack or poker, but most are exclusively slot rooms. Some have hotel rooms, but they are simply located above the ground-floor casinos—there are no separate hotel towers. A parking garage that serves many of the casinos is hidden behind the main street and is disguised as an additional block of storefronts. All casinos strictly adhere to regulations that require them to preserve (or create) pre–World War I architecture. The result is a small town of yesteryear containing the latest multiline video slots. The amenities (free drinks and popcorn) would exasperate those accustomed to dining at four-star restaurants on the Strip, but the genuinely urban feel of the Cripple Creek casinos is an attraction that casino resorts cannot offer: one has the freedom to walk across the street without meandering through porte cocheres or negotiating pedestrian overpasses. These casinos have created jobs and enhanced state revenues, but, with their low-stakes wagering, they are not as profitable as Strip casinos. The large Las Vegas–based operators have therefore stayed out of Cripple Creek.

In Black Hawk, on the other hand, casino operators have taken a less literal approach to respecting the requirements for pre-1914 architecture. Driving into that town, the first thing one sees is the concrete parking garage of the Riviera Black Hawk. Many of the casinos look like scaled-down casino resorts. They do not huddle behind renovated storefronts; rather, they dominate the street as freestanding modern buildings. Larger operators like Fitzgerald's and Hyatte have opened casinos in Black Hawk. These look and feel like miniature Strip resorts. It will be interesting to see if the nonresort casinos of Cripple Creek eventually give way to the mini-Vegas casinos of Black Hawk. If not, they may provide a viable alternative for casino development.

As of today, though, existing casinos have been profitable across the heartland. The riverboat casinos of the Middle West and South have generated significant revenue and development. Mississippi, considered the leader among "emerging" (i.e., not Nevada or Atlantic City) gaming markets, has been so successful at creating jobs and revenue that promoters speak of the "Mississippi Miracle." By any quantifiable measure, casinos have poured money into the state. In 2001, casinos generated over $1 billion in direct and indirect wages, paid nearly $330 million in gaming taxes, and spent about $2.23 billion more on operating expenses and other spending. Tunica County, once one of the nation's most impoverished rural counties, has become the nation's third-largest casino destination.[28] Not every state has seen a turnaround this dramatic, but on the whole casinos have delivered on their promises to create jobs and generate revenue.

Riverboat gambling, though, is not necessarily a strong anchor for a diversified tourist economy. By their design, riverboats are more self-contained than even traditional casino resorts. In states where boats are required to sail, it is physically impossible for casino visitors, on impulse, to leave the casino and stroll down the block. Even where dockside gambling permits patrons to come and go at will, riverboats tend to pull their visitors from within a relatively small market; they are no more tourists than are shoppers at the local mall. In their consideration of the feasibility of riverboat gambling as a tourist attraction, Sabina Deitrack, Robert A. Beauregard, and Cheryl Zarlenga Kerchis concluded that adding a waterborne casino to a large city with a diversified tourist market, such as Los Angeles, New York, or San Francisco, would have little impact, and that to propose riverboat casinos as a core tourism strategy for an undeveloped or moribund tourist region was to "place hope far beyond reality."[29] These authors are correct in asserting that riverboat gaming, as it has developed over the past decade, draws on local rather than national markets. Though it certainly can generate jobs and revenue, it cannot replicate the booming success of Las Vegas's gambling, entertainment, and convention-based tourist economy.

The proliferation of riverboat and land-based casinos throughout the Midwest, Mountain West, and central South has other problems as well. They prompt states to compete for gaming by offering operators greater inducements. Illinois, for example, might feel compelled to offer potential operators more beneficial terms and less of a tax burden than originally planned, lest they and their tax revenue go to Indiana. Once states begin competing for casino gaming, the logical end is a marked liberalization of state regulation everywhere and a wider development of casino gaming. In the end, this may lead to both overdevelopment of the industry and a loss of public confidence following scandals that would follow a relaxation of regulation. Although this cycle is unlikely to turn into a complete prohibition of casino gaming, the untrammeled expansion of casino gaming may force a reactive contraction of the industry in the future.

Through casinos on riverboats, depressed small towns, and Indian land, economically marginalized areas profit at the expense of more developed areas. They forthrightly state their intention to lure gamblers from nearby metropolitan regions. All of this is easily justifiable to locals—after all, why do tourist industries exist if not to get rich from vacationers? Critics argue that casino resorts in these settings frequently cause social and economic dislocations in neighboring cities and states, areas that receive no tax benefits or employment from casino resorts.

To counter this trend, some cities are moving to recapture these revenues by legalizing casino resorts within their boundaries. The city of New Orleans, by the late 1990s, was located near several gaming markets, including Mississippi's Gulf Coast and riverboats in Louisiana itself. In order to bolster tourism in the Crescent City, Louisiana, lawmakers permitted the operation of a single land-based casino in New Orleans. When Harrah's Entertainment won the franchise to operate the casino in 1993, it was presumed to be a windfall, but the New Orleans casino has been dogged by structural and political difficulties. A temporary casino, Harrah's Jazz, filed for bankruptcy in 1995, and the permanent facility, Harrah's New Orleans, was forced into bankruptcy, unable to meet the state's $100 million tax take. In early 2001, Harrah's negotiated with the city and state for tax relief and fiscal concessions that would give the struggling property a lifeline.

Significantly, this beleaguered property was not a full-fledged casino resort, but a stand-alone casino; city merchants had lobbied the legislature to prevent the casino from offering lodging, entertainment, and dining. Given the casino's struggles and the specter of adding 3,000 casino employees to the unemployment lines, the city agreed, in early 2001, to permit Harrah's to expand into services traditionally found in casino resorts. The difficulties of Harrah's New Orleans as a stand-alone casino under a restrictive tax burden and its apparent success as a casino resort is yet another vindication for the integrated, insular casino resort, and it raises serious doubts about the casino resort's efficacy in a major city.

But just as the Battle of New Orleans came too late to affect the settlement of the War of 1812, not everyone has heeded the lessons of Harrah's New Orleans. Other large cities have begun to flirt with legalized casino gaming. Detroit has gone so far as to embrace casinos. Like New Orleans, it had been pulled toward casinos by the presence of nearby casino dollar drainers, in this case the Casino Windsor, a 100,000 sq. ft., 400-room casino resort immediately across the Detroit River in Canada. The Casino Windsor, owned by the Province of Ontario, opened in 1994 and fed the appetites of Detroiters for gambling. To capture revenues that were otherwise leaving the city, Michigan lawmakers chose to permit three casino licenses within the city of Detroit under very specific circumstances. The Detroit casinos could operate "temporary" casinos for four years while the city acquired waterfront land, which would ultimately house the three casinos. Land prices, higher than expected, have precluded the city from acquiring the land, and as of this writing, municipal authorities are negotiating with the casinos on an alternate plan.[30]

Interestingly, the "temporary casinos," located in urban areas and without hotels, are seen as less desirable than "permanent" ones, which would include hotel towers, restaurants, and convention space. Present programs that allow patrons to redeem points on their players cards for meals at nearby restaurants would seem to be a needed stimulus for the local business community, but the casinos and civic leaders insist that only a full-blown casino resort can bring the kinds of visitors that will generate economic growth. Thus, the Detroit experiment is yet another vindication of the concept of the casino resort as the optimal form of legalized gambling. The nationalization of the gaming market is also clear in Detroit; two of the three casinos are owned by major Las Vegas–based operators, MGM MIRAGE and Mandalay Resort Group, while the third is owned by the Sault Sainte Marie tribe of Chippewa Indians and a consortium of local investors. As in Atlantic City, Mississippi, and other markets, the large national operators and integrated casino resorts clearly have a competitive advantage.

While the casino resort became ubiquitous throughout the nation, it found new footholds in the Silver State. Even in its oldest homes, gambling has been transformed by the casino resort. When Las Vegas began to overshadow Reno in the 1950s, Reno establishments still had the flavor of urban "gambling factories," which offered easy odds and little more. But as the Strip innovation of the insular casino resort began to pull ahead in

Southern Nevada, northern operators could not help but notice. In the 1970s and 1980s, existing Virginia Street gambling halls began to add hotel towers, moving toward the casino-resort model.

Casino resorts also sprouted in areas that were not traditionally tourist-oriented or, indeed, were barely in existence. One such modern casino boomtown is Laughlin, situated to the south of Las Vegas across the Colorado River from Bullhead City, Arizona, and thirty miles north of Needles, California. With the introduction of casino gaming in 1981, rapid commercial development of the city began, and within a decade Laughlin had ten casinos. In contrast to Las Vegas's fervent excitement, Laughlin promoted itself as casual and inexpensive.[31]

Because there was no existing urban structure, casinos could not be blamed for removing dollars from the local economy. In fact, the casino resorts provoked a boom in ancillary commercial and residential development. The rapid success of casinos in Laughlin caused, in turn, a shortage of schools, social services, and affordable housing, problems similar to those encountered by Las Vegas in the 1950s and, indeed, any rapidly growing city. As a marginal jurisdiction, Laughlin's success with casino resorts is not at all surprising. Exploiting a niche market underutilized by Las Vegas has enabled Laughlin to repeat, on a smaller scale, the casino-driven prosperity of its northern neighbor.[32] Casino resorts have also successfully implanted themselves along Interstate 15, the major highway connecting Las Vegas to Los Angeles, at Jean and Primm, and to the north near the state line at Mesquite. That independent casino resorts can flourish so close to the epicenter of American casino gaming is as strong a commentary as any on their resiliency. On the water or in the desert, it seems, casinos can thrive.

A bus person's millennium

Despite their myriad locations, casinos are remarkably alike in their internal design and function. The structural and operational systems that developed on the Strip dominate. With a few cosmetic adjustments, they have been exported across the nation. The new megaresorts of the Strip, such as Mandalay Bay, Paris, or the Bellagio, certainly push the envelope of ornate design, but they are not that different from any of the Stern-derivative casino resorts that have become ubiquitous across America. The casino floor of the Riviera is almost interchangeable with that of Palace Station or Harrah's Lake Tahoe or the Atlantic City Hilton. An archipelago of slot machines and table games has been spread across the continent.

Economists and other social scientists disagree whether this casino archipelago is a good or bad thing. Robert Goodman devotes *The Luck*

Business to assailing the "chaser governments" who vie for casino development. Goodman's argument, that casinos siphon money away from more beneficial sectors of the economy, has been countered by casino proponents who argue that money spent in a casino would otherwise be spent on other forms of entertainment, none of which is taxed as heavily as casino gaming. Thus, casinos can theoretically help a state by drawing in more tax revenue than comparable forms of entertainment.

Unsurprisingly, there is no consensus on the ultimate efficacy of the casino resort as a form of development. Still, interested parties should heed the lessons to be learned from the checkered pattern of development based on the casino resort. The casino resort began as a nonurban institution whose primary goal was to isolate patrons within it for a maximum amount of time. Such an institution is obviously ill-suited for a classic urban downtown, as every inch of its design is dedicated to attracting and retaining patrons. When compared with, say, a sports arena, a casino resort is a very poor neighbor. An arena draws people into it for a single, defined event, usually a few hours in duration. Before and after the event, visitors can budget time to dine, shop, and be entertained in the area around the arena. Restaurants and bars can schedule special promotions for ticket holders. The negatives associated with a large arena—crowds and parking shortages—are precisely the problems that most urban districts like to have. By contrast, a casino resort has no real "schedule." It is usually open around the clock, and its patrons rarely if ever leave for dining, shopping, or entertainment. Its employees, it is true, can patronize local businesses, but casinos, generally speaking, do not boost the businesses around them as much as other attractions might.

For these reasons, developers should no more consider dropping a casino resort into an existing urban framework than they would a shopping mall or any stand-alone attraction. Yet, casino resorts remain popular redevelopment options for several reasons, the most salient of which are revenue enhancement and job creation—very real and easily tabulated statistics. Additionally, many casino proponents argue that legalized casino gaming pulls money away from illegal gambling and thus weakens organized crime. In an age of taxpayer revolt, a doubtful economy, and diminished expectations, casino gaming offers an ostensibly painless way to raise revenue. Indeed, in virtually every campaign the proponents of casino gaming have argued that casinos will provide, directly or indirectly, tax relief for the middle class.

Casinos are also job factories that have effectively lowered unemployment rates in otherwise depressed areas. Large businesses employing several thousand workers themselves and with each of these workers in turn supporting a cobweb of ancillary services, casino resorts can add thousands to the employment rolls of a given jurisdiction. It is impossible to imagine that, without casino gaming, Atlantic City would have any industry directly employing over 50,000 workers, or that Indian reservations would be able to significantly lower their unemployment. For many, the jobs available are at the lower end of the scale—low wage, unskilled positions—but they still offer benefits and reasonable security, something that many workplaces no longer do.

The economic growth that casinos bring to a region is not "junk food development." Casinos bring with them real development—new tourist facilities, improved infrastructure, and national exposure—that has the potential to elevate an area as a tourist destination. Comparing Atlantic City with, say, Asbury Park demonstrates this. Atlantic City itself, it is true, still struggles with crime, unemployment, and other problems, but the region around the city has grown tremendously, and the city now has the potential, at least, to become again a national destination resort. Asbury Park, another seaside resort fallen on hard times, has had no real economic growth in years and, as far as many are concerned, little prospect for the future. Certainly an economy based solely on gaming and hospitality has its problems, but there are few who work in Atlantic City who would choose to look for work in Asbury Park. If casino resorts are used to promote economic growth in regions that have proven themselves incapable of industrial or commercial growth, they represent a valid form of development that is hard to refute.

So for state governments seeking to raise revenue and increase employment without hiking taxes or spending, the lure of gaming is almost irresistible. The goals of casino gaming legalization—lowered taxes, increased employment, and local redevelopment—are laudable, but politicians and policy analysts should be mindful that the history of casino resorts as institutions aloof from the city placed constraints on their feasibility as tools for urban redevelopment. All things being equal, casino resorts are better suited for marginal regions than more developed ones. Southern Nevada, Atlantic City, and some Indian reservations, in the absence of other forms of development, have made a de facto transition to economies based on insular casino resorts, something that, while it may not be ideal for everyone, at least gives these areas a chance at productivity. Major metropolises such as New Orleans or Detroit, make less suitable locations for casino resorts. Gambling should not be considered "the last resort" for dismal local economies, but planners and voters should carefully square the nature of the casino resort with the social and economic needs of a prospective site before making their decisions.

Whatever its ultimate impact on society, casino gaming, and indeed any form of legal, regulated gambling, forces states into a paradoxical position. Through regulation, states effectively sanction and promote casino resorts as safe, socially legitimate recreational areas. The development of a confident casino industry without regulation is unthinkable. To protect a valuable revenue stream, state governments are put into a position in which they must promote, sometime overtly, casino gaming; they actively help casinos lure more visitors who will hopefully lose more money. Yet states also have a responsibility to protect the social welfare of their citizens, something that is not aided by encouraging people to spend their spare time and money in casinos. In addition, problem gambling creates tremendous difficulties for the individual and for society. States may plow some of their casino revenue back into compulsive gambling treatment programs. But some critics charge that these efforts, where they exist, would not be necessary at all if states did not promote gambling.

The resorts that Americans enter have begun to change from vacation destinations to weekly, or even nightly, escapes. When a video poker session no longer entails a long flight or drive to Las Vegas, are these customers really tourists? One of the most common arguments of casino gaming advocates, that casino resorts encourage tourism and funnel money into a region's economy, is validated by figures from Las Vegas but not so clearly supported by the numbers from other jurisdictions. In 1999, Las Vegas had about 32.8 million available hotel room nights and about 33.8 million visitors; most visitors could have stayed overnight, as is typical in a destination resort. In Atlantic City, the Strip's closest rival in terms of gaming revenue, in that same year there were only 4.2 million available room nights but 33.6 million visitors. Most visitors drove or bussed to town, hit one or more casino resorts, and returned home, contributing little to the local economy outside of the portion of gaming expenditures recaptured by the state as taxes and plowed back into the region as payroll.[33]

The Atlantic City visitation statistics hit at the fundamental difference between casino resorts on the Las Vegas Strip and elsewhere. The Las Vegas Strip sits at the apex of a highly developed tourist destination; since the 1950s, guidebooks (and since the mid-1990s, web sites) have given prospective visitors a list of nearby attractions. None of them is likely to inspire a trip by themselves, but combined they present the perception that there is more to Las Vegas than gaming. On the "new" Strip, high-end retail and expanded entertainment give visitors another reason to stay a few days and "do" Las Vegas. Other gaming markets simply lack the facilities to do so. In many ways, it is a chicken and egg proposition—tourists will come for extended periods if there are a variety of attractions, but operators will invest in attractions only if there is a sizable overnight tourist market. Whereas Las Vegas, is filled with tourists who gamble thanks in part to the convention trade and fifty years of development and vigorous promotion as a vacation destination, the same is not necessarily true for other jurisdictions.

It is easier to speak of gambling commuters than gambling tourists in many areas. Casino patrons bussed into Atlantic City, for example, often follow a familiar pattern: get on a bus in their hometown or neighborhood (usually in the New York/New Jersey/Pennsylvania tristate area), disembark in a bus loading area, take chits for comps and coin, and spend a few hours in the casino resort before reboarding the bus and heading back to South Philadelphia or Staten Island. Gaming destinations reliant on extended "locals" markets don't really encourage tourism; they encourage repeat visitors, who are in essence commuters.[34]

If most casino patrons are commuters rather than tourists in the classic sense, the implications are tremendous. The original intention of the casino resort to provide a distant but accessible vacation retreat has been reversed. To the scores of patrons for whom a trip to the casino is a weekly, rather than annual, rite, the casino floor is as familiar as the local supermarket, shopping mall, or other outpost of consumer capital. Within the last ten years, the casino resort has lost its traditional position as an exotic pleasure dome to be visited occasionally. For most Americans, casino gaming is no longer about a brief immersion in the "Vegas experience"; it is about hours patiently banked at the tables or machines while accumulating points, to be redeemed later for complimentary food and entertainment. For some, gambling acquires a familiar rhythm; they are in the casino with such regularity that they might as well be punching a time clock. Everything but "the action" is unimportant, and whether the surrounding casino is in Davenport or Temecula hardly matters.

Though the gambling itself is indistinguishable, the casino markets of America, divided by divergent state or tribal regulations, remain dissimilar. The markets, scale, and operation of casino gaming on the Las Vegas Strip, Cripple Creek, and Foxwoods are so utterly different that to lump them under one category is nonsensical. Indeed, industry analysts are careful to differentiate between the many casino markets when offering predictions about future performance. Though these markets are very different, they share certain general trends; casino resorts employ many people, in a range of skilled and unskilled positions, and the jobs they create do promote regional development by creating jobs that lure new residents and ancillary services to an area. They function as Keynesean pump primers that bring dollars into a regional economy and stimulate further growth. They bring tax revenue into state coffers and profits to well-run operations, but they don't, as a rule, attract tourists who spend money outside of the casino resort.

Once loosed from its greenhouse on the Strip, the casino resort has continued, then, its remarkable track record of drawing visitors, pulling in revenue, and creating jobs. In 1976, the gaming industry in the United

States was, for all practical purposes, Las Vegas. Reno certainly had its share of the market, but the Strip defined American gambling. A *War Games* scenario, in which a pasty young Matthew Broderick unintentionally rained nuclear fire on Las Vegas, would have devastated the national gaming industry, robbing it of both its primary physical plant and its outstanding human capital. With the dramatic spread of casino resorts around the nation, that is clearly no longer true.

Beyond casino colonialism

At the beginning of the twenty-first century, then, it is possible to speak with confidence of a national gaming industry segmented into idiosyncratic markets, a far cry from the locally run casino resorts of the 1950s Strip. Though they might draw upon investors from around the country, on-site managers who were often part owners ran most Strip casino resorts. With the transition to publicly traded ownership and the gradual easing out of traditional syndicates, off-site ownership became an accepted reality. Initially, most of the corporations that bought Strip casino resorts were national hotel chains like Hilton, Ramada, or Holiday Inn, headquartered in Los Angeles or New York. But over the next twenty years, a series of events led to the domination of American gaming by an oligopoly of publicly traded gaming operators and manufacturers, usually based in Las Vegas.

In some ways, the emergence of Las Vegas as the capital of the national gaming industry reversed an earlier trend, in which national hospitality chains acquired Strip resorts. Holiday Inns, Inc., for example acquired Bill Harrah's casino properties, which included casinos in the northern part of Northern Nevada, in 1980. Even before the purchase, it is important to remember, Harrah's company had been listed on the New York Stock Exchange and had a national reputation. The resulting company eventually became Harrah's Entertainment, a casino operator based in Las Vegas.[35]

The migration of the Las Vegas Strip's Holiday Casino is itself a microcosm of the past generation of changes in casino-resort ownership. Opened in 1973 by Shelby and Claudine Williams of Las Vegas, the Holiday Casino was not originally directly affiliated with Holiday Inns, though that company eventually acquired the casino. The decision by Holiday Inns to acquire Harrah's northern Nevada casinos—and name—gave the hospitality giant an immediate gambling brand name and management team. The Holiday Casino, like other Strip properties that have escaped implosion, such as the Sahara and Riviera, was transmogrified by a series of expansions into an unrecognizable titan. In 1992, Harrah's erased the last vestiges of the Holiday era as the casino became Harrah's Las Vegas, with a

Casino resorts in Atlantic City seem somewhat incongruous on the pedestrian Boardwalk. Bally's Wild Wild West Casino overlooks the Atlantic Ocean, but imagines itself in the dusty wilds of the old American West. Courtesy UNLV Special Collections (Bally's Atlantic City Promotional File).

glitzy Mardi Gras theme in place of the original riverboat "ship on the Strip."[36] The cumulative changes were astounding. Former Holiday shift manager Robert Deiro, comparing the present Harrah's to the original casino, said, "It's no longer a hotel, it's a city."[37]

This story of the Holiday's transformation into the casino/city Harrah's Las Vegas is echoed along the Strip. Many other casinos passed from small syndicate ownership to absentee hotel landlords to companies specializing in casinos. Park Place Entertainment, the world's largest casino company, had a similar story, coming together as the fusion of the Hilton, Bally's, Grand Casinos, and Caesars empires—Caesars Palace itself having been owned by its original syndicate, Lum's, Caesars World, ITT, and Starwood Hotels before becoming a brand of Park Place Entertainment. While a period of these two casino giants' history involves outside ownership, their core management came from within the Nevada industry, belying the belief that outside corporations devoured native casinos, or that the "corporate era" of Las Vegas gaming has been a story of economic colonialism and outside control.

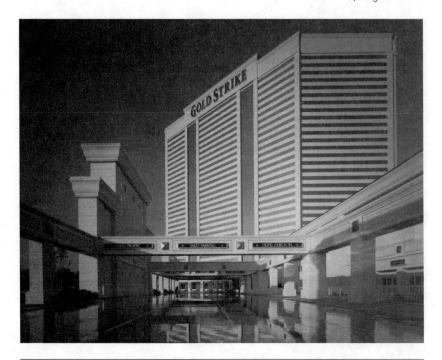

Riverboat casinos, while they would seem to be the polar opposite of the desert-locked resorts of the Strip, actually borrowed much of their integrated design. Like Strip casinos, this building is obviously designed with the automobile in mind. The Gold Strike Casino Resort, in Tunica, Mississippi, is the tallest structure in the state—a distinction that various Strip resorts have also claimed throughout their history in Nevada. The complex features a 1200-room hotel, convention facilities, restaurants and, of course, an "attached" casino. Courtesy UNLV Special Collections (Gold Strike Promotional File).

In fact, the two remaining members of the gaming oligopoly developed forthrightly from Las Vegas interests before expanding into other markets. Mandalay Resort Group is the erstwhile Circus Circus Enterprises's combination with Gold Strike Resorts; the former company slowly grew from William Bennett and William Pennington's Circus Circus (which they had acquired from founder Jay Sarno), and the second was founded by a group of Circus Circus dissidents and later reacquired. MGM MIRAGE combines Kirk Kerkorian's MGM and Steve Wynn's Mirage companies; Kerkorian had owned casinos in Las Vegas since the 1960s, and Wynn built an empire starting from downtown's Golden Nugget.

While these corporations have impeccable Las Vegas lineages, they are still beholden to outside capital. The chief difference between them and earlier ownership syndicates is their easy access to Wall Street investment

houses and other sources of megainvestment dollars, thus enabling them
to build the super-sized casino resorts that have come to define the Las
Vegas Strip. Charting the rise of the current industry leader reinforces the
notion that corporate ownership is better defined as a more mature stage
of earlier casino management structures. While it is largely captained from
Las Vegas, the modern casino industry is, in some ways, more thoroughly
determined by the ebbs and flows of the finance markets than by actual
casino performance—something that, again, ties it to the mainstream of
American business life.

The oligopoly of gaming operators, which mirrors similar trends toward
consolidation throughout American business, gives investors a steady, diversified, group of players. Together, the four largest gaming operators command an impressive share of the gaming market. On the Las Vegas Strip, they
own a majority of the high-profile casino resorts. Their collective hold on
the Strip south of the Flamingo intersection is broken only by the Aladdin
and Tropicana, and the only major new casinos of the 1990s Strip not currently among their ranks are the Aladdin, Venetian, and Stratosphere. This
speaks to the difficulty of operating in such a competitive market, but it also
reveals the tremendous regulatory and capital barriers raised to new casino
projects.

In Atlantic City, a more bounded market with greater regulatory and financial barriers to entry, the picture of consolidation is even starker. Of the
city's twelve operating (as of early 2003) properties, four were owned by
Park Place Entertainment, two by Harrah's Entertainment, and three by
Trump Hotels and Casino Resorts. Together, these three companies owned
almost three-quarters of the nation's second-largest gaming market. National operators with smaller portfolios controlled the balance of the market, as Aztar Corporation owned one casino, and financier Carl Icahn,
owner of the Stratosphere and two other Las Vegas properties, another.
The only proposed casinos on the horizon are planned by Las Vegas–based
companies. The Borgata, under construction in early 2003, is a joint effort
of MGM MIRAGE and Boyd Gaming, and MGM MIRAGE is contemplating
an independent project nearby. The situation is similar in other commercial gaming markets. New Orleans's sole land-based casino is partly owned
and managed by Harrah's and two of Detroit's three casinos are managed
by Las Vegas–based gaming operators.

Around the nation, smaller-sized gaming operators have also found
market niches. Some have a portfolio of casinos in a single area, such as Las
Vegas–based Station Casinos. Others, such as Isle of Capri, have more far-
flung holdings; that company owns a franchise chain of Isle of Capri casinos throughout the South and Midwest. While these smaller companies
may be headquartered outside of Las Vegas, they are still dependent on

the fiscal wellsprings of the same investment communities that serve the larger, Las Vegas–based operators. Casino corporate structures, in addition to standardizing building designs, marketing strategies, and operating procedures, have also routinized the financing of casino resorts.

The standardization of the casino resort extends to the makeup of the casino floor itself. Increasingly, the slot machines that dominate the casino floors of American casino resorts are produced by an oligopoly of manufacturers. International Game Technology, the industry leader, has about a 70 percent market share in North America, a degree of domination rarely seen in any field.[38] Much as with casino ownership, regulatory barriers make the cost of entry into the field extremely high, limiting start-up competition. But though the number of slot manufacturers has remained small, the diversity of themed machines (usually based on television shows or other pop culture phenomena) has given casino floors the appearance of heterogeneity. Still, casinos have become, in spite of idiosyncratic themes and a range of eye-catching slot machines, increasingly standardized spaces.

This consolidation of the expanding casino gaming market has come about because the continuing operation of a casino requires deep pockets and top-level managers. The "Big Four" Las Vegas–based operators have a formidable advantage in the recruitment and training of the next generation of casino managers as well as a proven ability to obtain financing for new projects and renovations—an important asset in the always regenerating world of the casino. So although the casino archipelago has outcroppings throughout the nation, it looks and operates with increasing homogeneity. The typical bus person bound for Shreveport, magically transported to the Atlantic City Expressway, could be forgiven for not being unduly alarmed; the casino she stepped into at journey's end would look, feel, and run almost identically. The casino atmosphere had been successfully transformed from exotic to mundane, and only the most skillful of marketers can create a mystique compelling enough to transcend the commonplace.

From Highway to Boulevard: The Las Vegas Strip, reborn and redefined

Contemporaneous with the expansion of casino gaming across the United States came an equally striking redefinition of the casino resort's birthplace, the Las Vegas Strip. In the 1980s, Atlantic City outearned the Strip's gaming revenue and loomed as a burgeoning competitor. With a spate of riverboat, land-based, and Indian casino openings in the early 1990s, it was apparent that Nevada had surrendered its nearly half-century monopoly on legal casino gaming. The threat of new gaming jurisdictions seemed to bode ill for Las Vegas, as it was feared that, with gaming available closer to home, would-be visitors might not make the trek to the Mojave.

However, casino operators countered by building new casino resorts (and modernizing old ones) to reinvent the Strip as a unique tourist and convention destination. During the 1990s, successive waves of investment created a Las Vegas Strip that could legitimately sell itself as the "entertainment capital of the world." Most of the projects of the 1990s combined Stern-derivative integrated casino hotels with a hyper-theming that soars beyond anything Jay Sarno had imagined. The results have mesmerized architectural critics and casual tourists alike, often to the detriment of good analysis. The Strip, as it was re-created in the 1990s, was not a surreal pastiche of space and time; it was a series of well-engineered complexes comprising casinos, restaurants, hotel rooms, convention centers, and shopping arcades, garnished with thematic flourishes. The latest crop of Strip casinos are, essentially, business towers stacked with hotel rooms connected to warehouse-like casino/retail/dining facilities, all sprayed with painted plastic foam skin. The Strip of the twenty-first century may whisk credulous patrons to the streets of Paris or the markets of Morocco, but its "fantasy architecture" is more often than not crafted in a North Las Vegas warehouse.

Amid all the sound and fury about the transformation of "Sin City" into a Disneyfied family retreat, the fact that Las Vegas has always courted families has been lost. Even in the booming, heady 1950s, the Last Frontier Village was an attraction for all ages and the Desert Inn sported a "Kachina Doll House," which was described as a miniature hotel for child guests. The 1970s saw the International/Hilton Youth Hotel. Of course, most casino resorts tilted toward Jay Sarno's original vision for Circus Circus—adult playlands—but the idea that Las Vegas was on the verge of becoming a full-fledged family resort was a minor trope in the city's promotional literature since the early 1950s.

Though the Strip, taken as a whole, seems to have been remarkably transformed, there has not been much change in the design of casinos. While it shares the same basic elements, the typical Strip casino of the 1990s is much larger than its predecessors, with more convention and retail space and far more hotel rooms. Park Place Entertainment's Paris, opened on the Strip in 1999, is typical of the new wave of casino development. It is a themed property owned by one of the "Big Four" operators. Smaller than the MGM Grand, without the all-suites cachet of the Venetian or the upscale buzz of Mandalay Bay, it is striking nonetheless. It would be the centerpiece of any other gaming market, but on the Strip it is "just" another casino resort. With just under 3,000 hotel rooms, 2,500 slots, and 100 table games, it is an average end-of-century Strip casino. Obviously much larger than the casinos of the weekend-tourist 1950s, which had perhaps 300 motel rooms, a few hundred slots, and two dozen or so table games, it is not really very different from them. Its structures are elaborated versions of what is found in any Stern-derived casino resort, and its functions are those of the original resorts of the Strip—to entertain, feed, and house gamblers while keeping them as close as possible to the casino.

Since the expansion of the Strip in the 1990s and the application of technological innovations, the Strip, and casino resorts elsewhere, are more than ever artificial green felt gardens, almost striking in their synthetic order. A range of adventures is available, each with a specified price. A ride to the top of the Eiffel Tower will cost $9; a whirl through the virtual reality of Star Trek: The Experience is priced at $25 ($20 for Nevada residents and other special, marginalized groups). Of course, this is no innovation of the gaming industry; increasingly in the United States, consumers expect to exchange money for an intangible experience.

It is telling that the casino industry has been viewed, in some quarters, as a real innovator in this process. In a sense this is true; all of the IMAX theaters, erupting volcanoes, and theme restaurants to decorate the Strip are nothing more than elaborations of earlier lures. Casinos have always had gimmicks, from dancing waters to dancing girls. These gimmicks were nothing more than ways to encourage tourists to visit a specific casino. After all, with many competitors on the Strip, casinos had to work hard to make their property a "must see" that patrons would unfailingly visit. With the gradual sophistication of American entertainment, it is only natural that casinos have also become more interesting places.

So the operators of the Strip turned to a theming so ridiculously garish and over-the-top that it is almost taken seriously. "Is Las Vegas so fake its real?" asked *Preservation* magazine in 2000 in an article about the fabricators of the new themed resorts, such as the Venetian. Since visitors know that the façade is not real, it is not disingenuous to pass it off as genuine. For many, this kind of "genuine artificial" touch is more honest than the artificially genuine ambience of other themed attractions such as the House of Blues, a restaurant/nightclub masquerading as a weathered, vintage Chicago blues club—directly off the floor of the obviously new, luxurious Mandalay Bay. But not all casino resorts will be overthemed; at the start of the twenty-first century, nonthemed properties are making a resurgence. Resorts such as the Palms, just off of the Strip at Flamingo, and Steve Wynn's plans for Le Reve, his anticipated masterwork on the site of the closed Desert Inn, eschew themes for the kinds of general vacation elegance that made Strip resorts attractive in the 1950s, though today's resorts have an opulence and scale previously unimaginable.

Outside of the crowded Las Vegas Strip market, most casino resorts are not the ballyhooed edifices of postmodernity that attract so much attention. Many visitors, having read about the giddy euphoria of the casino environment, are disappointed after visiting most casino resorts around the country. Beyond the neon sunburst of the porte cochere and outside signage, they are rather prosaic: banks of slot machines, a pit or two of table games, a few restaurants (rarely straying from the tripartite gourmet room, coffee shop, and buffet model), a showroom, and a hotel tower with a few hundred passable hotel rooms and perhaps a clutch of suites. Far from the faux fantasy world of the south Strip, this is the casino that most Americans visit and work in.

Even within Las Vegas, many casino resorts are the pedestrian models described above. Although some of these are located in the "tourist zones" of Fremont Street and the Strip, an increasing number of casino resorts are located outside these traditional areas. Some of these market themselves to nonlocal tourists, such as the Rio a few blocks to the west of the Strip or the Rampart Casino at Summerlin far to its northwest. But most areas of Las Vegas now boast at least one neighborhood casino. These are a far cry from the smoky video poker parlors that blight most Southern Nevada strip malls. They are full-service casino resorts, offering a gambling casino but also several hundred hotel rooms, restaurants, and shopping. The affluence created by the business of the casino resort has created a major urban center in an otherwise inhospitable corner of the Mojave Desert; neighborhood casinos such as the Orleans and a host of Station casinos (Palace, Texas, Sunset, et al.) exist because many Las Vegas residents want to gamble. In this desire they are no different from millions of other visitors to Las Vegas. But the deepest implication of the "neighborhood" casino resort is that even in Las Vegas the traditional space of the casino resort—isolated desert suburb—has collapsed into the city it has improbably created.

Indeed, the entire urban space of the Las Vegas Strip has been inverted. What once was a dusty, hot desert roadway dotted with casino resorts is now a pedestrian-friendly thoroughfare with an interconnected hive of casino development. This change is best read in the renaming of the thoroughfare. As the Los Angeles Highway, it meant a means of getting to Southern California rather than a destination in itself, and a road with no greater presence in Las Vegas than in Barstow. But "Las Vegas Boulevard" suggests an urbane, possibly even elegant, avenue at the center of Las Vegas. Indeed, the Strip has become urban. Pedestrian overpasses span the Strip and its intersectors, obviating footraces across the street. Wonderstruck tourists now march down the Strip to gape at the Bellagio's water show, the Mirage's exploding volcano, and Treasure Island's pirate show— all attractions designed to interface with pedestrians outside the casino, something unthinkable even in the 1970s. The casino resorts of Las Vegas Boulevard have abandoned their earlier sine qua non of a spacious front parking lot as they have encroached upon the sidewalks of the Strip. Casinos that retain substantial setbacks, such as the Mirage, Caesars Palace, and

Bally's, have installed people movers to draw pedestrian traffic from the busy Strip.

Interestingly, it seems that Americans, who have now lived predominantly suburban lives for over a generation, are going to places like Disney and casino resorts to enjoy the very commodity that they left behind in the cities: shared social space. This is perhaps why a Disney promotional pamphlet advertises "Downtown Disney: Uptown Fun!" This new "Downtown Disney District," sandwiched between the Disneyland theme park and Disney's California Adventure is, according to its promoters, "a bazaar of the truly unique," which takes its visitors from "traditional to virtual." In their study of suburban sprawl, architects Andres Duany, Elizabeth Palter-Zyberk, and Jeff Speck concluded that suburbanites didn't go to Disney parks for rides (the average visitor spending an estimated 3 percent of his time on rides and shows) but for the mixing. Disney provides what most suburban developments do not: "pleasant, pedestrian-friendly, public space" and the opportunity to socialize in it.[39] New developments such as Downtown Disney show that the corporation itself is mindful of this. The Las Vegas Strip, cut from the same cloth, has always offered the same kind of sociability, only now the resorts themselves are more gregarious, opening up to each other and building an infrastructure that permits pedestrian access.

The casino resort has been, throughout its history, an unlikely stepchild and an object lesson in the law of unintended consequences. Nurtured unwittingly by antigambling critics who shuttered competing jurisdictions, the refuge for suburban middle-class Americans came to embody the underside of American sleaze. Designed as deliberately aloof, insular structures, casino resorts have not only created a major city in the least likely of places but they have also meshed into a remarkable simulacrum of urban space. Once, one needed a car or taxi to traverse the open desert between Strip resorts—now, tourists freely walk down the Strip, snapping photos at landmarks along the way. In the strangest of ironies, downtown's Fremont Street has survived only by malling itself into a canopied light show, the Fremont Street Experience—it discarded its own urban heritage. Though the casino resorts themselves have become simulacra of urban space, Las Vegas itself remains a disjointed collection of subdivisions and strip malls—the quintessence of Sunbelt suburban sprawl.

But the greatest apparent paradox of the gaming industry at the turn of the millennium is that the expansion of casino gaming throughout the continental United States has only stoked the growth of the Las Vegas Strip. When Californians voted to permit Indian tribes to run "Vegas-style" casinos, most analysts predicted that the presence of a multibillion dollar gaming industry in the state that sends more gamblers to Nevada than any other would not adversely affect the Strip's growth. This is because the

Strip casino resorts have reached a level of sophistication far beyond any others. More capital, financial and human, has been poured into the Strip casinos since 1990 than any other jurisdiction. The result is the series of meretricious pleasure palaces etched into the popular imagination as the unrivaled Las Vegas Strip.

Casual observers, looking at the disparity between Las Vegas and its closest rival, Atlantic City, wonder how many years it will take for the casino capital of the East to catch up to Las Vegas. What they don't understand is that, in a very significant way, the Atlantic City casino market is older than the Las Vegas Strip's. Stacked up against downtown Las Vegas, or even the relatively stagnant upper edge of the Strip, Atlantic City compares quite well. But there is no real comparison to the southern Strip because most of it was built after Atlantic City's 1980s building boom. This is nothing unique to gaming; all other things being equal, a newer hotel or entertainment venue has a definite competitive edge over an older one. But in the historically volatile gaming industry, the pressure to resurrect or fall behind is particularly keen. This translates into the constant retooling of individual resorts and a collective character that is distinctively protean.

But that Strip business has expanded dramatically despite far greater competition cannot be explained solely by its superior physical plant. The Strip, as a whole, has written itself into the global consciousness as the center of the gaming and tourism world, a must-see for even the idle curious whose hearts don't quicken while slot reels spin. By providing a variety of attractions besides gambling, it has made itself almost unique. Within three hours of their homes, most Americans could find "Vegas-style" gambling, be it on a riverboat, Indian reservation, or land-based casino. But they have to go to Las Vegas to soak in the "Las Vegas Experience" as it has been promoted for half a century in advertising campaigns, films, and news stories. Just as an evening at the local repertory theater is no substitute for a Broadway musical, a few hours in a casino in Tunica or Gary doesn't have the same resonance as a Vegas vacation. The far-flung archipelago of casino resorts are not Strip competitors, much as they would like to think they are; rather, they are feeder markets.

So, at the end of a half-century of development, where is the casino resort? Given free reign in Southern Nevada, it created Las Vegas as a "neon metropolis." For mid-century suburbanites, it handily solved the dilemma of gambling by preserving it for relatively affluent vacationers while antigambling crusaders smashed the networks of illegal gambling in the cities. Individual operators found casino resorts explosively profitable businesses that held out the hope of legitimacy for their otherwise illicit vocation. And middle- and upper-class Americans, apparently, found vacationing and gambling in Strip resorts to their liking, as the new industry arced upward from the late 1940s to the end of the century.

But the last two decades of the twentieth century saw a fundamental transformation in the casino resort, as it was plucked from its dusty birthplace to redevelop a series of marginal jurisdictions, beginning with Atlantic City. Still, casino resorts, though no longer isolated, remained insular. While they transcended their original role as desert vacation spas for a mostly suburban audience, their original functions remained intact; they still functioned as ruthlessly efficient machines dedicated to keeping visitors inside and near the casino. Whether this makes a desirable neighbor will be, along with the legality of in-home Internet gambling, the preeminent question of the public policy of gambling in the early twenty-first century.

Epilogue
Odds against Tomorrow
Now that the game is everywhere, the rules have changed

Follow me into the desert
As thirsty as you are.
Soundgarden, "Burden in my Hand," 1996

In the first decade of the twenty-first century, Americans feel very differently about gambling than they did a scant generation earlier. Fortuitously, the changing nature of casino gaming has been captured by yet another federal study. The federal government's third look at gambling took place in the late 1990s when the National Gaming Impact Study Commission (NGISC) surveyed the current state of American gaming. Congress created the NGISC with an act signed into law by President Clinton in 1996. The group met from 1997 to 1999, delivering its final report on June 18, 1999. The NGISC was charged with looking at the legal, regulatory, political, social, and economic effects of gambling, from the impact of problem gambling upon individuals and families to the importance of gaming revenues to states. Its report reflected favorably on the commercial gaming industry, concluding that casino gaming created jobs, increased state revenue, and reduced unemployment. It did find that problem gambling was calamitous for those afflicted, but it recommended further study and treatment programs rather than a gambling prohibition.

Significantly for the casino resort, the NGISC found that "destination type resorts" were responsible for most of the social benefits traced to gambling expansion, whereas "convenience-style" gambling, such as video lottery terminals and Internet gambling, carried the potential to unleash a

209

landslide of social ills. In many respects, the NGISC's "Final Recommendations" endorsed the casino resort as an economic generator and social balm for distressed regions. Cynics sneered that the commercial gaming industry had "bought" the NGISC through skillful lobbying, but in fact the report's recommendations squared with what a host of Americans, both casino employees and casino patrons, had intuitively known: that the casino resort, as it has developed, has been used to harness Americans' desires to gamble into legal channels that are seen as socially constructive, and that unrestricted "convenient" gambling is undesirable.

The NGISC report signaled a profound shift in the federal government's policy toward casino resorts. The Kefauver Committee saw in casino resorts social and moral sickness incarnate. The resorts of the Strip were imagined as outposts in legitimate business for criminal syndicates and the "nest egg" of the criminal underworld. The committee's investigation into the status of Nevada gaming was, from the outset, meant to condemn rather than understand. The 1970s Committee to Review the National Policy on Gambling looked at gambling with a far less jaundiced eye, but the committee had only the Strip resorts to analyze, as the committee's work immediately predated the explosion in casino gaming. The NGISC was the first study of gambling conducted by the federal government when a majority of states had legal gaming. That its report was favorable to casino resorts, even though it was chartered partially because of antigambling sentiment, indicates that the perception of them as innocuous forms of gambling, cultivated so artfully in the 1950s, remains.

During the first generation of its development, only the most diehard gamblers visited casinos more than a few times a year, if that. Today, this cannot be said. The casino resort is no longer a vacation curiosity for most Americans. More states in the continental United States have legal casino gaming than do not. Gaming is an inextricable part of the daily lives of the half-million or so Americans who work in casino resorts. And an increasing number of people choose to visit casinos; in 1998, U.S. households visited casinos 161.3 million times, up from 78.5 million a mere five years earlier. The average visitor saw the inside of a casino an average of once every seven weeks.[1] As much as the NGISC railed against convenience gambling, the national spread of the casino resort has made a weekly or even daily session at the slots a possibility for millions of Americans throughout the nation. What was once exotic has become familiar.

When the casino resort was taken out of the Las Vegas Strip, it ceased to be a regional phenomenon. This was never more obvious than in the aftermath of September 11, 2001. With the airline industry paralyzed, the Strip resorts centered on fly-in visitors were threatened with disaster. But around the nation, after a few days of uncertainty, casino numbers quickly improved. Indeed, by January 2002, aggregate national gaming revenues moderately outperformed the previous year's, while four states saw impressive double-digit growth.[2] Americans no longer needed the time and money for a vacation to Nevada to gamble; they now only needed the inclination to endure a bus or car trip. The worst terrorist attacks to date in the nation's history caused barely a stutter in overall casino attendance—as stark a reminder as any that, like it or not, casino resorts have become an almost universal part of American life.

Better than staying at home?

If people do enjoy casino gaming, it is not for any easily quantifiable motivation. Individuals are drawn to casinos for a variety of contradictory reasons. Hope and despair, excitement and boredom equally draw patrons into casinos. On the surface, most patrons claim to enjoy their trips to the casino. Their gambling losses are rationalized as the cost for a day's or weekend's diversion. For some, the nine to five world of timecards, computer consoles, and fluorescent eyestrain does not offer enough excitement. The action in a casino gives these patrons their needed doses of adrenaline. An entire cohort of retirees shows up at the casino for sheer lack of other diversions. For others, a trip to the casino brings much-needed social contact. Whatever the individual motivations, casino marketers agree that it is wisest to sell the casino experience as one that promises fun, not profit. People for the most part do not go to casinos to get rich; they fly, drive, and bus themselves there to have a good time.

Prescient operators always stressed the "good time" of a trip to the casino over winning. Bill Moore and Tommy Hull were selling "casino entertainment" in the mid-1940s, though they did not call it that. Still, they pioneered the idea of providing gambling customers with a unique experience unattainable elsewhere. They sold the package vacation (sunshine, entertainment, and dining), not the gambling itself. Patrons rationalized gambling losses as the cost of the ostensibly complimentary fine dining and floorshows. Losing at the tables seemed a fair bargain for a fun weekend.

The difference now is that the gambling experience *is* the package for many early-twenty-first-century casino goers. Thousands of visitors trek to the slot machines in Atlantic City, Tunica, Gary, and other cities without laying eyes on a swimming pool, health spa, gourmet restaurant, or even a hotel room. Casinos now sell a compressed packet of excitement and customer service. A gambler quoted in Gold Strike Resorts's newsletter *Casino Express* lauded the staff of the downtown Las Vegas Pioneer Club for their hospitality, which he deemed more important to his experience than actually winning. "Of course I didn't leave a winner," he concluded, "but they made me feel very comfortable."[3] Outside of the Las Vegas Strip, most casino resorts don't have to offer patrons much in the way of amenities outside of a modicum of comfort. Players are less interested in winning, or in seeing great entertainment, than they are in simply playing.[4]

Or so they claim. But it is easy to see deeper motivations for the sharp rise in casino visits in the late twentieth century. An unknown number may have skimmed money from their own private businesses, gotten untaxed cash payouts, or have profited in illegal enterprises and need a way to legitimately "earn" this money.[5] Others may be problem gamblers who cannot control their need to gamble. Still others may have nothing better to do. As one patron, when questioned on her occasional casino trips, stated: "It's better than sitting at home." The casino is simultaneously a world of real high-stakes wagering and a refuge from the tensions of the real world. For most Americans, this paradoxical escape has become available increasingly closer to home in the last twenty years.

The National Gambling Impact Study Commission reported that, ultimately, it was unable to identify the social consequences of expanded gambling or even surmise whether gambling triggered social problems. That is because the true "costs" of gambling are difficult to measure, whereas the "profits" of gambling, as far as state governments are concerned, are easy to tabulate. Revenues generated by gambling taxes are analyzed and released for public consumption, and jobs created by casinos represent very real opportunities for people who might not otherwise have work. It is much harder to conclusively demonstrate that the opening of a specific casino caused x amount of slides into problem gambling or y amount of bankruptcies. It is impossible to say with any true certainty whether casino gaming, rather than any other form of legal or illegal gambling, causes an increase or decrease in the desire to gamble.

Because of this, the true opportunity costs of gambling are impossible to chart. Who knows where the money spent on gambling might have gone had there been no casino to capture it? It may have been put to more productive use, but it is impossible to say for sure. Similarly, those who spend their leisure hours in casinos may have spent more time with their families or devoted a few hours to volunteer work. Or, they might have simply sat in front of the television. It is even more likely that they would have traveled a bit farther to visit a casino in a neighboring state.

Opponents of gambling expansion don't have the graphs showing created jobs and lowered taxes that proponents do, and they are armed with little more than the nagging feeling that allowing more casinos to open is somehow wrong. Those against expansion might be thought irrational in light of the fact that casinos have been successfully harnessed for jobs and revenue for years. But arguments against expansion make historical sense.

After all, Estes Kefauver rode antigambling sentiment into the political limelight for a reason—Americans were frustrated at rampant gambling in the cities. Intelligent and sensible citizens clearly sided against convenient gambling in the 1950s, and there is no reason to believe that, eventually, Americans fifty years later may make the same decision.

Worse than going out? Internet gaming and the next frontier

When casino gambling could be found only on the Las Vegas Strip, gambling opponents sneered but did not protest too vigorously. If Nevada wanted to put up with gambling, and people wanted to vacation there, the conventional wisdom ran, what business was it of anyone else? With the opening of casinos around the nation, though, the antigambling banner is being gripped a bit tighter—a bit of the panic about widespread gambling seen in the late 1940s is beginning to return. For those against the spread of casinos, the past twenty years, when casino gambling has become a $20 billion a year business and an integral part of many regional economies, have not been good ones. Even more distressing to the foes of legal casino gambling, the emergence of the Internet has rendered any debate about the "expansion of gambling" via casinos all but academic. Online casinos have ensured that anyone with Internet access can place a virtual bet with ease. In the same decade when Americans began to accept legal casino gambling outside of Nevada and New Jersey, the sudden proliferation of online casinos completely changed the dynamics of gambling. The containment of gambling in space, strained by the expansion of casinos across the landscape, completely collapsed with the introduction of Internet gambling. American homes, formerly "protected" against gambling by its banishment within casinos, now became potential gambling parlors themselves.

In theory, Internet gambling is not that different from earlier extensions of gambling. New technologies have always made possible expansions of gambling. The transportation revolution and the popularity of steamboat travel created the milieu of the riverboat gambler. With the emergence of rail travel in the mid-nineteenth century, many riverboat shapers moved from the Mississippi to the rails, where they found willing victims. Bookies used telegraphs and telephones in the early and middle twentieth century to facilitate their betting businesses. Indeed, it is the Wire Act of 1961, a now-archaic statute designed to stop the transmission of horse racing results via the telegraph, that provides the federal basis for anti-Internet gambling efforts. The Internet is simply the latest technology to become a conduit for gambling, and there is nothing about the Internet that makes it intrinsically different from any other kind of gambling. The medium is not the message.

But Internet gambling presents new problems for individuals and society. If a casino within an hour's drive of home can lead some to gamble uncontrollably, a casino within the home itself is undoubtedly a greater temptation. One of the many proposed solutions for problem gamblers, self-exclusion, can conceivably work in brick-and-mortar casinos: casino personnel can be instructed to refuse entrance or deny the credit of those who agree that they have no business gambling. In an online casino, this is impossible; even if a problem gambler could get one casino to stop accepting his credit card, there are about 1,800 other casinos waiting to offer him play. That Internet gambling is a private activity, conducted away from peers and family, could encourage irresponsible gambling; without the moderating influence of others, Internet gamblers can literally gamble for days. For those without gambling problems, online wagering has few apparent returns. Internet casinos offer the gambling of casino resorts (and presumably the social and economic costs associated with gambling) with few of the benefits: job creation, revenue enhancement, and increased tourism. Unless Internet gambling is regulated, it becomes a tax suction, pulling taxable gaming revenue out of a jurisdiction.

Proposed solutions to the problems of Internet gambling range from unfeasibly draconian (and impossible to enforce) bans on all Internet gambling to state regulation and sponsorship. Once the province of tiny Caribbean nations best known as tax shelters, Internet gaming has now been embraced by major nations such as Australia and the United Kingdom. In the United States, lawmakers have shuffled from indignant efforts to "ban" Internet gambling to cautious pragmatism, best seen in Nevada's 2001 decision to regulate Internet gambling—if the federal government decriminalizes it first.[6]

In contemplating Internet gambling, policymakers would do well to heed some lessons from the history of casino resorts. When gambling is available, Americans will patronize it, even if they have to cross borders. One cannot imagine the California state legislature, disturbed at the increasing numbers of Angelenos gambling in Las Vegas in the 1950s, passing a law forbidding its constituents from traveling to Nevada to gamble, or even slapping a punitive state tax on gambling winnings. Such a scheme would be unworkable at best and ridiculous at worst. Similarly, it is hard to marshal arguments against allowing Americans to spend their money as they see fit. If Internet gaming operators are able to implement identification verification technology that could prove an online gambler is not underage nor a self-excluded problem gambler, there seems little reason to stop them from accepting bets.

As is often the case, technology does not wait patiently for the law to catch up. Purveyors and consumers of Internet gambling have entrenched themselves in cyberspace. Gambling has become one of the most popular uses of the Internet. Before Americans considered creating a legal and regulatory framework, Internet casinos opened and thrived. As a result, American voters and lawmakers now must face a serious set of decisions about Internet gambling. The lessons of the Strip are relevant here: casinos resorts allowed affluent Americans to safely indulge their desires to gamble in distant oases, something that presumably kept the cities safe from the ravages of uncontrolled gambling. The only state to permit and regulate casino gaming reaped a bonanza, and the city whose boosters encouraged the most extensive casino development became a major metropolis. Providing an outlet for gambling proved profitable for mid-century Nevadans; abandoning the online field to offshore casinos may prove a costly misstep for twenty-first-century Americans.

Eyes in the sky

Despite the growing popularity of Internet gambling, the brick-and-mortar industry continues to grow in both its distribution and its size. As casinos have become more prevalent geographically, they have also become more routinized environments. The changes in the casino experience for patrons can be quickly summarized as depersonalization and standardization. In the "good old days" of the 1950s and 1960s on the Las Vegas Strip, a player's trip to a casino resort could be a profoundly personal adventure. He might have known a casino manager or high-level employee from his hometown who invited him to play at "his" casino, offering him a range of complimentaries solely on the basis of this personal connection. As the corporate hegemony fastened itself to the casino resort, complimentaries became a little more rationalized, but not much more. Casino managers' best resources for determining complimentaries were the observations and judgments of their employees who watched and rated players.

With dramatic increases in visitation and advances in technology, this system has become all but obsolete. It is hard to imagine any method by which a small staff of casino marketing personnel could keep tabs on the 30 million plus gamblers who visit Las Vegas each year. Computerized player-tracking systems emerged in the 1970s and came to prominence in the 1980s. Since then, they have evolved into sophisticated programs that use computers to track casino play and assign complimentaries.

Harrah's Entertainment has been the industry leader in taking this technology to the next level. It's initiative in developing a national, cross property brand loyalty program based on a player card is the envy of the other multiproperty gaming operators. Through the Total Rewards program, which allows players to use a single card at its twenty-first properties, Harrah's management can collect information about patron betting patterns. Marketing personnel then compare the patron's actual gaming habits with expected betting levels and offer appropriate comps. Players know that the more they play, the more points they earn toward free meals, shows, and rooms.[7] Using kiosks located in and around the casino floor, they can chart how many points they have earned and learn how many they need to garner desired comps. They can even print out their own comps at these self-serve kiosks, a perfect adaptation to the ATM-familiar consumers of today.

This system allows casino marketing personnel to make rational, impersonal decisions about comps in a way that was not possible before. That the player tracking system is national is, obviously, a result of the expansion of gambling. Though they may seem to be radical new ways to break a patron's casino experience down into coldly mathematical formulas of predicted versus actual wagering, players card programs such as Total Rewards constitute little more than extensions of traditional casino marketing techniques to encompass new realities in information technology and new demands in customer service.

Underneath the surface promotion of player card technology as the latest in customer convenience, there is an ominous undertone in reading about the certainty with which casino managers can now predict gambling behavior. It may be a feeling familiar to anyone who has looked carefully enough at the ceiling of a casino to see the dozens of opaque domes dotting it. These domes, as anyone who has seen *Rain Man* knows, hide closed circuit television cameras that, at the direction of surveillance personnel, silently observe and record. Because of the importance of tracking money on the casino floors and, in many cases, the state-mandated requirements that casino staff be able to see everything, everywhere, the floor of a casino resort has become the ultimate panopticon. Perhaps it is the harbinger of a surveillance state.

It is no great secret that the internet has aided the ability to monitor behavior. Whether they realize it or not, web surfers' viewing habits—consumer and otherwise—become grist for "data mining," in which their choices are recorded and analyzed for the benefit of marketing. In the aftermath of the terrorist attacks of September 11, 2001, many Americans have expressed a tolerance, and even desire, for more strenuous surveillance, visual and documentary, by government authorities. Biometric systems that can digitally identify subjects via surveillance cameras, embraced as a panacea for event and airport security, first found their customers in casino resorts eager to identify known cheaters and evictees. So Americans who want to live in a more controlled society would do well to spend some time in a casino—because these venues have already realized visual and behavioral surveillance systems that mainstream business and law enforcement are only beginning to understand.

In the final analysis, the compartmentalized gambling world that Americans created in the last century has collapsed. The casino resort has become a fixture in every section of the nation, and the Internet has allowed casino-style gambling into Americans' homes. In this world, the solutions to yesterday's problems no longer work—gambling is no longer spatially contained. It is overstating the case to say that the casino resort "saved" gambling as a legal public diversion in America, but the re-creation of gambling within the casino resort was the most striking development of American gambling in the twentieth century. With the success of Nevada and, later, New Jersey authorities in casino regulation, Americans began to believe that gambling could be controlled and a portion of its profits redirected toward the public good. The Las Vegas Strip was the fulcrum for this profound historical change. Cloning the Las Vegas Strip in three or four places did not substantially change the casino resort paradigm—the first casino outposts were still relatively isolated—but the appearance of a Boulder Strip, whose casinos have few amenities and are geared to locals, in every major metropolitan area in the United States, will make Americans rethink the basic idea of the casino resort. They may decide that the casino resort is no longer a "safe" place that contains gambling, culturally and spatially.

This prospect leads back to the crisis in American gambling that originally led to the creation of the casino resort on the Las Vegas Strip: how to contain the problems caused by widespread gambling. At the time of the mid-century antigambling movement, Americans discovered a solution, geographic isolation, haphazardly and through the absence of a national policy on gambling. In the 1950s, the nascent gaming industry seized on one of Nevada's attributes, its remoteness, and turned it to its advantage. Suburban citizens throughout the nation, though they made periodic trips to the Strip, steadfastly refused to legalize gaming in their own areas, thus containing the feared social ill-effects of gaming in the desert. But once other jurisdictions sought to transplant the casino resort near major population centers, the idea that casino gaming could be kept safe through containment was ended. Consequently, reports of problem gambling nationwide have climbed precipitously since the late 1980s. The economic boons of casino gaming have helped to increase revenues and create jobs, but serious questions about gambling are asked more loudly as gambling expands: How much is too much? Is nontourist gambling a viable solution to revenue shortfalls?

But in many ways the suburbs of America share the same dilemma as the casino resort. Originally developed as alternatives to crowded, dirty urban living, they have created problems of their own, including sprawl and gridlock caused by overdevelopment. Once-serene bedroom communities that sent wage earners off to the city in the mornings and welcomed them back in the evening have themselves evolved into metropolitan areas of their own, with industrial and commercial development to rival many cities. The suburbs that casino resorts courted in the 1950s are no more. Though the casino resort has survived, it is now in a position completely unimaginable in its earliest years—far larger and less isolated than had ever been conceived.

It is not surprising that the casino resort, specifically tailored to suburban Southern Nevada, has not been a perfect fit in other settings. Casino resorts become yet another suburban node in a metropolitan area, but they cannot become centers of thriving urban development. This is directly linked to the ways that the casino resort developed on the Strip in the postwar period. The mixed results of the casino resort as an urban redeveloper are the legacy of its suburban genesis.

After over a half-century of development, the casino resort has created much good: the development of Las Vegas as a major American city, the containment of gambling in a socially and politically acceptable form, and the creation of jobs and opportunity for hundreds of thousands of hardworking people. But one cannot help but remember that the very success of 1950s "boss gambler" syndicates eventually priced their owners—the true industry pioneers—out of the casino market. Those with a stake in the contemporary casino business should be careful where expansion takes them. Abundant prosperity may, for the second time, prove too much to handle.

Notes

Introduction

1. The presentation book, along with much of Stern's other work, is on file in UNLV Special Collections. I used it as the basis for my online exhibit *Paradise Misplaced: The Xanadu Hotel Casino*, which you can find at http://gaming.unlv.edu/Xanadu.
2. Sally Anne Fowler, *How to Become a Casino Cocktail Waitress* (Las Vegas: Sally Anne Fowler, 1983), 5.
3. Mike Velardo, *Oral History*. William Velardo, collector, Untranscribed interview. University of Nevada Oral History Project, Las Vegas 1977.
4. Until the 1970s, virtually all members of the dealers' hierarchy were men. As the profession has become inclusive of women, the word "floorperson" has become accepted. Then, and now, dealers often contracted the word, looking for advice from or receiving a reprimand from "the floor."
5. Shannon Bybee, "Which Is It: Gambling or Gaming?" *International Gaming and Wagering Business* 5, no. 10 (2002): 91–92.
6. John Hannigan wrote persuasively about the rise of theme parks as nonurban entertainment in *Fantasy City* (London and New York: Routledge, 1998).

Chapter 1

1. For more on popular gambling in the nineteenth century, see Ann Fabian, *Card Sharps, Dream Books, and Bucket Shops: Gambling in 19th-Century America* (Ithaca, N.Y.: Cornell University Press, 1990).
2. See *The Victims of Gaming; Being Extracts from the Diary of an American Physician* (Boston: Weeks, Jordan & Company; New York: J. S. Taylor [etc., etc.]; 1838).
3. U.S. Department of Justice Central File 5-23-987, cited in personal communication with Mark Haller, December 1996.
4. Milton Leekoff, "Brooklyn Badlands," in Noah Sarlat, ed., *America's Cities of Sin* (New York: Lion Books, 1951), 19.
5. Mark H. Haller, "The Changing Structure of American Gambling in the Twentieth Century," in Eric H. Monkkonen, ed., *Crime and Justice in American History*. Vol. 8: *Drugs, Gambling, and Organized Crime* (Munich and London: K.G. Saur, 1992), 315, 336.
6. Haller, "Changing Structure," 336.

7. "Delinquency Link to Pinballs Seen," *New York Times,* June 24, 1948. This should give pause to anyone who thinks that linking video games to teen violence is a recent novelty.

8. August Hecksher with Phyllis Robinson, *When LaGuardia Was Mayor: New York's Legendary Years* (New York: W. W. Norton and Company, 1978), 107.

9. Carlisle and Carlisle, "The Big Slot-Machine Swindle," *Collier's Magazine,* 26, 60.

10. Carlisle and Carlisle, 58.

11. W. E. Farbstein, "Devilish Devices," *New York Times Magazine,* March 12, 1950, 58. Apparently, sedentary lifestyles, smoking, and cholesterol-rich diets were only part of the problem.

12. Norman Carlisle and Madelyn Carlisle, "The Big Slot-Machine Swindle." *Collier's Magazine,* 123 February 9, 1949, 26. This would break down to an average of $15,000 per machine per year, or about $41 a day per machine. On nickel machines, a common denomination, this would amount to 820 coins per day or 34 per hour, if the machine were used 24 hours daily. Quarter machines, the other chief denomination, would average 164 coins per day or only approximately 7 per hour. If the estimate of 200,000 slots is accurate (it seems reasonable), this is a good and perhaps conservative estimate. Since most slot machines returned between 60 and 90 percent of coins played, though, the profits were considerably less than $3 billion.

13. W. E. Farbstein, "Devilish Devices," *New York Times Magazine,* March 12, 1950, 58.

14. "Gamblers Anonymous: New Club, Similar to 'Alcoholics,' Aims at Another Vice," *New York Times,* January 4, 1947.

15. See William Howard Moore. *The Kefauver Committee and the Politics of Crime, 1950–1952* (Columbia: University of Missouri Press, 1974), introduction, for a more complete analysis of the national policy toward gambling at mid-century.

16. For greater detail on the debate surrounding the entrance of Nevada into the Union, see Russell R. Elliott, *History of Nevada* (Lincoln: University of Nebraska Press, 1987), particularly chapt. 5.

17. Elliott, *History of Nevada,* 44.

18. Nevada Gaming Commission and State Control Board, *Gaming Nevada Style* (Carson City: early 1980s). 7.

19. Eric N. Moody, "Nevada's Legalization of Casino Gambling in 1931," *Nevada Historical Society Quarterly* 37 no. 2 (summer 1994): 81–82.

20. Moody, "Nevada's Legalization," 95.

21. Moody, "Nevada's Legalization," 84.

22. Stanley W. Paher, *Las Vegas: As It Began—as It Grew* (Las Vegas: Nevada Publications, 1971), 14.

23. The eponymous six companies were: Utah Construction Company (which also built the infamous Hetch Hetchy dam outside San Francisco), Morrison-Knudsen Company, J.F. Shea, Company, Pacific Bridge Company, MacDonald and Kahn, Incorporated, and Bechtel, Kaiser, and Warren, itself an amalgamation of three corporations (W.A. Bechtel, Henry J. Kaiser Company, and the Warren Brothers Construction Company). Most observers agree that Henry Kaiser was the driving force behind Six Companies.

24. Joseph E. Stevens, *Hoover Dam: An American Adventure* (Norman: University of Oklahoma Press, 1988), 222–24.

25. Sharon Zukin, *Landscapes of Power: From Detroit to Disney World* (Berkeley: University of California Press, 1991), 52.

26. For the most in-depth treatment of the development of Las Vegas, see Eugene Moehring. *Resort City in the Sunbelt: Las Vegas, 1930–1970* (Reno and Las Vegas: University of Nevada Press, 1989).

27. Zukin, *Landscapes of Power,* 142.

28. Herbert Gans, *The Levittowners: Ways of Life and Politics in a New Suburban Community* (New York: Columbia University Press, 1967), 284.

29. John Hannigan. *Fantasy City: Pleasure and Profit in the Postmodern Metropolis* (London and New York: Routledge, 1998), 34–43. For a further discussion of the decline of downtowns, see Robert M. Fogelson, *Downtown: Its Rise and Fall, 1880–1950* (New Haven, Conn.: Yale University Press, 2001).

30. Gilbert Millstein, "Mr. Coward Dissects Las Vegas," *New York Times Magazine,* June 20,

1955, 41. There is no extant comment from Carl Degler on this "everyman his own vaca-tioner" interpretation of Las Vegas.

Chapter 2

1. Most of the contemporary accounts of the origins of the Strip, including those of Best and Hillyer, Ralli, and Scott describe mysteriously parallel versions of the origins of the El Rancho, Last Frontier, and Flamingo. Whether any of these stories is "true" is not as important as the effect they were intended to have on visitors to casino resorts. Interestingly, every such story features an unexpected visit to a barren desert highway and a revelation of incredible profits to be earned there. This is a curious capitalist twist on the Native American vision quest.
2. Deke Castleman, *Las Vegas* (New York: Fodor's Travel Publications, 1997), 50.
3. George Stamos, Jr., "El Rancho Vegas," *Las Vegas Sun Magazine*, April 1, 1979.
4. Stamos, "El Rancho Vegas."
5. Castleman, *Las Vegas*, 50.
6. Stamos, "El Rancho Vegas."
7. Goldie Spicer, *Oral History*. Elmer Heeren, collector, untranscribed interview, University of Nevada Oral History Project, Las Vegas, 1977.
8. See Joseph E. Stevens, *Hoover Dam: An American Adventure* (Norman: University of Okla-homa Press, 1988), 223–24.
9. Elaine Tyler May, *Homeward Bound: American Families in the Cold War Era* (New York: Basic Books, Inc., 1988), 11.
10. For more about the surge of growth in the Sunbelt, see David C. Perry and Alfred J. Watkins, eds., *The Rise of the Sunbelt Cities* (Beverly Hills, Calif.: Sage Publications, 1977).
11. Mark Gottdiener, *The New Urban Sociology* (New York: McGraw Hill, Inc., 1994), 66.
12. Dick Pearce, "Pleasure Palaces," *Harper's Magazine*, February 1955, 82.
13. John Hannigan, *Fantasy City: Pleasure and Profit in the Postmodern Metropolis* (London and New York: Routledge, 1998), 4.
14. Barbara and Myrick Land, *A Short History of Reno* (Reno: University of Nevada Press, 1995), 101–102. Reno's city council struggled to enforce the redline even as casino resorts brought prosperity to Southern Nevada. Despite the dogged efforts of casino operator Ernest Primm, Reno gambling remained mostly confined until the 1960s, by which time the Strip had irrevocably become the nation's gambling center.
15. Ernest Havemann, "Gamblers Paradise Lost," *Life*, October 25, 1954, 67–68.
16. Kenneth T. Jackson, *The Crabgrass Frontier: The Suburbanization of the United States* (New York: Oxford University Press, 1985), 257–59.
17. Richard P. Horwitz, *The Strip: An American Place* (Lincoln: University of Nebraska Press, 1985), 9–11.
18. William Moore, *Oral History*. Elizabeth Nelson Patrick, interviewer, University of Nevada Oral History Project, Reno, 1981, 54.
19. Katherine Best and Katherine Hillyer, *Las Vegas, Playtown, USA* (New York: David McKay Company, 1955), 64–65.
20. Castleman, *Las Vegas*, 50.
21. Paul Ralli. *Viva Vegas* (Hollywood, Calif.: House-Warven Publishers, 1953), 223–24; see also "Last Frontier Hotel is Sold," *New York Times*, August 25, 1951.
22. Moore, *Oral History*, 5. See figure 8.
23. Best and Hillyer, *Las Vegas*, 61.
24. Moore, *Oral History*, 13.
25. Moore *Oral history*, 34. See figure 10.
26. Ralli, *Viva Vegas*, 169.
27. "Old West Display," *New York Times*, January 28, 1951.
28. Morton Saiger, *Oral History*. R.T. King, collector, University of Nevada Oral History Pro-ject, Reno, 1985, 36.
29. Moore, *Oral History*, 38–39.
30. Hannigan, *Fantasy City*, 3.
31. Hannigan, *Fantasy City*, 3.

32. Richard P. Horwitz, *The Strip: An American Place*, 5.

33. Ferris A. Scott, *The Las Vegas Story* (Santa Ana, Calif.: Western Resort Publications, 1957). Unpaginated pamphlet.

34. John M. Findlay, *People of Chance: Gambling in American Society from Jamestown to Las Vegas* (New York: Oxford University Press, 1986), 3–4.

35. Saiger, *Oral History*, 41–42.

36. W. R. Wilkerson III, *The Man Who Invented Las Vegas* (Los Angeles: Ciro's Books, 2000), 43.

37. Wilkerson, *The Man Who Invented Las Vegas*, 81.

38. Best and Hillyer, *Las Vegas*, 62.

39. "Flamingo Hotel Plays Host to Film Luminaries," *Las Vegas Review-Journal*, December 30, 1946.

40. Thelma Coblentz, *Oral History*. Uncredited collector, untranscribed interview, University of Nevada Oral History Project, Las Vegas, 1977. See also "Flamingo Resort Hotel Jammed at Opening," *Las Vegas Review-Journal*, December 27, 1946, for an offbeat description of the opening.

41. For an analysis of the importance of Siegel and the Flamingo, see James F. Smith, "'Bugsy's' Flamingo and the Modern Casino Hotel, in William R. Eadington and Judy A. Cornelius, eds., *Gambling and Public Policy: International Perspectives*, (Reno: Institute for the Study of Gambling and Commercial Gaming, 1991), 499–518.

42. Even the claim that Siegel's murder prompted Nevada authorities to "clean up" the gaming law is inaccurate. Nevada's gaming laws have been evolving, since the reestablishment of legal gambling in 1931, to administer to an expanding and changing industry. While there were some changes in Nevada,s gaming code in the late 1940s, the most sweeping changes didn't happen until 1955. Dick Pearce, "Pleasure Palaces," *Harper's Magazine*, February 1955, 81.

43. U.S. Senate, *Hearings before the Special Committee to Investigate Organized Crime in Interstate Commerce*, 81st Congress, 2nd Session, 1950, 181–82.

44. *Hearings*, 91.

45. Noah Sarlat, *America's Cities of Sin*, (New York: Lion Books, 1951), 75.

46. The most famous cinematic portrayal of Siegel is Barry Levinson's 1991 Warren Beatty vehicle *Bugsy*. Buying into decades of Siegel hype, *Washington Post* film critic Hal Hinson described the biopic as "the Francis Ford Coppola story 'Tucker' with tommy guns" and an essentially accurate account of Siegel and the Flamingo. See Hinson's review, *Washington Post*, December 20, 1991. Popular accounts of the Mafia and Las Vegas, in which Siegel is a central or peripheral figure, describe him in much the same way.

47. Mario Puzo and Francis Ford Coppola, *The Godfather Part Two*. Paramount Pictures, 1974.

48. Saiger, *Oral History*, 12.

49. Lucius Beebe, "Nevada," in *American Panorama: West of the Mississippi* (Garden City, N.Y.: Doubleday and Company, Inc., 1960), 161.

50. Saiger, *Oral History*, 15–16.

51. Coblentz, *Oral History*.

52. A female dealer, for example, wrote a tell-all article for the May 13, 1950, *Saturday Evening Post* titled, "I Was a Gambling House Dealer," that completely stripped any pretensions of glamour from the position. The June 20, 1955, issue of *Life* magazine, by contrast, featured a cover story on Las Vegas that lavished praise on the young, lovely dancers and waitresses of the Strip. The cover photo was, predictably, dancers on stage at the Moulin Rouge.

53. For the ladies, news articles and guidebooks of the early Strip were less expansive on the possibilities of transient pleasure, though they often hailed casino resorts as husband-hunting havens. Later guidebooks were equally explicit for men and women, informing each where they could find hustlers, prostitutes, and swingers of any persuasion.

54. Jefferson Graham, *Vegas, Live and in Person* (New York: Abbeville Press, 1989), 148, 166.

55. Sands Collection, in UNLV Special Collections, box 23, folder 11.

56. Barbara Ehrenreich, *The Hearts of Men: American Dreams and the Flight from Commitment* (New York: Anchor Books, 1983).

57. Paul Ralli, *Nevada Lawyer* (Culver City: Murray and Gee, Inc., 1949), 214–16. Ralli, who handled many divorce cases, devoted much of his book to tales of divorcées, and the prominent role they play in his Las Vegas underlines the importance of women to the development of the casino resort.

58. Ed Reid and Ovid Demaris, *The Green Felt Jungle* (New York: Trident Press, 1963), 112–16.

59. In 1954, Hank Greenspun's *Las Vegas Sun* conducted an undercover investigation of local politicos and police, in which a private detective posed as a "hood" from back East looking to buy influence. The investigation revealed a motherlode of corruption, ensnaring officials as high as Lieutenant Governor Clifford Jones in an influence-peddling scheme that also revealed Meyer Lansky as a secret owner of the Thunderbird casino.

Chapter 3

1. Noah Sarlat, *America's Cities of Sin* (New York: Lion Book, 1951), 18.
2. See Thomas Albini, *The American Mafia: Genesis of a Legend* (New York: Irvington Publishers, 1979). Throughout this book, Albini explains the history of the "mafia" in terms of this framework, and he explicitly and compellingly lays it out in chapter 3, "The Social Locale."
3. William Howard Moore, *The Kefauver Committee and the Politics of Crime, 1950–1952* (Columbia: University of Missouri Press, 1974), 25–26.
4. Quoted in Moore, *Kefauver Committee*, 25.
5. For a book-length distillation of this genre, see Fred Cook, *A Two-Dollar Bet Means Murder* (New York: Dial Press, 1961). This book was based on the February 15, 1960, edition of *The Nation*, in which Cook strenuously denounced gambling and gamblers.
6. Moore, *Kefauver Committee*, 12–13.
7. "Gaming Total Put Over Housing Cost," *New York Times*, January 28, 1950.
8. Moore, *Kefauver Committee*, 35–39.
9. "Voters Set Policy on 164 Proposals," *New York Times*, November 9, 1950.
10. For a more complete analysis of Kefauver's political career, see Joseph Bruce Gorman, *Kefauver: A Political Biography*, (New York: Oxford University Press, 1971).
11. Moore, *Kefauver Committee*, 49.
12. See Jerome E. Edwards, *Pat McCarran: Political Boss of Nevada* (Reno: University of Reno Press, 1982), chapter 9, for a detailed discussion of McCarran's role in restraining congressional antigambling action.
13. It is an interesting historical aside that Joe McCarthy attempted to steer the crime investigation to his Special Investigations Committee but was stymied by Kefauver's persistent lobbying. Less than a month after accession of the crime turf to Kefauver, McCarthy, speaking before a Republican women's group in Wheeling, West Virginia, made public his scandalous discovery of "205" known communists working for the State Department. It would make an interesting exercise in speculative historical fiction to hypothesize about how the fabric of the postwar era would have been changed had McCarthy turned his talents toward fighting crime instead of hunting communists.
14. It has been alleged that committee members kept on asking questions that they knew wouldn't be answered, making it appear that witnesses were being evasive. This fueled conspiracy theories about the scope of gambling and organized crime. It also contrasts with events fifty years later when Enron executives "asserted their Constitutional rights" and declined to answer any questions about that firm's accounting practices—after establishing that a witness wouldn't talk, the committee simply thanked him, validated his parking ticket, and let him go on his way.
15. Estes Kefauver. *Crime in America* (Garden City, N.Y.: Doubleday, 1951), 12–16.
16. *Hearings before the Special Committee to Investigate Organized Crime in Interstate Commerce*. Part 10, Nevada-California (Washington: U.S. Government Printing Office, 1951), 97–88.
17. "Gamblers Anonymous: New Club, Similar to 'Alcoholics,' Aims at Another Vice," *New York Times*, January 4, 1947.
18. Halley's words, when questioning Jones. *Hearings before the Special Committee to Investigate Organized Crime in Interstate Commerce*, 33.
19. This view of Siegel's murder contrasts with the most widely accepted one, that it was inspired by skimming and/or failure at the Flamingo. The Kefauver Committee spent a great deal of time and energy tracing the tentacles of the race wire service and regarded Nevada gaming as a minor part of the national criminal conspiracy, which may explain Kefauver's conclusion that the wire service and not the Flamingo was behind Siegel's death. According to most sources, however, Siegel's wire service partners were also investors in the Flamingo, which makes the question one of "why" rather than "who."

20. *Third Interim Report of the Special Committee to Investigate Organized Crime in Interstate Commerce* [Kefauver Committee] (New York: Arco Publishing Company, 1951), 2.

21. *Third Interim Report*, 90–92.

22. "Gamblers Lie Low in Gale of Reform, *New York Times*, December 6, 1951.

23. Rufus King, *Gambling and Organized Crime* (Washington, D.C.: Public Affairs Press, 1969), 147.

24. "Slot Machine Bill Signed by Truman," *New York Times*, January 3, 1951.

25. For an in-depth discussion of the effects of the antigambling movement in New York City, see George Walsh, *Public Enemies: The Mayor, the Mob, and the Crime That Was* (New York: W.W. Norton and Company, 1980), part 6, "1952–1973: Aftermath." The antigambling movement had a similar impact in most jurisdictions. For an account of the earlier stages, see Walter Arm, *Pay-Off: The Inside Story of Police Corruption* (New York: Appleton-Century-Crofts, Inc., 1951).

26. Robert Lacey, *Little Man: Meyer Lansky and the Gangster Life* (Boston: Little, Brown, and Company, 1991), 310.

27. Wallace Turner, *Gamblers' Money: The New Force in American Life* (Boston: Houghton Mifflin Company, 1965), 78–79.

28. Turner, *Gamblers' Money*, 77–78.

29. King, *Gambling*, 121.

30. Anthony Downs, "The 'Issue-Attention Cycle,'" *The Public Interest* 28 (1972): 38–50.

31. Scott, *Las Vegas Story*.

32. Las Vegas Chamber of Commerce Research and Statistical Bureau, *The Las Vegas Report*, 1959 (Las Vegas, Chamber of Commerce, 1959), 30.

33. Scott, *Las Vegas Story*.

34. Alan Brinkley and Ellen Fitzpatrick, *America in Modern Times, since 1890* (New York: McGraw-Hill, 1997), 406–409.

35. The years 1953–55 saw a boom in casino construction in Clark County, with dollar amounts totaling $48.4 million, $62.9 million, and $57.8 million, respectively. By 1956, new construction accounted for only $26.9 million as the market suffered an overcrowding that would not be mitigated until the construction of the Convention Center and the growth of Las Vegas as a convention town in the early 1960s. Statistics from Las Vegas Chamber of Commerce Research and Statistical Bureau. *The Las Vegas Report*, 1959, 23.

36. See Mark Gottdiener, *The Theming of America: Dreams, Visions, and Commercial Space* (Boulder, Colo.: Westview Press, 1997), 26–32.

37. Deke Castleman, *Las Vegas* (New York: Fodor's Travel Publications, 1997), 94.

38. The inherent incompatibility of the casino resort and urban space resulted in the malling of Fremont Street in 1995. In order to "revitalize" the downtown casino district, Las Vegas enclosed a several-block stretch of Fremont Street under a canopy that "performs" a light show nightly on the hour. There are few examples in current urban geography of a more blatant "malling of America."

39. Nevada Gaming Commission and State Control Board, *Gaming Nevada Style* (Carson City: Nevada Gaming Commission, 22.

40. Nevada Gaming Commission, *Gaming Nevada Style*, 12.

41. A. L. Higginbotham, *Legalized Gambling in Nevada: Its History, Economics, and Control* (Carson City: Nevada Gaming Commission, 1970), 11.

42. Higgenbotham, *Legalized Gambling*, 11.

43. Higgenbotham, *Legalized Gambling*, 11.

44. See Gene Burd, "The Selling of the Sunbelt: Civic Boosterism in the Media," in David C. Perry and Alfred J. Watkins, eds., *The Rise of the Sunbelt Cities* (Beverly Hills, Sage Publications, 1977), 129–49, for an in-depth discussion of the role that favorable media has played in promoting the Sunbelt cities.

45. Gladwin Hill, "Klondike in the Desert," *New York Times*, June 26, 1953.

46. Kent Ruth, How to Enjoy Your Western Vacations. (Norman: University of Oklahoma Press, 1956), 226.

47. Al Freeman, Memo in Sands Collection, box 3, folder 9.

48. "Visit Las Vegas," Pamphlet in Sands Collection, UNLV Special Collections, box 47, folder 11.

49. Donn Knapp, *Las Vegas: Entertainment Capital*, (Menlo Park, Calif.: Lane Publishing, 1983), 53.

50. See Robert Sonnett, *Sonnett's Guide to Las Vegas* (Las Vegas: Sonnett, 1969).

Chapter 4

1. Dick Pearce, "Pleasure Palaces," *Harper's Magazine*, February 1955, 81.

2. Taken from advertisements in *Fabulous Las Vegas* Magazine, October 22, 1955.

3. Jefferson Graham, *Vegas, Live and in Person* (New York: Abbeville Press, 1989), 148–49.

4. "History of the Folies Bergère" (Las Vegas: Tropicana Public Relations Office, 1999). Personal correspondence with Tropicana Public Relations Office. See figure 26.

5. Kim Krantz, *Oral History*. Joyce Marshall, collector, Las Vegas Women in Gaming and Entertainment Oral History Project, University of Nevada, Las Vegas. 1996, 4.

6. Lee Fisher, "Boom Times Continue in Las Vegas for 16th Consecutive Year," in Dunes Collection, box 1, folder 18, UNLV Special Collections

7. Count Guido Roberto Deiro, *Oral History*. David Schwartz, collector, University of Nevada, Las Vegas, Special Collections, 2002, 24–25.

8. "Eight Days to Win," *Time*, January 13, 1958, 83–84.

9. A. Gottesman statement. In Dunes Collection, box 2, folder 5. UNLV Special Collections.

10. "Whose Glitter Gulch?" *Newsweek*, September 29, 1958. 72.

11. Files in Sands Collection, UNLV Special Collections, box 40, folder 6.

12. *Stardust Hotel and Golf Club: The Hotel That Made Conventions Popular in Las Vegas*, in Stardust Hotel/Casino Promotional and Publicity Files, News Releases 1969–1992 folder, UNLV Special Collections.

13. Correspondence in Sands Collection, UNLV Special Collections, box 1, folder 5.

14. Al Freeman, Las Vegas Convention Center promotional pamphlet (Las Vegas: Las Vegas Convention Center 1959).

15. Freeman, promotional pamphlet.

16. Freeman, promotional pamphlet.

17. Dick Pearce, "Pleasure Palaces," *Harper's Magazine*, February 1955, 81.

18. See David Johnston, *Temples of Chance: How America, Inc., Bought Out Murder Inc. to Win Control of the Casino Business* New York: Doubleday, 1992).

19. Leon Mandel, *William Fisk Harrah* (Garden City, N.Y.: Doubleday, 1982), 59–61.

20. For a full treatment of Harrah's career, see Leon Mandel, *William Fisk Harrah* (Garden City, N.Y.: Doubleday, 1982). For an in-depth analysis of Harrah the man and Harrah the businessman, see William A Douglass, "William F. Harrah: Nevada Gaming Mogul," in Richard O. Davies, ed., *The Maverick Spirit: Building the New Nevada* (Reno: University of Nevada Press, 1999). See also R. T. King, ed. *Every Light Was On: Bill Harrah and His Clubs Remembered* (Reno: University of Nevada Oral History Program, 1999).

21. Mandel, *William Fisk Harrah*, 207.

22. Reid and Demaris, *Green Felt Jungle*, 233–34.

23. Alan Balboni. Beyond the Mafia: Italian Americans and the Development of Las Vegas. (Reno: Univ. of Nevada Press, 1996), 30–31.

24. Ernest Havemann, "Gamblers Paradise Lost," *Life*, October 25, 1954, 69.

25. Tom Alexander, "What Is Del Webb up to in Nevada?" *Fortune Magazine*, May 1965, 185.

26. Alexander, "What Is Del Webb up to in Nevada?" 186.

27. For more on the Del Webb Corporation, see Margaret Finnerty. *Del Webb: A Man, a Company* (Flagstaff, Ariz.: Heritage Publishers, 1991).

28. "Del Webb Group Presentation," in Del Webb Promotional and Publicity Material, News/Press Releases Folder, UNLV Special Collections.

29. Estes Kefauver, *Crime in America* (Garden City, N.Y.: Doubleday, 1951), 231.

30. Kefauver, *Crime in America*, 231.

31. Robert Lacey. *Little Man: Meyer Lansky and the Gangster Life*. (Boston: Little, Brown, and Company, 1991), ii.

32. Ralph C. James and Estelle Dinerstein James, *Hoffa and the Teamsters: A Study of Union Power* (Princeton, N.J.: D. Van Nostrand and Company, Inc., 1965), 245.

33. James and James, *Hoffa and the Teamsters*, 247.
34. James and James, *Hoffa and the Teamsters*, 260.
35. Steven Brill, *The Teamsters* (New York: Simon and Schuster, 1978), 210.
36. General Accounting Office, *The Department of Labor's Oversight of the Management of the Teamsters' Central States Pension and Health and Welfare Funds.* (Washington: General Accounting Office, 1985), 3, 16.
37. Peter Wiley and Robert Gottlieb, *Empires in the Sun: The Rise of the New American West* (Tucson: University of Arizona Press, 1982), 198–99.
38. John G. Edwards, "E. Parry Thomas," in *The First 100: Portraits of the Men and Women Who Shaped Las Vegas* (Las Vegas: Huntington Press, 1999), 157.
39. Wiley and Gottlieb, *Empires in the Sun*, 1999.
40. *Hearings before the Special Committee to Investigate Organized Crime in Interstate Commerce.* Part 10: Nevada-California (Washington, D.C.: U.S. Government Printing Office, 1951), 24.
41. Robert Lacey, *Little Man: Meyer Lansky and the Gangster Life* (Boston: Little, Brown, and Company, 1991), 294–95.
42. Bill Friedman, *Casino Management.* (Seacaucus, N.J.: Lyle Stuart Inc., 1974), 30.
43. Bill Friedman, *Casino Management.* (Seacaucus, N.J.: Lyle Stuart Inc., 1974), 243.
44. Bill Friedman, *Casino Management.* (Seacaucus, N.J.: Lyle Stuart Inc., 1974), 243–44.
45. Bill Friedman, *Casino Management.* (Seacaucus, N.J.: Lyle Stuart Inc., 1974), 244. The notion of the slot zone as a happy, magic place is laughable for anyone who has ever actually watched slot players grind at the machines for hours on end.
46. Bill Friedman, *Casino Management.* (Seacaucus, N.J.: Lyle Stuart Inc., 1974), 227–32. For an account of the methods and career of an actual slot theft "team" of the 1970s and 1980s, see Jim Sloan, *Nevada: True Tales from the Neon Wilderness* (Salt Lake City: University of Utah Press, 1993), chap. 2.
47. Bill Friedman, *Casino Management.* (Seacaucus, N.J.: Lyle Stuart Inc., 1974), 250.
48. CJH, box 2, "Biographical Sketch."
49. Untitled speech fragment, in Charles J. Hirsch Collection, box 2, University of Nevada, Las Vegas, Special Collections. Collection subsequently cited as CJH.
50. Jack Rice, "His Eye on Figures in Las Vegas Casino," *St. Louis Post-Dispatch*, October 29, 1961. From CJH.
51. "Engineering: Square Bones," *Newsweek*, July 3, 1961. From CJH.
52. Jack Rice, "His Eye on Figures in Las Vegas Casino," *St. Louis Post-Dispatch*, October 29, 1961. From CJH.
53. CJH, box 2.
54. Roy Thompson, "Las Vegan Defends Honor of His City," *Winston-Salem Journal*, March 3, 1971. From CJH.
55. CJH, box 2.
56. CJH, speech fragment, box 2.
57. CJH, untitled press clipping, box 2.

Chapter 5

1. For more on Sinatra and constructions of masculinity, see Roger Gilbert, "The Swinger and the Loser: Sinatra, Masculinity, and Fifties Culture," in Leonard Mustazza, ed., *Frank Sinatra and Popular Culture: Essays on an American Icon* (Westport, Conn.: Praeger, 1998), 38–49.
2. Mustazza, *Sinatra*, 144, 150.
3. Lawrence J. Quirk and William Schoell. *The Rat Pack! The Hey-Hey Days of Frank and the Boys.* (Dallas: Taylor Publishing Company, 1998. 234. All the true Rat Pack films had numbers in their titles.
4. It is more or less accepted that Martin and Sinatra's "ownership" interests in the casino were in fact held for deeper investors who could not get licenses. However, this did not stop them from acting as if they owned the place.
5. Al Freeman, Promotional notes. In Sands Collection, box 1, folder 5.
6. For a detailed description of the plot, cast, and critical reception of *Ocean's Eleven*, see Gene Ringgold and Clifford McCarty, *The Films of Frank Sinatra* (New York: The Citadel Press, 1971), 163–67.

7. Harry Brown and Charles Lederer, *Ocean's Eleven* final script. Warner Brothers, 1960, 78.

8. Brown and Lederer, *Ocean's Eleven* final script, 131.

9. Brown and Lederer, *Ocean's Eleven* final script, 131.

10. Katherine Best and Katherine Hillyer. Las Vegas: *Playtown USA.* (New York: David McKay Company, 1955), 136.

11. James B. McMillan, *Fighting Back: A Life in the Struggle for Civil Rights* (Reno: University of Nevada Oral History Program, 1997), 92–97.

12. McMillan, *Fighting Back,* 98.

13. Mort Saiger, *Oral History.* R. T. King, collector, University of Nevada Oral History Project, Reno, 1985, 23.

14. Photographs and notes in Sands Collection, UNLV Special Collections, box 56 folder 6.

15. *Caesars Palace Press Release,* 1986. In promotional and publicity material of Caesars World, Inc., UNLV Special Collections.

16. *Las Vegas Sun,* August 2, 1966. If the figure of $40,000 included capital costs and debt servicing as well as daily expenses, the profit expected was astronomical.

17. Eugene Moehring, *Resort City in the Sunbelt: Las Vegas, 1930–1970.* (Reno: University of Nevada Press, 1989), 117.

18. Westward Ho pamphlet in Circus Circus Promotional and publicity material, UNLV Special Collections.

19. For more on the place of theming in postwar culture, see Mark Gottdiener, *The Theming of America: Dreams, Visions, and Commercial Space* (Boulder, Colo.: Westview Press, 1997).

20. "Pleasure Palaces," *Harper's Magazine,* February 1955, 81.

21. See Robert Venturi, Denise Scott Brown, and Steven Izenour, *Learning from Las Vegas: The Forgotten Symbolism of Architectural Form* (Cambridge: The MIT Press, 1977), 18–72. Also Mark Gottdiener, *The Theming of America: Dreams, Visions, and Commercial Space* (Boulder, Colo.: Westview Press, 1997), 98–109.

22. Las Vegas Chamber of Commerce Research and Statistical Bureau, *The Las Vegas Report,* Las Vegas: Chamber of Commerce Research and Statistical Bureau, 1967), 11, 32.

23. It's difficult to speak of most Atlantic City casinos as having hyper-theming; they, too, suggest rather than imitate colonial India (Trump Taj Mahal) or the Mississippi (the Showboat). Bally's Wild Wild West, though, is hyper-themed, as are planned developments that seek to vastly expand the city's market. Laughlin casinos either eschew theming or feature subdued Western themes, and most Indian and riverboat casinos are not elaborately themed. The almost ridiculous hyper-theming of the casino resort seems to be a structural adaptation to the crowding of the Southern Nevada market.

24. In 1976, the Black Book's official designation was changed to the politically correct "List of Excluded Persons" following a complaint by an African-American activist. Ed Olsen's claim that the name "Black Book " is due to an excess of heavy stock black paper, which led the state printer to bind the books in black covers, may be somewhat disingenuous. Since the eleven were effectively blacklisted, it only made sense to put them in a "black book."

25. Ronald A. Farrell and Carole Case, *The Black Book and the Mob: The Untold Story of Nevada's Casinos* Madison: University of Wisconsin Press, 1995), 8. While the original Black Book also listed the colorful nicknames of those listed, I feel that it merely sensationalizes the men's personas, so I am consciously not including them.

26. Nevada Gaming Control Board, June 13, 1960. Cited in Farrell and Case, *Black Book and the Mob,* 31.

27. Edward A. Olsen. "The Black Book Episode—An Exercise in Muscle," in Eleanore Bushnell, ed., *Sagebrush and Neon* (Reno: University of Nevada Bureau of Governmental Research, 1976), 3–4.

28. Olsen, "Black Book Episode," 5–6. Marshall was, of course, trying to bait casino executives into denying him entrance so he could sue them and the Gaming Commission, but the itinerary still is impressive and revealing.

29. Olsen, "Black Book Episode," 7.

30. Olsen, "Black Book Episode," 7. Olsen notes a surreal moment in the Marshall tragicomedy when Desert Inn executives, interrupted from a private Halloween party, arrived in the pits to deal with the issue. "The incongruous sight of grown men in Halloween costumes," Olsen writes, "heatedly arguing with the feisty Abbaticchio in the middle of an elegant gambling pit tickled the funnybone of many an observer." Olsen's account of the challenges

to the Black Book is one of the most articulate and absorbing texts on the casino industry that this author has read.

31. Farrell and Case, *Black Book and the Mob,* 42–43. For a better description of the judicial process, see Olsen, "Black Book Episode," 11–21.

32. According to Giancana's younger brother Chuck, he actually planned to wiretap the Cal-Neva, supposedly a favorite haunt of the Kennedys, to spy on JFK and RFK. See Sam and Chuck Giancana, *Double Cross: The Explosive, Inside Story of the Mobster Who Controlled America* (New York: Warner Books, 1992), 271–73. Works like these fuel the fires of conspiracy theorists everywhere.

33. Wallace Turner, Gambler's money: *The New Force in American Life.* Boston: Houghton Mifflin Company, 1965, 161–63.

34. Jerome H. Skolnick, *House of Cards: The Legalization and Control of Casino Gambling* (Boston: Little, Brown, and Company, 1978), 124–26.

35. Olsen, *Oral History,* 338–39.

36. Skolnick, *House of Cards,* 129.

37. For an in depth analysis of Robert Kennedy as attorney general, see Victor Navasky, *Kennedy Justice* (New York: Athenum, 1977).

38. Navasky, *Kennedy Justice,* 9–80.

39. Olsen, *Oral History,* 346–48.

40. Mark H. Haller, "The Changing Structure of American Gambling in the Twentieth Century," in Eric H. Monkkonen, ed., *Crime and Justice in American History. Vol. 8. Prostitution, Drugs, and Organized Crime. Part I,* (Munich: K.G. Saur, 1992), 315–16.

41. In his 1953 article "Crime as an American Way of Life," Daniel Bell makes much the same argument for the rise to political and economic of Italian Americans in the years after Prohibition and the entrance of the next generation into the American mainstream. In Las Vegas, former illegal practitioners found the "organized illegality" of gambling, which served as their "stepladder of social ascent," perfectly legal. Thus, the "social development" of the Italian or Jewish "gangster" was accelerated. Moe Dalitz, whose past connections with organized crime would cause him licensing difficulties into the 1980s, was hailed as "Mr. Las Vegas" and a leading public citizen. See Daniel Bell, "Crime as an American Way of Life," in Nikos Passas, ed., *Organized Crime* (Brookfield, Vt.: Dartmouth Publishing Company, 1995), 131–54.

42. *Las Vegas Review-Journal,* April 8, 1954.

43. Best and Hillyer, *Las Vegas: Playtown USA,* 85. This account reflects the typical honest gambler/crooked hoodlum dichotomy that canonized Wilbur Clark while demonizing the Desert Inn syndicate, and the authors were either unaware of Roen's origins or chose to conceal them by omission.

44. Wallace Turner, *Gambler's money: The New Force in American Life.* Boston: Houghton Mifflin Company, 1965, 91.

45. *Las Vegas Review-Journal,* April 14, 1961; March 19, 1962; December 12, 1964.

Chapter 6

1. There are several slightly different accounts of the arrival in Las Vegas extant, some with machine gun-toting guards, others with the stretcher as a decoy. This version, taken from Robert Maheu's autobiography, is supported by the less outrageous of the accounts and seems historically accurate. See Robert Maheu and Richard Hack, *Next to Hughes: Behind the Power and Tragic Downfall of Howard Hughes by His Closest Advisor* (New York: Harper-Collins, 1992), 155–57. The male nurses comprised the inner cadre of what was called the "Mormon Palace Guard," though one of them was not a Mormon.

2. Omar V. Garrison, *Howard Hughes in Las Vegas* (New York: Lyle Stuart, 1970), 47–50. What were the DI's liabilities? Although this casino was always popular, it was also perennially in debt because of its constant expansions and remodelings.

3. Michael Drosnin, *Citizen Hughes* (New York: Holt, Rinehart, and Winston, 1985), 45–46. By contrast, Steve Wynn paid $270 million when he bought the resort in 2000, something that shows the dramatic increase in value in Strip real estate.

4. Maheu and Hack, *Next to Hughes,* 163.

5. Garrison, *Howard Hughes in Las Vegas*, 56.

6. "Mark on Nevada by Hughes Staggering," *Las Vegas Review-Journal*, April 6, 1976.

9. Garrison, *Howard Hughes in Las Vegas*, 67–68.

8. Maheu and Hack, *Next to Hughes*, 198–99.

9. Drosnin, *Citizen Hughes*, 55.

10. Garrison, *Howard Hughes in Las Vegas*, 75.

11. Nancy Sinatra, *Frank Sinatra: An American Legend* (Santa Monica, Calif.: General Publishing Group, 1995), 203.

12. For a full-length biography of Kerkorian that is largely complimentary, see Dial Torgerson, *Kirk Kerkorian: American Success Story* (New York: The Dial Press, 1974). The quote is Steve Wynn's from his 2001 Global Gaming Expo keynote address.

13. Full-page advertisement, *Las Vegas Now*, July 1970.

14. George Stamos, Jr., "Landmark," *Las Vegas Sun Magazine*, December 9, 1979.

15. Mort Saiger, *Oral History*. R.T. King, collector, University of Nevada Oral History Program, Reno, 1985, 48. Saiger felt so out of place at the Landmark that he requested, and received, a transfer back to the Frontier, where he had started in the early 1940s.

16. George Stamos, Jr., "MGM Grand," *Las Vegas Sun Magazine*, December 23, 1979. Note: the original MGM Grand, at the corner of Flamingo and the Strip, was purchased by Bally's Gaming (now Park Place Entertainment) in 1985 and renamed Bally's Las Vegas. The casino now called the MGM Grand, at the corner of Tropicana and the Strip, was built from the ground up by Kerkorian in 1994. Its 5,005 rooms ensured that, for a while at least, the MGM Grand would again be the world's largest hotel.

17. For a strenuously documented Elvis biography and critical analysis of other Presley biographies, see Patsy Guy Hammontree, *Elvis Presley: A Bio-Bibliography* (Westport, Conn.: Greenwood Press, 1985), 61–70. Hammontree's book chronicles the resurgence in Las Vegas and Presley's broadened fan base.

18. International Hotel. Promotional mailing, Las Vegas, March 1969. In Las Vegas Hilton promotional and publicity materials at UNLV Special Collections.

19. For an analysis of the imitator phenomenon and a detailed depiction of Elvis imitator Tony Roi, see Jefferson Graham, *Vegas, Live and in Person* (New York: Abbeville Press, 1989), 178–81.

20. A. L. Higgenbotham, *Legalized Gambling in Nevada: Its History, Economics, and Control* (Carson City: Nevada Gaming Commission, 1970), 12.

21. Jimmy Newman, *Oral History*. Maureen Kelly Ryan, collector, University of Nevada Oral History Project, Las Vegas, 1978, 14.

22. Nevada Gaming Commission, *Gaming Nevada Style* (Carson City: Nevada Gaming Commission, 1981), 13–14.

23. Economic Research Section, *Nevada Gaming Abstract* (Carson City: Nevada State Gaming Control Board, 1972).

24. Nevada State Gaming Control Board Economic Research Division, *Direct Levies on Gaming in Nevada* (Carson City: Gaming Control Board, 1971); *Direct Levies on Gaming in Nevada* (Carson City: Gaming Control Board, 1977).

25. "Chronology of Key Events," Caesars Palace Press Release, 1986. Reminder of a world without political correctness: the Centurion Tower expansion featured "an exquisite Japanese steak house, appropriately named Ah So and totally manned by Oriental personnel." In Caesars World Promotional and Publicity Files, UNLV Special Collections.

26. "Caesars Palace Purchased by Lum's," *Las Vegas Sun*, October 1, 1969.

27. Ramada Inns, Incorporated, *1979 Annual Report* (Phoenix: Ramada Inns, Incorporated, 1979), 12. In Tropicana Promotional and Publicity files, UNLV Special Collections.

28. In *Temples of Chance*, journalist David Johnston gives a grimmer tale of Ramada's entrance into the casino business, charging that they defrauded the Tropicana's previous owner, Mitzi Briggs. See David Johnston, *Temples of Chance: How America, Inc., Bought Out Murder Inc. to Win Control of the Casino Business* (New York: Doubleday, 1992), 60–66.

29. Economic Research Section, *Nevada Gaming Abstract* (Carson City: Nevada State Gaming Control Board, 1976), 1, I–1.

30. Newman, *Oral History*, 14.

31. Stamos, "Las Vegas Hilton," *Las Vegas Sun Magazine*, November 18, 1979; and Dominick and Dominick, "Prospectus: International Leisure Corporation."

32. Newman, *Oral History*, 26.
33. "Caesars Palace Purchased by Lum's," *Las Vegas Sun*, October 1, 1969.
34. Tony Grasso, *Oral History*. Colleen Seifert, collector, untranscribed interview, University of Nevada Oral History Project, Las Vegas 1980.
35. Aladdin "Magic Holiday Air Tour Vacation Package" brochure, Las Vegas, 1977. In Aladdin Hotel and Casino Publicity and Promotional Materials at UNLV Special Collections.
36. Sam Boyd, *Oral History*. Ralph Roske, collector, University of Nevada Oral History Project, Las Vegas 1977, 21.
37. Flamingo advertisement, 1976. In Flamingo Hotel and Casino Promotional and Publicity Materials at UNLV Special Collections.
38. Flamingo advertisement, 1977. In Flamingo Hotel and Casino Promotional and Publicity Materials at UNLV Special Collections.
39. The corporate administration's uneasy relationship with the Flamingo's gangster past was chronicled in newspaper accounts of the Flamingo's fiftieth anniversary. See "After 50 Years, Siegel Legend Haunts Resort," *Las Vegas Sun*, December 20, 1996, and "Bugsy's Place Turns 50," *Las Vegas Review Journal*, December 20, 1996. Flamingo Hilton president Horst Dziura stated in the *Review-Journal* article that "our company feels the stigma we had years ago it something you don't want to highlight, but history is history." Despite this seeming reticence, references to the Flamingo's past, which were initially allusive, such as the Speakeasy restaurant, became more forthright with the passage of time. By 1996, the Flamingo Hilton featured "Bugsy's Bar," "Bugsy's Deli," and "Bugsy's Celebrity Theater."
40. Newman, *Oral History*, 25.
41. Mike Velardo, *Oral History*. William Velardo, collector, untranscribed interview, University of Nevada Oral History Project, Las Vegas, 1976.
42. Edward Thorp. *Beat the Dealer*. New York: Random House, 1962.
43. Grasso, *Oral History*.
44. John Haines, *Oral History*. Thomas S. Hager, Jr., collector, University of Nevada Oral History Project, Las Vegas, 1972, 10.
45. Jimmy Gay, *Oral History*. Joyce M. Wright, collector, University of Nevada Oral History Project, Las Vegas, 1979, 9.
46. Newman, *Oral History*, 23.
47. Las Vegas Department of Community Development, *Let's Take a Look at Downtown Las Vegas* (Las Vegas: Department of Community Development, 1975), 2.
48. Department of Community Development, 7. Emphasis original.
49. Department of Community Development, 8. Emphasis original.
50. *First Interim Report of the Commission on the Review of the National Policy toward Gambling* (Washington, D.C.: U.S. Government Printing Office, 1975), 1–5.
51. Commission on the Review of the National Policy toward Gambling *Final Report: Gambling in America* (Washington, D.C.: U.S. Government Printing Office, 1976), 78. For an analysis of the CRNPG's role in the legitimization of Nevada gaming, see Jerome E. Edwards, "Nevada Gambling: Just Another Business Enterprise," *Nevada Historical Society Quarterly* 37, no. 2 (Summer 1994): 101–114.
52. Commission on the Review of the National Policy toward Gambling, *Final Report*, 78.

Chapter 7

1. For a somewhat smug analysis of Atlantic City in the Gilded Age, see Charles Funnell, *By the Beautiful Sea: The Rise and High Times of That Great American Resort, Atlantic City* (New York: Alfred A. Knopf, 1975).
2. Davis, *Atlantic City Diary: A Century of Memories 1880–1985* (McKee City, N.J.: Atlantic Sunrise Publishing Company, 1986), 67.
3. Cited in Robert Goodman, *The Luck Business: The Devastating Consequences and Broken Promises of America's Gambling Explosion* (New York: The Free Press, 1995), 19.
4. *New Jersey Legislative Statues*. 5:12–1, 12.
5. For an exhaustive survey of the intents and expectations of the builders of New Jersey's regulatory regime, see *Report and Recommendations on Casino Gambling by the Commission of Investigation of the State of New Jersey* (Trenton: State of New Jersey cite, 1978).

6. For an in-depth analysis of the transformation of the Mary Carter Paint Company into Resorts International, the casino's operating company, and the opening of Resorts, see Gigi Mahon, *The Company That Bought the Boardwalk: A Reporter's Story of How Resorts International Came to Atlantic City* (New York: Random House, 1980).

7. As of April 2002, it had 85,738 sq. ft. of casino space, with 2,863 slots and 97 table games.

8. Bear Stearns Equity Research, *Atlantic City at the Jumping-Off Point* (New York: Bear Stearns, 2000), 5.

9. Bear Stearns Equity Research, *Atlantic City at the Jumping-Off Point* (New York: Bear Stearns, 2000), 5.

10. For an optimistic assessment of the economic impact of casino gaming on Atlantic City, see Dan Heneghan, "Economic Impacts of Casino Gaming in Atlantic City," in Cathy H. C. Hsu, ed. *Legalized Casino Gaming in the United States: The Economic and Social Impact* (New York: The Hapworth Hospitality Press, 1999). For a book-length exploration of Atlantic City circa 1991, see John Alcamo, *Atlantic City: Behind the Tables* (Grand Rapids, Mich.: Gollehon, 1991).

11. Denis P. Rudd, "The Social Impacts of Atlantic City Casino Gaming," in Cathy H. C. Hsu, ed., *Legalized Casino Gaming in the United States: The Economic and Social Impact*, 213.

12. "At CCC, a Pause to Mark 25 Years," *Press of Atlantic City*, October 10, 2002.

13. William N. Thompson, "History, Development, and Legislation of Native American Casino Gaming," in Cathy H. C. Hsu, ed., *Legalized Casino Gaming in the United States: The Economic and Social Impact*, 46–47.

14. Thompson, "History, Development, and Legislation," 47.

15. Thompson, "History, Development, and Legislation," 49–50.

16. Janet Plume, "Doing Big Business," *Casino Journal*, 14, no. 4 (April 2001): 32.

17. Carl A. Boger, Jr., Daniel Spears, Kara Wolfe, and Li-Chun Lin, "Economic Impacts of Native American Casino Gaming," in Cathy H. C. Hsu, ed., *Legalized Casino Gaming in the United States: The Economic and Social Impact*, 135–39.

18. Plume, "Doing Big Business," 33–34.

19. Merrill Lynch, *Beating the House—26 June 2001* (New York: Merrill Lynch, 2001), 20.

20. Boger, et al., "Economic Impacts," 136.

21. Cheryl Simrell King and Casey Kanzler, *Background to Dream: Impacts of Tribal Gaming in Washington State* (Olympia, Wash.: First American Education Project, 2002), 2, 18.

22. "Tribal Leaders Donate over $1Million to Aid White Mountain Apache Tribe," *Indian Gaming*, August 2002, 28.

23. Donald L. Barlett and James Steel, "Look Who's Cashing in at Indian Casinos," *Time*, December 8, 2002.

24. See Liz Benston, "Suicide Study Finds No Link with Gambling," *Las Vegas Sun*, July 15, 2002. <http://www.lasvegassun.com/sunbin/stories/sun/2002/jul/15/513713837.html>, and American Gaming Association, "Myths and Facts," <http://www.americangaming.org/casino_entertainment/myths_facts/ sub_myths.html.>.

25. Cathy H. C. Hsu, "The History, Development, and Legislation of Riverboat and Land-Based Non-Native American Casino Gaming" in Cathy H. C. Hsu, ed. *Legalized Casino Gaming in the United States: The Economic and Social Impact*, 64–71.

26. For a detailed study of the impact of gaming in South Dakota and Colorado, see Katherine Jensen and Audie Blevins, *The Last Gamble: Betting on the Future in Four Rocky Mountain Mining Towns* (Tucson: University of Arizona Press, 1998).

27. Dave Ellingson, "Bountiful Black Hawk," *Casino Journal* 14 no. 4 (April 2001): 46. Interestingly, the state legislature, not wanting to taint the state's educational system with gaming revenues, earmarked a portion of state gambling taxes not to schools but to historic preservation. Casinos have thus underwritten the unparalleled efforts of Colorado to catalog and preserve its history.

28. Roger Gros, "Ten Years After," *Global Gaming Business* 1 no. 3 (August 1, 2002): 20–23.

29. Sabina Deitrack, Robert A. Beauregard, and Cheryl Zarlenga Kerchis, "Riverboat Gambling, Tourism, and Economic Development," in Dennis R. Judd and Susan S. Fainstein, eds., *The Tourist City* (New Haven, Conn.: Yale University Press, 1999), 244.

30. Morgan Stanley Dean Witter, *Snapshot of the Detroit Market*, New York, April 2001, 2–3.

31. Given the resort's proximity to Arizona, its focus on retirees is not surprising; during the winter, approximately 80 percent of visitors are over fifty. Summertime attractions, which

include water-skiing, fishing, and boating, draw a slightly younger crowd in the summer, but the town has made a name for itself as a resort for the Western cousins of Atlantic City bus people. State of California, Governor's Office of Planning and Research, *California and Nevada: Subsidy, Monopoly, and Competitive Effects of Legalized Gambling* (Sacramento: Office of Planning and Research, 1992), 18.

32. State of California, Governor's Office of Planning and Research, *California and Nevada: Subsidy, Monopoly, and Competitive Effects of Legalized Gambling* (Sacramento: Office of Planning and Research, 1992), 19.

33. Bear Stearns Equity Research. *Atlantic City at the Jumping-Off Point* (New York: Bear Stearns, 2000), 23.

34. Some bus people have turned these junkets into a virtual cottage industry. One frequent rider interviewed in 2002, for example, lived in a $10-a-night hostel in Queens, N.Y. After paying $11 for a bus ticket, she was given a voucher for $20, putting her $9 ahead and "only a dollar short of rent." Eschewing the slots, she dined in a church soup kitchen, watched other people gamble and, presumably, found a way to earn one dollar. While the casinos can't abide free riders who receive vouchers but don't gamble, such programs have become virtual entitlements that, should they be taken away, would engender a public outcry. See "Chinese Immigrants Rely on Free Casino Cash," *Online Casino News*, <http://www.onlinecasinonews.com/ocn/article/article.asp?id=1736>.

35. The Holiday Inns, Inc. parent company subsequently changed its name to the more general "Holiday Corporation," reflecting its entrance into the casino business as well as its range of hotel brands. The Holiday Corporation, in turn, later spun off some of its brands, including Harrah's (by now a multistate casino operator) into the Promus Companies. The Promus Companies, in 1996, spun off its remaining hotel brands into the Promus Hotel Corporation and the residual company, now consisting only of Harrah's casinos, morphed into Harrah's Entertainment.

36. *Harrah's Timeline*, Harrah's Entertainment <http://www.harrahs.com/about_us/timeline/timeline.html>.

37. Count Guido Roberto Deiro, *Oral History*. David G. Schwartz, collector, University of Nevada Oral History Project, Las Vegas, 2002, 49.

38. Jason Ader, Marc J. Falcone, and Danielle M. McElley, *The Slot Floor of the Future* (New York: Bear Stearns Equity Research, 2000), 63.

39. Andres Duany, Elizabeth Palter-Zyberk, and Jeff Speck, *Suburban Nation: The Rise of Sprawl and the Decline of the American Dream* (New York: North Point Press, 2000), 63.

Epilogue

1. American Gaming Association, *State of the States: The AGA Survey of Casino Entertainment* (Washington, D.C.: American Gaming Association, 1999), 22.

2. Jason Ader et al., *Gaming Intelligence Report, March 2002* (city: Bear Stearns Equity Research, 2002), 26.

3. "Gold Strike Resorts," *Casino Express* 1, no. 2 (December 1988/January 1989).

4. The proliferation of multiline nickel machines bears out this hypothesis. These pay smaller jackpots than larger denominations (thus lessening the chance of a life-changing jackpot), but they allow the patron to play for longer before losing.

5. A dollar or patron amount here is necessarily impossible to quantify, but money laundering or tax evasion may be a motivation for many.

6. For more on the legal status of Internet gambling, see Mark Balestra, ed., *Internet Gambling Report V.: An Evolving Conflict between Technology, Policy, & Law* (St. Charles, Mo.: The River City Group, 2002).

7. For more on the information technology behind Total Rewards, see Meredith Levinson, "Harrah's Knows What You Did Last Night," *Darwin Magazine*, May 2001.

Selected Bibliography

"I Never Sold Any Bibles," *Time* vol. 54 no 22, November 28, 1949.

Albini, Joseph L. *The American Mafia: Genesis of a Legend.* New York: Irvington Publishers Inc., 1979.

Alcamo, John. *Atlantic City: Behind the Tables.* Grand Rapids, MI: Gollehon, 1991.

Alvarez, A. *The Biggest Game in Town.* Boston: Houghton Mifflin Company, 1983.

American Panorama: West of the Mississippi. A Holiday Magazine Book. Garden City, NY: Doubleday and Company, Inc., 1960.

Arm, Walter. *Pay-off: The Inside Story of Big City Corruption.* New York: Appleton-Century-Crofts, Inc., 1951.

Asbury, Herbert. *Sucker's Progress: an informal history of gambling in America from the colonies to Canfield.* New York: Dodd, Mead & Co., 1938.

Atlantic County, NJ. *Growth Trends.* Atlantic City, 1994.

Bailey, William. *The Oral History of William H. (Bob) Bailey.* Elizabeth Nelson Patrick, editor. Las Vegas: University of Nevada Oral History Project, 1978.

Balboni, Alan. *Beyond the Mafia: Italian Americans and the Development of Las Vegas.* Reno: University of Nevada Press, 1996.

Barlett, Donald L. and James B. Steele. *Empire: The Life, Legend, and Madness of Howard Hughes.* New York; W.W. Norton, 1979.

Barnhart, Russell T. *Gamblers of Yesteryear.* Las Vegas: GBC Press, 1983.

Barnhart, Russell T. *Gambling in Revolutionary Paris—The Palais Royal 1789–1838* Las Vegas: R.T. Barnhart, 1990.

Berger, Arthur Asa. *Pop Culture.* Dayton, OH: Pflaum/Standard, 1973.

Best, Katharine and Katharine Hillyer. *Las Vegas: Playtown USA.* New York: David McKay Company, 1955.

Bracey, Earnest N. "The Moulin Rouge Mystique: Blacks and Equal Rights in Las Vegas." *Nevada Historical Quarterly,* 39:4 (Winter 1996), 272–288

Brennan, Bill. *The Frank Costello Story.* Derby, CT: Monarch Books, 1962.

Brill, Steven. *The Teamsters.* New York: Simon and Schuster, 1978.

Brinkley, Alan and Ellen Fitzpatrick. *America in Modern Times, since 1890.* New York: McGraw-Hill, 1997.

Browne, Ray and Marshall Fishwick, eds, *Icons of America.* Bowling Green, OH: Popular Press, 1978.

Bushnell, Eleanor ed. *Sagebrush and Neon.* Reno: University of Nevada Bureau of Governmental Research, 1976.

233

Cahlan, John F. *Reminiscences of a Reno and Las Vegas, Nevada Newspaperman, University Regent, and Public-Spirited Citizen.* Reno: University of Nevada Oral History Project, 1970.

Carlisle, Norman and Madelyn. "The Big Slot-Machine Swindle." *Collier's Magazine*, 123 (February 9, 1949).

Castleman, Deke. *Las Vegas.* Oakland: Fodor's Travel Publications, 1997.

Chafetz, Henry. *Play the Devil: A History of Gambling in the United States from 1492 to 1955.* New York: Bonanza Books, 1960.

Committee on Small Business, House of Representatives. *National Impact of Casino Gambling Proliferation.* Washington: US Government Printing Office, 1995.

Davies, Richard O. ed. *The Maverick Spirit: Building the New Nevada.* Reno: University of Nevada Press, 1999.

DeArment, Robert K. *Knights of the Green Cloth: The Saga of the Frontier Gamblers.* Norman: University of Oklahoma Press, 1982.

Department of Housing and Urban Development, Federal Housing Administration. *Analysis of the Las Vegas, Nevada housing market, as of August 1, 1971.* Washington, DC: FHA, 1972.

Dombrink, John and William N. Thompson. *The Last Resort: Success and Failure in Campaigns for Casinos.* Reno: University of Nevada Press, 1990.

Downs, Anthony. "The 'Issue-Attention Cycle,'" *The Public Interest.* N28, 1972. 38–50.

Drosnin, Michael. *Citizen Hughes.* New York: Holt, Rinehart, and Winston, 1985.

Dulles, Foster Rhea. *A History of Recreation: America Learns to Play.* New York: Appleton-Century-Crofts, 1965.

Eadington, William R. "Gambling: Philosophy and Policy," *Journal of Gambling Studies.*

Eadington, William R. "Regulatory Objectives and the Expansion of Casino Gambling." *Nevada Review of Business and Economics.* v VI, n 3. Fall 1982.

Eadington, William R. "The Development of Corporate Gambling in Nevada." in *Nevada Review of Business and Economics.* v VI, n 1, Spring 1982.

Eadington, William R. and Judy A. Cornelius, eds. *Gambling and Public Policy: International Perspectives.* Reno: Institute for the Study of Gambling and Commercial Gaming, 1991.

Eadington, William R. ed. *Gambling and Society: Interdisciplinary Studies on the Subject of Gambling.* Springfield, IL: Thomas, 1976.

Edwards, Jerome E. *Pat McCarran: Political Boss of Nevada.* Reno: University of Nevada Press, 1982.

Ehrenreich, Barbara. *The Hearts of Men: American Dreams and the Flight from Commitment.* New York: Anchor Books, 1983.

Eisenberg, Dennis, Uri Dan, and Eli Landau. *Meyer Lansky: Mogul of the Mob.* New York: Paddington Press LTD, 1979.

Eisner-Stewart Associates. *Proposed General Plan: Las Vegas Valley, Clark County, Nevada.* South Pasadena, 1966.

Elliott, Russell R. *History of Nevada.* Lincoln: University of Nebraska Press, 1987.

Erenberg, Lewis A. and Susan E. Hirsch, eds, *The War in American Culture: Society and Consciousness during World War II.* Chicago: University of Chicago Press, 1996.

Fabian, Ann. *Card Sharps, Dream Books, and Bucket Shops: Gambling in 19th Century America.* Ithaca: Cornell University Press, 1990.

Farbstein, W.E. "Devilish Devices." *New York Times* Magazine, March 12, 1950.

Farrell, Ronald A and Carole Case, *The Black Book and the Mob: The Untold Story of Nevada's Casinos.* Madison: University of Wisconsin Press, 1995.

Findlay, John. *Magic Lands: Western Cityspaces and American Culture after 1940.* Berkeley: University of California Press, 1992.

Findlay, John. *People of Chance: Gambling in American Society from Jamestown to Las Vegas.* New York and Oxford: Oxford University Press, 1986.

Fishman, Robert. *Bourgeois Utopias: The Rise and Fall of Suburbia.* New York: Basic Books, Inc., 1987.

Flink, James J. *The Car Culture.* Cambridge, MA: The MIT Press, 1975.

Florida Governor's Council on Organized Crime. *1986 Report on Organized Crime in the Casino Gambling Industry.* Tallahassee, 1986.

Fowler, Sally Anne. *How to Become a Casino Cocktail Waitress.* Las Vegas: Sally Anne Fowler, 1983.

Fox, Richard W. and T.J. Jackson Lears, *The Culture of Consumption: Critical Essays in American History, 1880–1980.* New York: Pantheon Books, 1983.

Friedman, Bill. *Casino Management* Seacaucus, NJ: Lyle Stuart Inc., 1974.

Frost, Lionel. *The New Urban Frontier: Urbanisation and City Building in Australasia and the American West.* Kensington: New South Wales University Press, 1991.

Gage, Nicholas. *The Mafia is not an Equal Opportunity Employer.* New York: McGraw-Hill, 1971.

Garreau, Joel. *Edge City: Life on the New Frontier.* New York: Anchor Books, 1991.

Garrison, Omar V. *Howard Hughes in Las Vegas.* New York: Lyle Stuart, 1970.

General Accounting Office. *The Department of Labor's Oversight of the Management of the Teamsters' Central States Pension and Health and Welfare Funds.* Washington: General Accounting Office, 1985

Gerber, Albert. *Bashful Billionaire: An Unauthorized Biography of Howard Hughes.* New York: Lyle Stuart, Inc., 1967

Giancana, Sam and Chuck. *Double Cross: The Explosive, Inside Story of the Mobster who Controlled America.* New York: Warner Books, 1992.

Glass, Mary Ellen. *Nevada's Turbulent 50s: Decade of Political and Economic Change.* Reno: University of Nevada Press, 1981.

Goffman, Erving. *Interaction Ritual: Essays on Face-to Face Behavior.* New York: Pantheon Books, 1967.

Gold, Susan. "Man on the Move: Kirk Kerkorian." *Signature,* v 4 n9, September 1969. V 11 (1), Spring 1995.

Goldsmith, Raymond W. *The National Wealth of the United States in the Postwar Period.* Princeton: Princeton University Press, 1962.

Goodman, Robert. *The Luck Business: The Devastating Consequences and Broken Promises of America's Gambling Explosion.* New York: The Free Press, 1995.

Gorman, Joseph Bruce. *Kefauver: A Political Biography.* New York: Oxford University Press, 1971.

Gottdiener, Mark. *The New Urban Sociology.* New York: McGraw Hill, Inc., 1994.

Gottdiener, Mark. *The Theming of America: Dreams, Visions, and Commercial Space.* Boulder, Westview Press, 1997

Graham, Jefferson. *Vegas, Live and in Person.* New York: Abbeville Press, 1989.

Haden-Guest, Anthony. *The Paradise Program: Travels through Muzak, Hilton, Coca-Cola, Texaco, Walt Disney and other World Empires.* New York: William Morrow and Company, 1975.

Halberstam, David. *The Fifties.* New York: Villard Books, 1993.

Hammontree, Patsy Guy. *Elvis Presley: A Bio-Bibliography.* Westport, CT: Greenwood Press, 1985.

Harrah, William F. *My Recollections of the Hotel-Casino Industry and as an Auto Collecting Enthusiast.* Reno: University of Nevada Oral History Project, 1978.

Hearings before the Special Committee to Investigate Organized Crime in Interstate Commerce. Part 10: Nevada-California. Washington: United States Government Printing Office, 1951.

Hecksher, August, with Phyllis Robinson. *When LaGuardia Was Mayor: New York's Legendary Years.* New York: W.W. Norton and Company, 1978.

Hess, Alan. *Viva Las Vegas: After-Hours Architecture.* San Francisco: Chronicle Books, 1993.

Hill, Gladwin. "Klondike in the Desert." *New York Times Magazine,* June 26, 1953.

Horwitz, Richard P. *The Strip: An American Place.* Lincoln: University of Nebraska Press, 1985.

Hraba, Joseph and Gang Lee, "Gender, Gambling, and Problem Gambling," *Journal of Gambling Studies.* V 12 (1) Spring 1996.

Hsu, Cathy H. C. ed. *Legalized Casino Gaming in the United States: The Economic and Social Impact.* New York: The Hapworth Hospitality Press, 1999.

Huizinga. Johan. *Homo Ludens: A Study of the Play Element in Culture.* Boston: The Beacon Press, 1950.

Jackson, Kenneth T. *The Crabgrass Frontier: The Suburbanization of the United States.* New York: Oxford University Press, 1985.

James, Ralph C. and Estelle Dinerstein James. *Hoffa and the Teamsters: A Study of Union Power.* Princeton: D. Van Nostrand Company, 1965.

Jennings, Dean. *We Only Kill Each Other: The Life and Bad Times of Bugsy Siegel.* Engelwood Cliffs, NJ: Prentice Hall, Inc., 1968.

Johnson, Lubertha. *Oral History Interview: Civil rights efforts in Las Vegas, 1940s-1960s.* Edited by Jamie Coughtry and R.T. King. Reno: University of Nevada Oral History Project, 1988.

Johnston, David. *Temples of Chance: How America, Inc., Bought Out Murder Inc. to Win Control of the Casino Business.* New York: Doubleday, 1992.

Kefauver, Estes. *Crime in America.* Garden City, NY: Doubleday and Company, 1951.

King, Robert Thomas. *Fighting Back: A Life in the Struggle for Civil Rights.* From oral history interviews with Dr. James B. McMillan; conducted by Gary E. Elliott; a narrative interpretation by R.T. King. Reno: University of Nevada Oral History Program, 1977.

King, Rufus. *Gambling and Organized Crime.* Washington, DC: Public Affairs Press, 1969.

Klein, Norman and Martin Schiesl, eds. *20th Century Los Angeles: Power, Promotion, and Social Conflict.* Claremont, CA: Regina Books, 1990

Knapp, Donn. *Las Vegas: Entertainment Capital.* Menlo Park, CA: Lane Publishing, 1983.

Kowinski, William Severini. *The Malling of America: an inside look at the great consumer paradise.* New York: W. Morrow, 1985.

Kranes, David. "Play Grounds," *Journal of Gambling Studies.* V11 (1), Spring 1995.

Lacey, Robert. *Little Man: Meyer Lansky and the Gangster Life.* Boston: Little, Brown, and Company, 1991.

Las Vegas Chamber of Commerce Research and Statistical Bureau. *Statistical Data and Supplement to the "Story of Southern Nevada."* Las Vegas, 1952.

Las Vegas Chamber of Commerce Research and Statistical Bureau. *The Las Vegas Report, 1959.* Las Vegas, 1959.

Las Vegas Chamber of Commerce Research and Statistical Bureau. *The Las Vegas Report, 1967.*

Las Vegas Chamber of Commerce Research and Statistical Bureau. *The Las Vegas Report, 1972.*

Las Vegas Department of Community Development. *Let's Take a Look at Downtown Las Vegas.* Las Vegas: 1975

Leach, William. *Land of Desire: Merchants, Power, and the Rise of a New American Culture.* New York: Pantheon Books, 1993.

Lewis, Oscar. *Sagebrush Casinos: The story of legal gambling in Nevada.* Garden City, N.Y., Doubleday, 1953

Limerick, Patricia. *The Legacy of Conquest: the unbroken past of the American West.* New York: Norton, 1987.

Maas, Peter. *The Valachi Papers.* New York: Putnam, 1968.

Maheu Robert and Richard Hack. *Next to Hughes: Behind the Power and Tragic Downfall of Howard Hughes by his Closest Advisor.* New York: HarperCollins, 1992

Mahon, Gigi. *The Company that Bought the Boardwalk: A reporter's story of how Resorts International came to Atlantic City.* New York: Random House, 1980.

Malone, Michael P. and Richard Etulain. *The American West: a twentieth-century history.* Lincoln: University of Nebraska Press, 1989.

Mandel, Leon. *William Fisk Harrah: The Life and Times of a Gambling Magnate.* Garden City, NY: Doubleday and Company, Inc. 1982.

May, Elaine Tyler. *Homeward Bound: American Families in the Cold War Era.* New York: Basic Books, Inc., 1988.

McCraw, Thomas K. *Prophets of Regulation: Charles Francis Adams, Louis D. Brandies, James M. Landis, Alfred E. Kahn.* Cambridge, MA: Belknap Press of Harvard University Press, 1984.

McCraw, Thomas K. ed. *Regulation in Perspective: Historical Essay.* Cambridge: Harvard University Press, 1981.

McGrath, Roger D. *Gunfighters, Highwaymen and Vigilantes: Violence on the Frontier.* Berkeley: University of California Press, 1984.

McMillan, James B. *Fighting Back: A Life in the Struggle for Civil Rights.* Reno: University of Nevada Oral History Program, 1997.

McMillen, Jan ed. *Gambling Cultures: Studies in History and Interpretation.* Routledge: London and New York, 1996.

Millstein, Gilbert. "Mr. Coward Dissects Las Vegas." *New York Times Magazine,* June 20, 1955.

Milner, Clyde A. Carol O'Connor, and Martha Sandweiss, eds. *The Oxford History of the American West.* New York: Oxford University Press, 1994.

Moehring, Eugene. *Resort City in the Sunbelt: Las Vegas, 1930–1970.* Reno and Las Vegas: University of Nevada Press, 1989.

Monkkonen Eric H., ed. *Crime and Justice in American History. Volume 8: Drugs, Gambling, and Organized Crime.* Munich and London: K.G. Saur, 1992.

Monkkonen, Eric H. *America Becomes Urban: the development of U.S. cities & towns, 1780–1980.* Berkeley : University of California Press, 1988.

Moore, William Howard. *The Kefauver Committee and the Politics of Crime, 1950–1952.* Columbia: University of Missouri Press, 1974.

Moore, William. *Oral History.* Elizabeth Nelson Patrick, interviewer. Reno: University of Nevada Oral History Project, 1981.

Munting, Roger. *An Economic and Social History of Gambling in Britain and the USA.* New York: St. Martin's Press, 1996.

Mustazza, Leonard ed. *Frank Sinatra and Popular Culture: Essays on an American Icon.* Westport, CN: Praeger, 1998.

Nasaw, David. *Going Out: The Rise and Fall of Public Amusements.* New York: Basic Books, 1993.

Nash, Gerald D. *The America West in the Twentieth Century: A Short History of an Urban Oasis.* Englewood Cliffs, NJ: Prentice-Hall, Inc., 1973.

National Institute of Law Enforcement and Criminal Justice. *Development of the Law of Gambling, 1776–1976.* Washington: November 1977.

Navasky, Victor. *Kennedy Justice.* New York: Athenum, 1977.

Nevada Gaming Commission and State Gaming Control Board. *Gaming Nevada Style.*

Nevada Writers Program. *Nevada: A Guide to the Silver State.* (American Guide Series) Portland: Binfords and Mort, 1940.

NJ Department of Labor and Industry, Division of Planning and Research. *Atlantic County Wage Survey of Selected Occupations: Casino versus Noncasino Wages.* July-September 1980. Trenton, July 1981.

Olsen, Edward A. *My Careers as a Journalist in Oregon, Idaho, and Nevada, in Nevada Gaming.* Reno: University of Nevada Oral History Project, 1972.

Paher, Stanley W. *Las Vegas: As it began—as it grew.* Las Vegas: Nevada Publications, 1971.

Puzo, Mario. *Inside Las Vegas.* New York: Grosset and Dunlap, 1977.

Quirk, Lawrence J. and William Schoell. *The Rat Pack: The Hey-Hey Days of Frank and the Boys.* Dallas: Taylor Publishing Company, 1998.

Ralenkotter, Rossi ed. *A Decade of Growth: 10 Year Summary • 1970–1979.* Las Vegas: Convention/Visitors Authority, 1980.

Ralli, Paul. *Viva Vegas.* Hollywood: House-Warven Publishers, 1953.

Ralli, Raul. *Nevada Lawyer: A Story of Life and Love in Las Vegas.* Culver City, CA: Murray and Gee, Inc., 1969.

Reid, Ed and Ovid Demaris. *The Green Felt Jungle.* New York: Trident Press, 1963.

Report and Recommendations on Casino Gambling by the Commission of Investigation of the State of New Jersey. Trenton: State of New Jersey, 1978.

Ringgold, Gene and Clifford McCarty. *The Films of Frank Sinatra.* New York: The Citadel Press, 1971.

Roemer, William F. jr., *War of the Godfathers: The Bloody Confrontation between the Chicago and New York Families for Control of Las Vegas.* New York: Donald I. Fine, 1990.

Rosecrance, John D. *The Degenerates of Lake Tahoe: A Study of Persistence in the Social World of Horse Race Gambling.* New York: Peter Lang, 1985.

Roth, Leland M. *A Concise History of American Architecture.* New York: Harper and Row Publishers, 1979.

Rothman, Hal. *Devil's Bargains: tourism in the twentieth-century American West.* Lawrence: University Press of Kansas, c1998.

Rothman, Hal. *Neon Metropolis: How Las Vegas Started the 21st Century.* New York: Routledge, 2002.

Ruth, Kent. *How to Enjoy Your Western Vacations.* Norman: University of Oklahoma Press, 1956. 225.

Saiger, Morton, *An interview with Morton Saiger.* Conducted by R.T. King. Reno: University of Nevada Oral History Project, 1985.

Scott, Ferris A. *The Las Vegas Story.* Santa Ana: Western Resort Publications, 1957.

Scriven, Michael. "The Philosophical Foundations of Las Vegas," *Journal of Gambling Studies.* V 11 (1), Spring 1995.

Shepperson, Wilbur S., ed. *East of Eden, West of Zion: Essays on Nevada.* Reno: University of Nevada Press, 1989.

Sinatra, Nancy. *Frank Sinatra: An American Legend.* Santa Monica: General Publishing Group, 1995.

Skolnick, Jerome. *House of Cards.* Boston: Little, Brown, 1978

Sloan, Jim. *Nevada: True Tales from the Neon Wilderness.* Salt Lake City: University of Utah Press, 1993.

Sonnett, Robert. *Sonnett's Guide to Las Vegas.* Las Vegas: Sonnett, 1969.

Sorkin, Michael, ed. *Variations on a Theme Park: The New American City and the End of Public Space.* New York: Hill and Wang, 1992.

State Gaming Control Board Staff, eds. *Legalized Gambling in Nevada: Its History, Economics, and Control (second revised edition).* Nevada, 1971.

State of California, Governor's Office of Planning and Research. *California and Nevada: Subsidy, Monopoly, and Competitive Effects of Legalized Gambling.* Sacramento: Office of Planning and Research, 1992.

State of New Jersey Gambling Study Commission. *Report to the Governor and Legislature.* February, 1973.

Steele, David Ramsay. "Yes, Gambling is Productive and Rational," *Liberty,* September 1997, pp27–34.

Strate, Larry D. "The Statute of Anne in Nevada." *Nevada Review of Business and Economics.* v IX, n 2. Fall/Winter 1985.

Third Interim Report of the Special Committee to Investigate Organized Crime in Interstate Commerce [Kefauver Committee]. New York: Arco Publishing Company, 1951.

Torgerson, Dial. *Kirk Kerkorian: American Success Story.* New York: The Dial Press, 1974.

Turner, Wallace. *Gambler's Money: The New Force in American Life.* Boston: Houghton Mifflin Company, 1965.

US Commission of the Review of the National Policy Towards Gambling. *First Interim Report.* Washington: 1975.

US Commission on the Review of the National Policy Towards Gambling. *Gambling In America (Final Report and appendices).* Washington: October 1976.

Venturi, Robert, Denise Scott Brown, and Seven Izenour. *Learning From Las Vegas: The Forgotten Symbolism of Architectural Form.* Cambridge: MIT Press, 1977.

Vogliotti, Gabriel R. *The Girls of Nevada.* Seacaucus, NJ: The Citadel Press, 1975.

Wajcman, Judy. *Feminism Confronts Technology.* Cambridge, UK: Polity Press, 1991.

Walsh, George. *Public Enemies: The Mayor, the Mob, and the Crime that Was.* New York: W.W. Norton and Company, 1980.

Whaples, Robert C. and Dianne C. Betts, eds, *Historical Perspectives on the American Economy.* New York: Cambridge University Press, 1995.

White, Richard. *"It's Your Misfortune and None of My Own": A New History of the American West.* Oklahoma: University of Oklahoma Press, 1991.

Wiley, Peter and Robert Gottlieb. *Empires in the Sun: The Rise of the New American West.* Tucson: University of Arizona Press, 1982.

Wilson, Woodrow. *Race, Community and Politics in Las Vegas, 1940s-1980s: an oral history.* edited by Jamie Coughtry and R.T. King. Reno: University of Nevada Oral History Project, 1990.

Winston, Stuart and Harriet Harris. *Nation of Gamblers: America's Billion-Dollar-a-Day Habit.* Englewood Cliffs, NJ: Prentice Hall, Inc., 1984.

Wolf, George with Joseph DiMona. *Frank Costello: Prime Minister of the Underworld.* New York: William Morrow and Company, 1974.

Index